William Sandys

Christmastide

Its History, Festivities and Carols

William Sandys

Christmastide
Its History, Festivities and Carols

ISBN/EAN: 9783337379780

Printed in Europe, USA, Canada, Australia, Japan

Cover: Foto ©Lupo / pixelio.de

More available books at **www.hansebooks.com**

A Christmas Carol

WHEN the Holy Babe was born,
    Angels, singing, woke the morn,
  Chanting praises to our Lord,
Peace on earth and sweet accord;
For He came to set us free;
    He was born our Lord to be;
    From sin and pain to set us free.

Star-led kings their gifts unrolled,
Myrrh and frankincense and gold:
From the farthest East they came,
From the North and South they came,
    That all peoples of the earth
    Should pay homage at His birth,
    Prince of Peace and Lord of Earth.

Prince of Peace! Alas, the shame
That the blessedness He came
Yearning to bestow on men
Still no nearer seems than then!
    We it is who hinder peace;
    Through us sin and pain increase;
    He would give the whole world peace.

Holy Babe of Bethlehem,
Number us, we pray, with them
In whose heart is echoed still,
"Peace on earth, to men good-will:"
    That Thy will in us be done,
    Let our will with Thine be one;
    Then we shall not be undone.

Christmastide.

CHRISTMASTIDE

its History, Festivities, and Carols.

By WILLIAM SANDYS, F.S.A.

LONDON:
JOHN RUSSELL SMITH,
SOHO SQUARE.

London: Printed by E. TUCKER, Perry's Place, Oxford Street.

TO

WYNN ELLIS, ESQUIRE,

High Sheriff of Hertfordshire,

THE FOLLOWING WORK

IS GRATEFULLY INSCRIBED, AS A SMALL TRIBUTE

OF RESPECT FOR HIS PUBLIC, AND

ESTEEM FOR HIS PRIVATE

CHARACTER.

CONTENTS AND ILLUSTRATIONS.

Lithographs.

	PAGE
Play before Queen Elizabeth	*frontispiece*
Ushering in the Boar's Head	30
Pageant before Henry the Eighth	66
Lord of Misrule, G. Ferrers	86
New Year's Gifts to Queen Elizabeth	100
Temple Revels, temp. Charles the Second	130
The Wassail Bowl	134
Old Christmas Festivities	142
The Christmas Tree	152

Vignettes.

CHAP.		
1	Edward the First's Offering at the Epiphany	1
2	Froissart's Christmas Log	23
3	Merry Carol	45
4	Archie returning his Christmas Gift	63
5	Teonge's Twelfth Night at Sea	85
6	Charles the Second gambling at Christmas	103
7	Pepys' Wassail Bowl	127
8	Modern Christmas Plays	145
9	Three Kings offering	159
10	Carol Singers of old	173
11	Decorating with Evergreens	199

	PAGE
Carols	215
A Mock Play	292
Christmas Play of St. George and the Dragon, as represented in the West of England	298
Index to Carols	303
Index to principal matters	305
Index of References	306

Music.

A Virgin most pure	313
A Child this day is born	315
The Lord at first had Adam made	316
The first Nowell	318
This New Christmas Carol	319
God rest you, merry gentlemen	320
St. Stephen	321
God's dear Son	323
To-morrow shall be my dancing-day	324
I saw three ships	325
Joseph was an old man	226
In those twelve days	327

CHAPTER I.

T would not be consistent with the proposed character of this work to enlarge on the Christian dispensation, as connected with the sacred feast of Christmas; to show Christianity as old as the Creation; that the fall of man naturally involved his punishment; and hence the vicarious sacrifice of our Saviour to redeem us from sin and death. These are subjects to be entered on by those who have had opportunities, if not of thinking more, at least of reading more, relative to them, than the writer of these pages, whose leisure hours are few, and whose endeavour will be to give, in as popular and interesting a manner as his abilities will enable him, some

information respecting the mode of keeping this Holy Feast, particularly in England, in the olden times, and in the middle ages.

The Nativity is hailed by Christians of all denominations, as the dawn of our salvation; the harbinger of the day-spring on high; that promise of futurity, where care, sin, and sorrow enter not, where friends long severed shall meet to part no more; no pride, no jealousy, no self (that besetting sin of the world) intruding. Well, then, may we observe it with gratitude for the unbounded mercy vouchsafed to us; for the fulfilment of the promise pronounced in the beginning of the world, releasing us from the dominion of Satan. A promise which even the Pagans did not lose sight of, although they confused its import, as a glimmering of it may be traced through their corrupted traditions and superstitious ceremonies.

Has the early dream of youth faded away purposeless?—the ambition of manhood proved vanity of vanities? Have riches made themselves wings and flown away? or, has fame, just within the grasp, burst like a bubble? Have the friends, the companions of youth, one by one fallen off from thy converse; or the prop of advancing age been removed, leaving thee weak and struggling with the cares of life; or, has "the desire of thine eyes" been taken from thee at a stroke? Under these and other trials, the Christian looks to the anniversary of the Nativity (that rainbow of Christianity) as the commemoration of the birth of the Blessed Redeemer, who will give rest to the weary, and receive in his eternal kingdom all those who truly trust in him. And well may His name be called, "Wonderful, Counsellor, the Mighty God, the Everlasting Father, the Prince of Peace!"

The season of Christmas, however, was not only set apart

for sacred observance, but soon became a season of feasting and revelry; so much so, that even our sumptuary laws have recognised it, and exempted it from their operation. When Edward the Third, in his tenth year, endeavoured to restrain his subjects from over luxury in their meals, stating that the middle classes sought to imitate the great in this respect, and thus impoverished themselves, and became the less able to assist their liege lord, he forbade more than two courses, and two sorts of meat in each, to any person, except in the great feasts of the year, namely, " La veile et le jour de Noël, le jour de Saint Estiephne, le jour del an renoef (New Year's Day), les jours de la Tiphaynei et de la Purification de Nostre Dame," &c.

A cheerful and hospitable observance of this festival being quite consistent with the reverence due to it, let us—after having as our first duty repaired to the house of our Lord, to return humble thanks for the inestimable benefits now conferred—while preparing to enter into our own enjoyments, enable, as far as in our power, our dependants and poorer brethren, to participate in the earthly comforts, as they do in the heavenly blessings of the season. Remember the days of darkness will come, and who can say how soon, how suddenly? and if long and late to some, yet will they surely come, when the daughters of music are laid low, then the remembrance of a kindly act of charity to our neighbour will soothe the careworn brow, and smooth the restless pillow of disease. " Go," then, " your way; eat the fat and drink the sweet, and send portions unto them for whom nothing is prepared: for this day is holy unto our Lord."

A great similarity exists in the observances of the return of the seasons, and of other general festivals throughout the world; and indeed the rites and ceremonies of the various pagan religions have, to a great extent, the marks of a common origin; and the study of popular antiquities involves researches into the early history of mankind, and their religious ceremonies.

Immediately after the deluge, the religion of Noah and his family was pure; but a century had scarcely elapsed before it became perverted among some of his descendants. That stupendous pagan temple, the Tower of Babel, was built, and the confusion of tongues, and dispersion of mankind, followed. As the waves of population receded farther from the centre, the systems of religion—except with the chosen people—got more and more debased, and mingled with allegories and symbols. But still, even the most corrupt preserved many allusions to the fall of man, and his redemption; to the deluge, and the deliverance by the ark; and to a future state. Thus, whether in China, Egypt, India, Africa, Scandinavia, in the rites of Vitzliputzli in Mexico, and of Pacha Camac, in Peru, among the Magi, the Brahmins, the Chaldæans, the Gymnosophists, and the Druids, the same leading features may be traced. It has even been supposed, that amongst a chosen race of the priests, some traditionary knowledge of the true religion prevailed, which they kept carefully concealed from the uninitiated.

One of the greatest festivals was that in celebration of the return of the sun; which, at the winter solstice, began gradually to regain power, the year commenced anew, and the season was hailed with rejoicings and thanksgivings. The Saxons, and other northern nations, kept a feast on the 25th of December, in honour of Thor, and called it the *Mother-Night*, as the parent of other nights; also *Mid-Winter* It was likewise called *Gule, Gwyl, Yule,* or *Iul,* and half a dozen similar names, respecting the meaning of which learned antiquaries differ: Gebelin and others stating they convey the idea of revolution or wheel; while others, equally learned, consider the meaning to be festival, or holy-day. *Gwyl* in Welsh, and *Geol* in Saxon, both signify a holy-day; and as *Yule,* or *I-ol,* also signifies ale, an indispensable accompaniment of Saxon and British feasts, they were probably convertible terms. The word *Yule* may be found in many of our ancient metrical romances, and some of the old mysteries, as applied to Christmas, and is still so used in Scotland, and parts of England. The word *Gala* would seem to have a similar derivation. The curious in these matters may, however, refer to the learned Hickes's two folios, Gebelin's nine quartos, and Du Cange's ten folios, and other smaller works, and satisfy their cravings after knowledge.

The feast of the birth of Mithras was held by the Romans on the 25th of December, in commemoration of the return of the sun; but the most important heathen festival, at this period of the year, was the *Saturnalia,* a word which has since become proverbial for high-jinks, and all manner of wild revelry. The origin seems to be unknown, but to have been previous to the foundation of Rome, and to have had some reference to the happy state of freedom and equality in the golden age of Saturn, whenever that era of dreams existed; for, when we go back to the olden times, no matter how far, we find the archæologists of that age still looking back on their older times: and so we are handed back, not knowing where to stop, until we stumble against the Tower of Babel, or are stopped by the prow of the Ark, and then decline going any farther.

The Greeks, Mexicans, Persians, and other great nations of antiquity, including of course the Chinese, who always surpassed any other country, had similar festivals. During the Saturnalia among the Romans, which lasted for about a week from the 17th of December, not only were masters and slaves on an equality, but the former had to attend on the latter, who were allowed to ridicule them. Towards the end of the feast a king or ruler was chosen, who was invested with considerable powers, and may be supposed to be intimately connected with our Lord of Misrule, or Twelfth Night King,—presents also were mutually given, and public places decked with shrubs and flowers. The birth of our Saviour thus took place at that time of the year, already marked by some of the most distinguished feasts. And why should it not have been so? We know that, at whatever period of the year it took place, it would have been, for Christians, "The Feast of Feasts;" and it is surely no derogation to imagine, that it was appointed at this time as the fulfilment of all feasts, and the culmination of festivals. The rising of the Christian Sun absorbed in its rays the lesser lights of early traditions, and it has continued to illuminate us with its blended brilliancy. Abercrombie, in his work on the Intellectual Powers, has some able remarks on the value of an unbroken series of traditional testimony or rites, especially as applicable to Christianity. "If the events, particularly, are of a very uncommon character, these rites remove any feeling of uncertainty which attaches to traditional testimony, when it has been transmitted through a long period of time, and, consequently, through a great number of individuals. They carry us back, in one unbroken series, to the period of the events themselves, and to the individuals who were witnesses of them. The most important application of the principle, in the manner now referred to, is in those observances of religion which are intended to commemorate the events connected with the revelation of the Christian faith. The importance of this mode of transmission has not been sufficiently attended to by those who have urged the insufficiency of human testimony, to establish the course of events which are at variance with the common course of nature."

During the Commonwealth, some of the Puritan party endeavoured to show that the 25th of December was not really the Birth of our Saviour, but that it took place at a different time of the year. Thomas Mockett, in 'Christmas, the Christian's Grand Feast,' has collected the principal statements corroborative of this view—arguments they cannot be called; and after all, his conclusion is nothing more than, be the 25th of December the right day or not, Christians were not bound to keep it as a feast, because the supreme authority of the land, and ordinances of both Houses of Parliament, had directed otherwise. Parliament, however, cannot control the day of the Nativity, though it can do a great deal; having, on one occasion, according to tradition, nearly passed an act against the growth of poetry (an enactment perhaps not much wanted at present), though this was said to have been a clerical error; and, at another time, after inflicting a punishment of fourteen years' transportation, gave half to the king and half to the informer; this, as may be supposed, was subsequently repealed. If, however, it is safe to say anything against Parliament, even of two hundred years since, without fear of the pains and penalties of contempt, it might be presumed that, like the patient in the 'Diary of a Physician,' they had "turned heads." Dr. Thomas

Warmstry, in 'The Vindication of the Solemnity of the Nativity of Christ,' published three years previous to Mockett's tract, gives satisfactory replies to the objections made by the Puritans, and seems to have embodied the arguments against them, considering it sufficient for us that the Church has appointed the 25th of December for our great feast.

Whether the Apostles celebrated this day, although probable, is not capable of proof; but Clemens Romanus, about the year 70, when some of them were still living, directs the Nativity to be observed on the 25th of December. From his time to that of Bernard, the last of the Fathers, A.D. 1120, the feast is mentioned in an unbroken series; a tract, called 'Festorum Metropolis,' 1652, naming thirty-nine Fathers, who have referred to it, including Ignatius, Cyprian, Athanasius, Gregory Nazianzen, Ambrosius, Chrysostom, Augustine, and Bede; besides historians and more modern divines. 'The Feast of Feasts,' 1644, also contains many particulars of the celebration during the earlier centuries of Christianity. About the middle of the fourth century, the feasting was carried to excess, as may have been the case occasionally in later times; and Gregory Nazianzen wars against such feasting, and dancing, and crowning the doors, so that the temporal rejoicing seems to have taken the place of the spiritual thanksgiving. In the same age there occurred one of those acts of brutality, which throughout all ages have disgraced humanity. The Christians having assembled in the Temple at Nicomedia, in Bithynia, to celebrate the Nativity, Dioclesian, the tyrant, had it inclosed, and set on fire, when about 20,000 persons are said to have perished; the number, however, appears large.

The early Christians, of the eastern and western Churches,

slightly differed in the day on which they celebrated this feast: the Easterns keeping it, together with the Baptism, on the 6th of January, calling it the Epiphany; while the Westerns, from the first, kept it on the 25th of December; but in the fourth century the Easterns changed their festival of the Nativity to the same day, thus agreeing with the Westerns. The Christian epoch was, it is said, first introduced into chronology about the year 523, and was first established in this country by Bede. New Year's Day was not observed by the early Christians as the Feast of the Circumcision, but (excepting by some more zealous persons, who kept it as a fast) with feasting, songs, dances, interchange of presents, &c., in honour of the new year; though the bishops and elders tried to check these proceedings, which were probably founded in some measure on the Roman feast of the double-faced Janus, held by them on this day. According to Brady, the first mention of it, as a Christian festival, was in 487; and it is only to be traced from the end of the eleventh century, under the title of the Circumcision; and was not generally so kept until included in our liturgy, in 1550; although, from early times, Christmas Day, the Nativity, and Twelfth Day, were the three great days of Christmas-tide. Referring to the probability, that the feasting on New Year's Day might have been derived from the feast of Janus, it must be observed, that some of the early Christians, finding the heathens strongly attached to their ancient rites and customs, which made it difficult to abolish them (at least until after a considerable lapse of time), took advantage of this feeling, and engrafted the Christian feasts on those of the heathen, first modifying and purifying them. The practice may have been wrong, but the fact was so. Thus, Gregory

Thaumaturgus, bishop of Neocæsarea, who died in 265, instituted festivals in honour of certain Saints and Martyrs, in substitution of those of the heathens, and directed Christmas to be kept with joy and feasting, and sports, to replace the *Bacchanalia* and *Saturnalia*. Pagan temples were converted into Christian churches; the statues of the heathen deities were converted into Christian saints; and papal Rome preserved, under other names, many relics of heathen Rome. The Pantheon was converted into a Romish church, and Jupiter changed to St. Peter.

When Pope Gregory sent over St. Augustin to convert Saxon England, he directed him to accommodate the ceremonies of the Christian worship as much as possible to those of the heathen, that the people might not be too much startled at the change; and, in particular, he advised him to allow the Christian converts, on certain festivals, to kill and eat a great number of oxen, to the glory of God, as they had formerly done to the honour of the devil. St. Augustin, it appears, baptized no fewer than 10,000 persons on the Christmas day next after his landing in 596, and permitted, in pursuance of his instructions, the usual feasting of the inhabitants, allowing them to erect booths for their own refreshment, instead of sacrificing to their idols,—objecting only to their joining in their dances with their pagan neighbours. Thus several of the pagan observances became incorporated with the early Christian festivals; and to such an extent, that frequent endeavours were made, by different Councils, to suppress or modify them; as, in 589, the songs and dances, at the festivals of Saints, were prohibited by the Council of Toledo, and by that of Chalon, on the Saone, in 650. In after times, the clergy still found it frequently requisite to connect the remnants of pagan idolatry with Christianity, in consequence of the difficulty they found in suppressing it. So, likewise, on the introduction of the Protestant religion, some of the Roman Catholic ceremonies, in a modified state, were preserved; and thus were continued some of the pagan observances. In this manner may many superstitious customs, still remaining at our great feasts, and in our games and amusements, be accounted for.

The practice of decorating churches and houses with evergreens, branches, and flowers, is of very early date. The Jews used them at their Feast of Tabernacles, and the heathens in several of their ceremonies, and they were adopted by the Christians. Our Saviour Himself permitted branches to be used as a token of rejoicing, upon His triumphal entry to Jerusalem. It was natural, therefore, that at Christmas time, when His Birth, and the fulfilment of the promise to fallen man, were celebrated, that this symbol of rejoicing should be resorted to. Some of the early Councils, however, considering the practice somewhat savoured of paganism, endeavoured to abolish it; and, in 610, it was enacted, that it was not lawful to begirt or adorn houses with laurel, or green boughs, for all this practice savours of paganism. In the earlier carols the holly and the ivy are mentioned, where the ivy, however, is generally treated as a foil to the holly, and not considered appropriate to festive purposes.

> "Holly and Ivy made a great party,
> Who should have the mastery
> In lands where they go.
> Then spake Holly, I am friske and jolly,
> I will have the mastery
> In lands where they go."

But in after times it was one of the plants in regular use. Stowe mentions holme, ivy, and bays, and gives an account of a great storm on Candlemas Day, 1444, which rooted up a standard tree, in Cornhill, nailed full of holme and ivy for Christmas, an accident that by some was attributed to the evil spirit. Old Tusser's direction is "Get ivye and hull (holly) woman deck up thine house." The misletoe—how could Shakespeare call it the "baleful misletoe?"—was an object of veneration among our pagan ancestors in very early times, and as it is probable it was the golden branch referred to by Virgil, in his description of the descent to the lower regions, it may be assumed to have been used in the religious ceremonies of the Greeks and Romans. His branch appears to have been the misletoe of the oak, now of great rarity, though it is found on many other trees. It was held sacred by the Druids and Celtic nations, who attribute to it valuable medicinal qualities, calling it *allheal* and *guidhel*, and they preferred, if not selected exclusively, the misletoe of the oak. Vallancey says it was held sacred because the berries as well as the leaves grow in clusters of three united to one stalk, and they had a veneration for the number three; his observation, however, is incorrect as to the leaves, which are in pairs only. The Gothic nations also attached extraordinary qualities to it, and it was the cause of the death of their deity Balder. For Friga, when she adjured all the other plants, and the animals, birds, metals, earth, fire, water, reptiles, diseases, and poison, not to do him any hurt, unfortunately neglected to exact any pledge from the misletoe, considering it too weak and feeble to hurt him, and despising it perhaps because it had no establishment of its own, but lived upon other plants. When the gods, then, in their great assembly, amused themselves by throwing darts and other missiles at him, which all fell harmless, Loke, moved with envy, joined them in the shape of an old woman, and persuaded Hoder, who was blind, to throw a branch of misletoe, and guided his hand for the purpose; when Balder, being pierced through by it, fell dead. The Druids celebrated a grand festival on the annual cutting of the misletoe, which was held on the sixth day of the moon nearest their new year. Many ceremonies were observed, the officiating Druid being clad in white, with a golden sickle, and received the plant in a white cloth. These ceremonies kept alive the superstitious feelings of the people, to whom no doubt the Druids were in the habit of dispensing the plant at a high price; and as late as the seventeenth century, peculiar efficacy was attached to it, and a piece hung round the neck was considered as a safeguard against witches. In modern times it has a tendency to lead us towards witches of a more attractive nature; for, as is well known, if one can by favour or cunning induce a fair one to come under the misletoe he is entitled to a salute, at the same time he should wish her a happy new year, and present her with one of the berries for good luck; each bough, therefore, is only laden with a limited number of kisses, which should be well considered in selecting one. In some places people try lots by the crackling of the leaves and berries in the fire.

From the pagan Saturnalia and Lupercalia probably were derived those extraordinary but gross, and as we should now consider them, profane observances, the Feast of Asses and the Feast of Fools, with other similar burlesque festivals. In the early ages of Christianity, there were practices at the beginning of the year of men going about dressed in female attire or in skins of beasts, causing occasionally much vice and debauchery; but the regular Feast of Asses and Feast of Fools were not apparently fully established until the ninth or tenth century; a period when it was considered a sufficient qualification for a priest, if he could read the Gospels and understand the Lord's Prayer. All sorts of buffooneries and abominations were permitted at these representations; mock anthems and services were sung; an ass, covered with rich priestly robes, was gravely conducted to the choir, and provided from time to time with drink and provender, the inferior clergy, choristers, and people dancing round him and imitating his braying; while all sorts of impurities were committed, even at the holy altar. A hymn was sung, commencing—

> Orientis partibus
> Adventavit asinus;
> Pulcher et fortissimus,
> Sarcinis aptissimus.
> Hez, Sire Asnes, car chantez;
> Belle bouche rechignez;
> Vous aurez du foin assez.
> Et de l'avoine à planter.
> Lentus erat pedibus,
> Nisi foret baculus,
> Et cum in clunibus
> Pungeret aculeus.

and after several verses in this strain, finishing with—

> Hez va! hez va! hez va, hez!
> Bialx Sire Asnes car allez;
> Belle bouche car chantez.

On the mock mass being completed, the officiating priest

turned to the people and said, "Ite missa est," and brayed three times, to which they responded by crying or braying out, Hinham, Hinham, Hinham. This festival is said to have been in commemoration of the flight to Egypt; but there was one kept at Rouen in honour of Balaam's ass, where the performers, if they may be so called, walked in procession on Christmas Day, representing the prophets and others, as David, Moses, Balaam, Virgil, &c., just as General Wolfe may now be seen as a party in the Christmas play of St. George and the Dragon. Many attempts were made from the twelfth to the end of the sixteenth century to suppress these licentious abuses of sacred things; and although by that time they were abolished in the churches, yet they were continued by the laity, and our modern mummers probably have their origin from them. A pupil of Gassandi, writing to him as late as 1645, mentions having seen in the church at Aix, the Feast of Innocents (which was of a similar nature) kept by the lay brethren and servants in the church, dressed in ragged sacerdotal ornaments, with books reversed, having large spectacles, with rinds of scooped oranges instead of glasses. Louis the Twelfth, in the early part of the sixteenth century, ordered the representation of the gambol of the 'Prince des Sots' and the 'Mère sotte,' in which, according to a note to Rabelais, liv. i, c. 2, ed. 1823, Julius the Second and the Court of Rome were represented. This was about the time probably when the principality of Chauny wishing to have some swans (*cignes*) for the waters ornamenting their town, unluckily wrote to Paris for some *cinges* (singe being then written with a *c*), and in due time received a wagonful of apes. They could, therefore, have readily proffered their scribe as the prince des sots, excepting that it takes a wise man to make a good fool. At Angers, there was an old custom called Aquilanneuf, or Guilauleu, where young persons went round to churches and houses on the first of the year, to collect contributions, nominally to purchase wax in honour of the Virgin, or the patron of the church, crying out, *Au gui menez Rollet Follet, tiri liri mainte du blanc et point du bis;* they had a chief called *Roi Follet,* and spent their money in feasting and debauchery. An order was made by the synod there, in 1595, which stopped the practice in the churches, but another, in 1668, was necessary to modify and restrain it altogether.

Feasts of this description were not much in vogue in England, though they were introduced, as we find them prohibited at Lincoln, by Bishop Grosthead, in the time of Henry the Third; but towards the end of the following century they were probably abolished. There are traces of the fool's dance, where the dancers were clad in fool's habits, in the reign of Edward the Third. A full account of these strange observances may be found in Ducange, and in Du Tilliot's Mémoires de la Fête des Foux.

Christianity was introduced among the Britons at a very early period, but there are no records, that can be considered authentic, of their mode of keeping the feast of the Nativity, though it was doubtless observed as one of their highest festivals. Some of the druidical ceremonies might have been embodied, and even the use of the mysterious misletoe then adopted, the aid of the bards called in, and ale and mead quaffed in abundance. The great and veritable King Arthur, according to the ballad of the "Marriage of Sir Gawaine,"—

"...... a royale Christmasse kept,
With mirth and princelye cheare;
To him repaired many a knighte,
That came both farre and neare."

This, though ancient, is certainly of a date long subsequent to the far-famed hero; but it ought to be taken as authority, for, according to the modern progress of antiquarianism, the farther off we live from any given time or history, the more we know about it; the old Babylonians, Greeks, Romans, and Mediævals, knowing nothing respecting themselves and their next door neighbours, while we are as familiar as if we had been born and bred with them. By the same rule of remoteness, the modern chronicler, Whistlecraft (Frere), should be taken as authority, for the particulars of the ancient Christmas feast, on which he humorously thus dilates:—

"They served up salmon, venison, and wild boars,
By hundreds, and by dozens, and by scores,
Hogsheads of honey, kilderkins of mustard,
Muttons, and fatted beeves, and bacon swine,
Herons and bitterns, peacocks, swan, and bustard,
Teal, mallard, pigeons, widgeons, and, in fine,
Plum-puddings, pancakes, apple-pies, and custard,
And therewithal they drank good Gascon wine,
With mead, and ale, and cider of our own,
For porter, punch, and negus were not known."

After the conversion of the Anglo-Saxons to Christianity, Easter, Whitsuntide, and Christmas, were kept as solemn festivals; the kings living at those times in great state, wearing their crowns, receiving company on a large scale, and treating them with great hospitality. The Wittenagemots were also then held, and important affairs of church and state discussed. Knowing the affection of the early Saxons for their ale and mead, and that quaffing these from the skulls of their enemies, while feasting from the great boar Scrymer, was—notwithstanding the apparent sameness of the amusement—one of their anticipated joys in a future state, we can readily imagine that excesses frequently took place at these festivals. The wassail bowl, of which the skull of an enemy would thus appear to have formed their *beau idéal*, is said to have been introduced by them. Rowena, the fair daughter of Hengist, presenting the British king, Vortigern, with a bowl of wine, and saluting him with "Lord King Wass-heil;" to which he answered, as he was directed, "Drinc heile," and saluted her then after his fashion, being much smitten with her charms. The purpose of father and daughter was obtained; the king married the fair cup-bearer, and the Saxons obtained what they required of him. This is said to have been the first wassail in this land; but, as it is evident that the form of salutation was previously known, the custom must have been much older among the Saxons; and, indeed, in one of the histories, a knight, who acts as a sort of interpreter between Rowena and the king, explains it to be an old custom among them. By some accounts, however, the Britons are said themselves to have had their wassail bowl, or lamb's wool—*La Mas Ubhal*, or day of apple fruit—as far back as the third century, made of ale, sugar (whatever their sugar was), toast and roasted crabs, hissing in the bowl; to which, in later times, nutmeg was added. The followers of Odin and Thor drank largely in honour of their pagan deities; and, when converted, still continued their potations, but in honour of the Virgin Mary, the Apostles, and Saints; and the early missionaries were obliged to submit to this substitution, being unable to abolish the practice, which afterwards degenerated into drinking healths of other people, to the great detriment of our own. Strange! that even from the earliest ages, the cup-bearer should be one of the principal officers in the royal presence, and that some of the high families take their name from a similar office.

The feast of Christmas was kept in the same state on the Continent, and the bishops were accustomed to send their eulogies—*Visitationis Scripta*—on the Nativity, to kings, queens, and others of the blood royal. But it is foreign to the purpose of this work to refer to the customs abroad, unless it may be necessary to do so slightly, for the purpose of illustration. It may be mentioned, however, that at this festival, in 800, Charlemagne received from the pope, Leo the Third, the crown of Emperor, and was hailed as the pious Augustus the Great, and pacific Emperor of the Romans.

Alfred, as might be expected from his fine character, reverently observed the festival. On one occasion he gave to the celebrated Asser, by way of gift, an abbey, in Wiltshire, supposed to have been Amesbury; another, at Barnwell, in Somersetshire; a rich silk pall, and as much incense as a strong man could carry on his shoulder,—a truly princely New Year's gift. He directed Christmas to be kept for twelve days; so that now, if not at an earlier date, the length of the feast was defined, and the name, probably, of Twelfth-day given to the last day of it; though, in the old Runic festivals, among the ancient Danes, it appears to have been more correctly called the thirteenth day, a name which would sound uncouth to our modern ears: **Who would eat any thirteenth cake?** Alfred was commemorating this festival, with his army, at Chippenham, in 878, when he was surprised by Guthrum, and his Danes, and compelled to fly and conceal himself in the Isle of Athelney, his power fading away for a time, even like that of a twelfth-night king. Something similar happened a century before, when Offa, king of Mercia, about the year 790, was completing Offa's dyke. The Welsh, despising the solemnity of the time, broke through, and slew many of Offa's soldiers, who were enjoying their Christmas. The Danish kings kept the feast much in the same manner as the Saxons; and there is a story told of Canute, who had many good qualities about him, which shows the rudeness of the times, even in the royal circle, though such a scene may even now be realized in Oriental courts. While this monarch was celebrating his Christmas in London, A.D. 1017, Edric, earl of Mercia, who had treacherously betrayed and deserted Ethelred and Edmund Ironside, boasted of his services to Canute, who turned to Eric, earl of Northumberland, exclaiming, "Then let him receive his deserts, that he may not betray us, as he betrayed Ethelred and Edmund." The Norwegian immediately cut him down with his battle-axe, and his body was thrown from a window into the Thames. Such speedy justice would rather astonish a drawing-room now-a-days.

Dancing seems then, even as at present, to have been a favourite Christmas amusement, and certainly in one instance was carried to an extreme. Several young persons were dancing and singing together on Christmas Eve, 1012, in a churchyard, and disturbed one Robert, a priest, who was performing mass in the church. He entreated them in vain to desist: the more he begged the more they danced, and, we may conclude, showed him some of their best *entrechats* and capers. What would, in modern times, have been a case for the police, was then a subject for the solemn interference of the powers of the church. Robert, as they would not cease dancing, as the next best thing, prayed that they might dance without ceasing. So they continued without intermission, for a whole year, feeling neither heat nor cold, hunger nor thirst, weariness nor decay of apparel; but the ground on which they performed not having the same miraculous support, gradually wore away under them, till at last they were sunk in it up to the middle, still dancing as vehemently as ever. Sir Roger de Coverley, danced down the whole length of the Crystal Palace, would have been nothing to this. A brother of one of the girls took her by the arm, endeavouring to bring her away; the limb, however, came off in his hand, like Dr. Faustus's leg, in the hand of the countryman, but the girl never stopped her dancing, or missed a single step in consequence. At the end of the year Bishop Hubert came to the place, when the dancing ceased, and he gave the party absolution. Some of them died immediately after, and the remainder, after a profound sleep of three days and three nights, went about the country to publish the miracle.

It was at Christmas, 1065, that Westminster Abbey was consecrated, in the presence of Queen Edgitha, and a great number of nobles and priests, Edward the Confessor being himself too ill to attend; and indeed he died on the 5th of January, 1066, and was buried in the Abbey on the following day; his tomb there, and his name of the Confessor, given him by the priests, having caused him probably to be better known than any particular merits of his own deserve.

A great change was now about to take place in the government of our country: William of Normandy claimed it as his of right against Harold; and, having power to support his claim, in the space of a few months became King of England, placing his Norman followers in the high places of the land.

CHAPTER II.

 HE Anglo-Norman kings introduced increased splendour at this festival, as they did on all other occasions; the king wearing his crown and robes of state, and the prelates and nobles attending, with great pomp and ceremony, to partake of the feast provided by their monarch, and to receive from him presents, as marks of his royal favour; returning, probably, more than an equivalent. William the Conqueror, was crowned on Christmas day, 1066.

> " On Christmas day in solemne sort,
> Then was he crowned here,
> By Albert, Archbishop of Yorke,
> With many a noble peere."

There was some disturbance during the ceremony, owing to the turbulence or misconception of his Norman followers, who, as well as their master, were disposed to rule with a rod of iron. William gave a striking proof of how little his nature was capable of understanding "good will towards men," when he kept his Christmas at York, in 1069, with the usual festivities, and afterwards gave directions to devastate the country between York and Durham; thus consigning 100,000 people to death, by cold, hunger, fire, and sword. Well, perhaps some of us are William the Conquerors in heart; what else is a bully at school, or a bully in society, or, yet more, a bully in domestic life? Who can count the misery caused by one selfish, one imperious tyrant, whose victims dare not, or will not, complain; the crouching child, the trembling, submissive, broken-hearted, yet even still the loving wife? Oh! woman,—woman, how few amongst us are able to appreciate you! We see you fair and accomplished; we find you loving and affectionate; we know you virtuous and faithful; but, can we estimate your truthfulness, your negation of self, your purity of thought? Partakers of our joys, but partners indeed in our sorrows; how many a weary heart of man, crushed by the pressure of worldly cares and trials, have you not saved, and brought to the contemplation of better things! "She openeth her mouth with wisdom; and in her tongue is the law of kindness."

It would be easy to give a list of the different places where our monarchs kept their Christmasses, from the time of the Conquest, in nearly, if not quite, an unbroken series; but as this would be scarcely as amusing as a few pages in a well conducted dictionary, it will no doubt be considered to have been wisely omitted. It may be stated, in general terms, that the earlier kings occasionally passed Christmas in Normandy, and that some of the principal towns favoured, besides London and Westminster, appear to have been, Windsor, York, Winchester, Norwich, Worcester, Gloucester, Oxford, Eltham, and Canterbury; and in the time of the Tudors, Greenwich. Some examples of marked or distinguished Christmasses will be given in the following pages.

In 1085, William, who was fond of magnificence, kept his Christmas with great state at Gloucester, which was a favourite place with him and his son William. He was either in a particular good humour, or wished to perform what he might think an act of grace, and compensate the severity with which he treated his conquered, or rather semi-conquered new subjects, by showing favour to his own countrymen;—a sort of liberal disposition of public gifts to family friends, that may be seen occasionally even in modern times—so he gave bishoprics to three of his chaplains, namely, that of London to Maurice, of Thetford to William, and of Chester to Robert. There is a somewhat strange regulation among the constitutions of Archbishop Lanfranc for the government of the monks of his cathedral, which contain numerous injunctions respecting washing and combing, and other matters that would now surprise even a well-regulated boys' school. On Christmas Eve they are directed to comb their heads before they washed their hands, while at other times they were to wash first, and comb afterwards. We do not see the philosophy of this curious distinction.

William Rufus, the weak and profligate successor of the Conqueror, kept the Christmas in state, like his father, and Henry the First followed their example; even in 1105, which was "annus valde calamitosus," wherein he raised many tributes, he still kept his Christmas in state, at Windsor. In 1116, he kept it at St. Albans, when the celebrated monastery there was consecrated. In the Christmas 1126-7, which was held at Windsor, anticipating the struggle for the crown that would take place after his death, he assembled all the principal clergy and nobles (David, king of Scots, being also present), and caused them to swear that they would maintain England and Normandy for his daughter, the Empress Matilda, after his death. In these early times, however, a few oaths, more or less, were of little consequence; the "time whereof the memory of man runneth not to the contrary" was of very short date; a week sometimes making a man to forget utterly what he might previously have sworn to; and the vicar of Bray would have been by no means a reprehensible character.

King Stephen, after his accession, wore his crown and robes of state like the former kings, and kept his Christmas at London; but about the fifth year of his reign, the internal wars and tumults became and continued of such magnitude, that during the remainder of this troubled reign, the celebration of festivals was laid aside.

Henry the Second renewed the celebration of Christmas with great splendour, and with plays and masques; and the lord of Misrule appears to have been known at this time, if not at a much earlier date. In 1171, he celebrated the feast at Dublin, in a large wooden house erected for the purpose, and entertained several of the Irish chieftains, as well as the principal men of his own court and army; the Irish were much surprised at the great plenty and variety of provisions, and were especially amused at the English eating cranes; however, after a very short hesitation they joined readily in the feasting themselves, and history does not say that any ill effects followed. Cranes continued to be favourites at Christmas and aristocratic feasts for some time; at the celebrated and often quoted enthronisation banquet of Archbishop Nevil, in the time of Edward the Fourth, there were no less than 204 of these birds. There were some strange dishes, however, in vogue in the time of Henry the Second, as far as the names, whatever the actual merits of the compounds might have been. Dillegrout, karumpie, and maupigyrnun, may have far surpassed some of our grand sounding modern dishes, where the reality sadly disappoints the ear. This dillegrout also was rather an important dish, as the tenant of the manor of Addington, in Surrey, held it by service of making a mess of dillegrout on the day of the coronation. Fancy the anxiety on this ceremony, not only for the excellence of the dish, but that it shall not be proclaimed a failure, and thus risk the possession of the manor, and some more favoured tenant being put in possession, on the tenure of providing a plum-pudding every Christmas, or something similar, like the celebrated King George's pudding, still tendered to visitors at the Isle of Portland. This dillegrout, too, required some little skill to make it well, being compounded of almond milk, the brawn of capons, sugar and spices, chicken parboiled and chopped, and was called, also, ' le mess de gyron,' or, if there was fat with it, it was termed maupigyrnun

At Christmas, 1176, Roderick, king of Connaught, kept court with Henry at Windsor, and in 1183, Henry kept the feast at Caen, in Normandy, and there wished his son Henry (who died not long afterwards) to receive homage from his brothers; but the impetuous Richard would not consent, the "merry" Christmas was, therefore, sadly interrupted, and fresh family feuds arose; they had previously been but too frequent, Henry's life having been much embittered by the conduct of his sons.

When Richard himself came to the throne, he gave a splendid entertainment during Christmas, 1190, at Sicily, when on his way to the Crusades, inviting every one in the united English and French armies of the degree of a gentleman, and giving each a suitable present, according to his rank. Notwithstanding, however, the romance of Richard Cœur de Lion affirms that—

> "Christmas is a time full honest,
> Kyng Richard it honoured with gret feste;"

and an antiquary of course ought to consider these romances of equal authenticity with the old chronicles; yet one cannot help thinking that during Richard's short reign, his captivity and his absence from his kingdom must have interfered with his Christmas celebrations; in fact, he, of the lion-heart, seems to have been more ornamental than useful in the pages of history.

John celebrated the feast pretty regularly, but seems occasionally to have selected a city or town for the purpose, where some great personage was allowed to provide for the entertainment; as, for instance, the celebrated Hubert de Burgh, at Canterbury, in 1203. In 1213, he kept his Christmas at Windsor with great festivity, and gave many presents. He was accustomed to make a present to his chancellor, every Christmas, of two marks of gold, according to ancient custom, no doubt by way of New Year's gift, and gave him half that value at Easter and Whitsuntide. In

1214, he was keeping his Christmas at Worcester, when he was informed of the resolution of the barons to withdraw their allegiance, unless their claims were attended to. This information being ill-suited for the festivities then in progress, the king departed suddenly and shut himself up in the Temple; but the barons went to him on the Epiphany of 1215 with their demands, to which he promised a satisfactory answer at the ensuing Easter. The dissensions between himself and his barons, ending in Magna Charta, are well-known matters of history. In the following year the chief barons of the realm were under sentence of excommunication, and the city of London was under an interdict; but the citizens disregarded this, kept open their churches, rang their bells, enjoyed their turtle and whitebait (whatever the turtle and whitebait of that time might have been), drank their hippocras, ale, mead, and claret or clarré, and celebrated their Christmas with unusual festivity. The English had long been celebrated for their pre-eminence in drinking; as Iago says, "your Dane, your German, and your swag-bellied Hollander, are nothing to your English." They probably inherited the talent from the Saxons, for their kings had their wine, mead, cyder, ale, pigment, and morat, to which their Norman successors added claret or clarré, garhiofilac, and hippocras. Morat was made from honey and mulberries; claret, pigment, hippocras, and garhiofilac (so called from the girofle or cloves contained in it), were different preparations of wine mixed with honey and spices, no doubt very palatable; and hippocras particularly was indispensable at all the great feasts. Garhiofilac was probably made of white wine, and claret of red wine, as there is an order of Henry the Third in existence, directing the keepers of his wines at York, to deliver to

Robert de Monte Pessulano two tuns of white wine to make garhiofilac, and one tun of red wine to make claret for him at the ensuing Christmas, as he used to do in former years. These sheriffs were very useful persons in those times, and performed many offices for our olden monarchs that would somewhat surprise a modern high sheriff to perform now, when he is only called upon to attend to the higher duties of his office, and becomes officially one of the first men in his county. Henry the Third, in his twenty-sixth year, directed the sheriff of Gloucester, to cause twenty salmons to be bought for the king, and put into pies against Christmas; and the sheriff of Sussex to buy ten brawns with the heads, ten peacocks, and other provisions for the same feast.

In his thirty-ninth year, the French king, having sent over as a present to Henry (whether as a New Year's gift or not does not exactly appear) an elephant—"a beast most strange and wonderfull to the English people, sith most seldome or never any of that kind had beene seene before that time,"— the sheriffs of London were commanded to build a house for the same, forty feet long and twenty feet broad, and to find necessaries for himself and keeper.

The boar's head just referred to was the most distinguished of the Christmas dishes, and there are several old carols remaining in honour of it.

> "At the begynnyng of the mete,
> Of a borys hed ye schal hete,
> And in the mustard ye shal wete;
> And ye shal syngyn or ye gon."

The dish itself, though the "chief service in this land," and of very ancient dignity—probably as old as the Saxons,—

was not confined to Christmas; for, in 1170, when King Henry the Second had his son Henry crowned in his own lifetime, he himself, to do him honour, brought up the boar's head with trumpets before it, "according to the manner." It continued the principal entry at all grand feasts, and was frequently ornamented. At the coronation feast of Henry the Sixth there were boars' heads in "castellys of golde and enamell." By Henry the Eighth's time it had become an established Christmas dish, and we find it ushered in at this season to his daughter the Princess Mary, with all the usual ceremonies, and no doubt to the table of the monarch himself, who was not likely to dispense with so royal a dish; and so to the time of Queen Elizabeth, and the revels in the Inns of Court in her time, when at the Inner Temple a fair and large boar's head was served on a silver platter, with minstrelsy. At the time of the celebrated Christmas dinner, at Oxford, in 1607, the first mess was a boar's head, carried by the tallest of the guard, having a green scarf and an empty scabbard, preceded by two huntsmen, one carrying a boar spear and the other a drawn faucion, and two pages carrying mustard, which seems to have been as indispensable as the head itself. A carol was sung on the occasion, in the burden of which all joined. Queen's College, Oxford, was also celebrated for its custom of bringing in the boar's head with its old carol. Even in the present day, though brawn, in most cases, is considered as a sort of substitute, the boar's head with lemon in his mouth may be seen, though rarely, and when met with, may be safely recommended as a dainty; but some of the *soi-disant* boars' heads seen at Christmas in a pompous state of whiskerless obesity, may without disparagement, take Lady Constance's words literally and "hang a calf skin on their recreant limbs." Brawn is probably as old as boar's head; but the inventor of such an arrangement of hogsflesh must have been a genius, and would have been a patentee in our days, and probably have formed a joint-stock brawn association. We have just observed it in the time of Henry the Third, and the 'begging frere,' in 'Chaucer's Sompnoure's Tales,' says, "geve us of your braun, if ye have any," and it may be found in most of the coronation and grand feasts; even in the coronation feast of Katharine, queen to Henry the Fifth, in 1421, brawn and mustard appear, though the feast was intended to be strictly a fish dinner, and with this exception and a little confectionary, really was so, comprising, with other marine delicacies, "fresh sturgion with welks," and "porperous rosted," the whole bill of fare, however, would match even the ministerial whitebait dinner. This is not the only instance where brawn was ranked with fish; for when Calais was taken, there was a large quantity there; so the French, guessing it to be some dainty, tried every means of cooking it; they roasted it, boiled it, baked it, but all in vain, till some imaginative mind suggested a trial *au naturel*, when its merits were discovered. But now came the question, in what class of the animal creation should it be placed? The monks tasted and admired: "Ha! ha!" said they, "capital fish!" and immediately placed it on their list of fast-day provisions. The Jews were somewhat puzzled, but a committee of taste, of the most experienced elders, decided that it certainly was not any preparation from impure swine, and included it in their list of clean animals.

At the coronation of Henry the Seventh, a distinction was made between "brawne royall," and "brawne," the former probably being confined to the king's table. Brawn and mustard appear to be as inseparable as the boar's head and mustard, and many directions respecting them may be found at early feasts. In the middle of the sixteenth century brawn is called a great piece of service, chiefly in Christmas time, but as it is somewhat hard of digestion, a draught of malvesie, bastard, or muscadell is usually drunk after it, where either of them is conveniently to be had.

> " Even the two rundlets,
> The two that was our hope, of muscadel,
> (Better ne'er tongue tript over,) these two cannons,
> To batter brawn withal, at Christmas, sir,—
> Even these two lovely twins, the enemy
> Had almost cut off clean."

At the palace, and at the revels of the Inns of Court, it seems to have been a constant dish at a Christmas breakfast. Tusser prescribes it amongst his good things for Christmas, and it has so remained to the present time. The salmon recently mentioned, as having been ordered for the king, continued to be a favourite dish for this feast. Carew says—

> " Lastly, the sammon, king of fish,
> Fils with good cheare the Christmas dish."

There used to be a superstition at Aberavon, in Monmouthshire, that every Christmas Day, in the morning, and then only, a large salmon exhibited himself in the adjoining river, and permitted himself to be handled and taken up, but it would have been the greatest impiety to have captured him. One would not wish to interfere with the integrity of this legend, by calling on the salmon some Christmas morning, for fear that he may have followed the tide of emigration, or may have been affected by free trade.

The salmon, however, is not the only living creature, besides man, that is supposed to venerate this season.

> "Some say, that ever 'gainst that season comes
> Wherein our Saviour's birth is celebrated,
> The bird of dawning singeth all night long:
> And then, they say, no spirit can walk abroad;
> The nights are wholesome; then no planets strike;
> No fairy tales, nor witch hath power to charm,
> So hallow'd and so gracious is the time."

According to popular superstition the bees are heard to sing, and the labouring cattle may be seen to kneel, on this morning, in memory of the cattle in the manger, and the sheep to walk in procession, in commemoration of the glad tidings to the shepherds.

Howison, in his 'Sketches of Upper Canada,' mentions an interesting incident of his meeting an Indian at midnight, on Christmas Eve, during a beautiful moonlight, cautiously creeping along, and beckoning him to silence, who, in answer to his inquiries, said, "Me watch to see the deer kneel; this is Christmas night, and all the deer fall upon their knees to the Great Spirit, and look up."

In our notice of Christmas wines, we must not omit malt-wine or ale, which may be considered, indeed, as our national beverage.

> "The nut-brown ale, the nut-brown ale,
> Puts downe all drinke when it is stale,"

or, as it has been classically rendered, *alum si sit stalum.* The Welsh who are still famous for their ale, had early laws regulating it, while the steward of the king's household had as much of every cask of plain ale as he could reach with his middle finger dipped into it; and as much of every cask of spiced ale as he could reach with the second joint of his middle finger. As millers are remarkable for the peculiarity of their thumbs, no doubt these stewards were gifted with peculiarly long middle fingers. Ale, or beer, was afterwards divided into single beer, or small ale, double beer, doubledouble beer, and dagger ale; there was, also, a choice kind, called March ale; and our early statute books contain several laws regulating the sale of ale, which was to be superintended by an ale-taster, and the terrors of the pillory and cuckingstool held over misdemeanants.

It may be expected that "Christmas broached the mightiest ale," and Christmas ale has, accordingly, been famous from the earliest times.—

" Bryng us in good ale, and bryng us in good ale,
For our blyssd Lady sake, bring us in good ale,"

is a very old wassailing cry, and the wandering musicians always expected a black jack of ale and a Christmas pye. A favourite draught, also, was spiced ale with a toast, stirred up with a sprig of rosemary,—" Mark you, sir, a pot of ale consists of four parts: imprimis, the ale, the toast, the ginger, and the nutmeg." Mead, or metheglin, was another national drink, and here the steward was only allowed as far as he could reach in the cask with the first joint of his middle finger. That metheglin was so called from one Matthew Glinn, who had a large stock of bees that he wished to make profitable, must be considered more as a joke than a tradition.

Henry the Third generally kept his Christmasses with festivities. In 1230, there was a grand one at York, the

King of Scots being present; but four years afterwards he kept it at Gloucester, with only a small company, many of the nobles having left him in consequence of the great favour he was showing foreigners, to their injury. In 1241, he again offended them by placing the Pope's legate, at the great dinner at Westminster Hall, in the place of honour, that is, the middle, he himself sitting on the right-hand, the Archbishop of York (the Archbishop of Canterbury being dead) on his left-hand, and then the prelates and nobles, according to rank. This etiquette, as to place at table, is certainly as old as the Egyptians, and many a wronged or neglected individual's dinner has been spoilt, who has failed in getting such a place above the salt, or at the cross table, as he considered his merits entitled him to.

On one occasion, in his forty-second year, Henry rather took undue advantage of the custom of the season, and being distressed for money, required compulsory New Year's Gifts from the Londoners. His wars frequently distressed him for money, and in 1254, his queen sent him, to Gascoigne, 500 marks from her own revenues, as a New Year's Gift, toward the maintenance of them. In several instances, he kept his Christmasses at the expense of some of the great nobles, as Hubert de Burgh, and Peter, bishop of Winchester, who, in 1232, not only took all the expense upon himself, but gave the king and all his court festive garments; and, in another year, when Alexander, King of Scots, married his daughter Margaret, the Archbishop of York, where the feast was held, gave 600 fat oxen, which were all spent at one meal, and expended 1000 marks besides. This convenient practice saved the pocket of the sovereign, and gratified the ambition of the subject; but the great expense caused by such a favour, must have been something like the costly present of an elephant, by an Eastern despot, to a subject. In his later years, the king laid aside hospitality very much.

The three Edwards kept the feast much as before, and Edward the First is said to have been the first king who kept any solemn feast at Bristol, holding his Christmas there in 1284. In his wardrobe accounts, there are some valuable particulars of the custom of the king at this time. In pursuance of ancient usage, he offered at the high altar, on the Epiphany, one golden florin, frankincense, and myrrh, in commemoration of the offering of the three kings; a custom carried down with some variation to the present day. In the same accounts, some of the New Year's Gifts given to him are mentioned; among them, a large ewer set with pearls all over, with the arms of England, Flanders, and Barr, a present from the countess of Flanders; a comb and looking-glass of silver-gilt enamelled, and a bodkin of silver in a leathern case, from the countess of Barr; also, a pair of large knives of ebony and ivory, with studs of silver enamelled, given by the Lady Margaret, his daughter, duchess of Brabant.

The custom of giving New Year's Gifts existed from the earliest period, and as Warmstry, in his 'Vindication,' says, may be " harmless provocations to Christian love, and mutuall testimonies thereof to good purpose, and never the worse because the heathens have them at the like times." The Romans had their Xenia and Strenæ, during the Saturnalia, which were retained by the Christians, whence came the French term *étrennes*; a very ancient one, for in the old mystery, " Li Gieus de Robin et de Marion," in the thirteenth century, Marion says, she will play, " aux jeux qu'on fait aux étrennes, entour la veille de Noël." The Greek word strenæ, is translated in our New Testament, delicacies; so that, whether delicacies were called strenæ because such gifts were generally of an elegant or graceful nature, or the New Year's Gifts adopted a word previously applied to delicacies, seems immaterial, as the result is the same. These "diabolical New Year's Gifts," as some called them, were denounced by certain of the councils, as early as the beginning of the seventh century, though without effect. They were either in the nature of an offering from an inferior to his superior, who gave something in return, or an interchange of gifts between equals. Tenants were accustomed to give capons to their landlords at this season, and in old leases, a capon, at Christmas, is sometimes reserved as a sort of rent,—

> "Yet must he haunt his greedy landlord's hall,
> With often presents at ech festivall;
> With crammed capons ev'ry New Year's morne."

The practice of New Year's Gifts is of great antiquity in this country. In the twelfth century, Jocelin of Brakelond, when about to make a gift to his abbot, refers to it, as being according to the custom of the English; and, in very early times, the nobility, and persons connected with the court, gave these New Year's Gifts to the monarch, who gave in return presents of money, or of plate, the amount of which in time became quite a matter of regulation; and the messenger, bringing the gift, had, also, a handsome fee given him. How much kindly feeling is caused by the interchange of these gifts, and how much taste and fancy displayed at Fortnum and Mason's, and other places, to tempt us to purchase for the gratification of our younger friends, and receive our reward in the contemplation of their unfeigned pleasure and amusement!

Humorous and witty, as well as elegant, bon-bons and souvenirs, drawing the money from us like so many magnets; as Nasgeorgus says—

> "These giftes the husband gives his wife,
> And father eke the childe,
> And maister on his men bestowes
> The like, with favour milde."

There are some particulars in the wardrobe accounts of the New Year's Gifts of Edward the Second, and also payments made to him to play at dice at Christmas; a custom existing probably long before his time, and certainly continued down to a comparatively recent period, gambling at the groom-porter's having been observed as late as the time of George the Third. He also gave numerous gifts, being, as is well known, of extravagant and luxurious habits. In his eleventh year, especially, at Westminster, several knights received sumptuous presents of plate from him, and the king of the bean (Rex Fabæ) is mentioned as receiving handsome silver-gilt basins and ewers as New Year's Gifts. Two of the kings of the bean named, are, Sir William de la Bech, and Thomas de Weston, squire of the king's household. Edward kept several stately Christmasses, and one at Nottingham in 1324, with particular magnificence, glory, and resort of people. Even when a prisoner at Kenilworth in 1326-7, he kept up a degree of state, although his son, Edward the Third, then aged about sixteen years, was crowned on Christmas Day, 1326, the queen-mother keeping open court, with a great assembly of nobles, prelates, and burgesses, when it was decided to depose the father, whose melancholy fate is well known. Edward the Third became not only a great warrior, but, also, in many respects, a great monarch, and his Christmasses, with other feasts, were held with much splendour. One at Wells, where there were many strange and sumptuous shows made to pleasure the king and his guests, is particularly mentioned; but that at Windsor, in 1343-4, is by far the most distinguished in history, as the king then renewed the Round Table, and instituted the celebrated Order of the Garter, making St. George the patron; whether from the circumstance of the countess of Salisbury having dropped her garter (whence the old Welsh tune took its name of Margaret has lost her garter), cannot now be distinctly proved; but we may as well leave the balance in favour of gallantry. Suffice it, that never has any order of knighthood enrolled such a succession of royal, brave, and world-renowned characters. In 1347 at Guildford, and 1348 at Ottford, in Kent, there were great revellings at Christmas. In the first of these years, there were provided for the amusements of the court, eighty-four tunics of buckram, of divers colours; forty-two visors of different likenesses; twenty-eight crests; fourteen coloured cloaks; fourteen dragons' heads; fourteen white tunics; fourteen heads of peacocks, with wings; fourteen coloured tunics, with peacocks' eyes; fourteen heads of swans, with wings; fourteen coloured tunics of linen; and fourteen tunics, coloured, with stars of gold and silver. In the following year, quadrupeds were in the ascendancy, instead of the feathered creation, and amongst the things mentioned in the wardrobe expenses are, twelve heads of men, surmounted by those of elephants; twelve of men, having heads of lions over them; twelve of men's heads, having bats' wings; and, twelve heads of wodewoses, or wildmen. A good pantomime decorator would have been invaluable in those days. On

New Year's Eve 1358, Edward, with his gallant son, were in a different scene, fighting under the banners of Sir Walter de Mauny before the walls of Calais, which place the French thought had been betrayed to them; but the plot was counteracted, and they were defeated, and many French knights made captives, who were hospitably entertained by the English king on the following day, being New Year's Day.

The mummeries, or disguises, just referred to, were known here as early as the time of Henry the Second, if not sooner, and may have been derived originally from the heathen custom of going about, on the kalends of January, in disguises, as wild beasts and cattle, and the sexes changing apparel. They were not confined to the diversions of the king and his nobles; but a ruder class was in vogue among the inferior orders, where, no doubt, abuses were occasionally introduced in consequence. Even now, our country geese or guise dancers are a remnant of the same custom, and, in some places, a horse's head still accompanies these mummers. The pageants, in former times, of different guilds or trades, some of which still exist, and, at the Lord Mayor's shows, had all probably a common origin, modified by circumstances; but, with respect to those of the city, I must refer to Mr. Fairholt's account, printed for the Percy Society, where he has treated largely on the subject. Who knows how many juvenile citizens may not have been fired by ambition at the sight of these soul-stirring spectacles, to becoming common councilmen, aldermen, sheriffs, and lord-mayors themselves—to have at their beck, the copper-cased knights; the brazen trumpets; the prancing horses, bedecked with streamers; the marshalmen, in martial attire; gilded coach, with the sword of state looking out of window!—and then the charms of the dinner, in all the magnificence of turtle-soup, barons of beef, champagne, venison, and minced pies, with Gog and Magog looking benignly on; though they must miss the times, when the **Lord Mayor's Fool used to jump into a huge bowl of Almayn custard.**

Edward the Third gave and received New Year's Gifts, as former kings; and we find an instance of presents given to Roger Trumpony and his companions, minstrels of the king, in the name of the king of the bean. He also made the usual oblations at the Epiphany.

The continental usages were, in many places, similar to our own; but, as before intimated, they will be but slightly noticed. Charles the Fifth, of France, for instance, in 1377, held the feast of Christmas, or Noël as it was called, at Cambray, "et là, fist ses sérimonies impériaulx, selon l'usage," referring evidently to old customs; he also presented gold, incense, and myrrh, in three gilt cups. Not many years afterwards, the duke of Burgundy gave New Year's Gifts of greater value than any one, and especially to all the nobles and knights of his household, to the value of 15,000 golden florins; but there was probably as much policy in this, as any real regard for the sacred festival.

Richard the Second was young when he came to the throne, extravagant, fond of luxury and magnificence, and the vagaries of fashion in dress were then, and for a long time after, unequalled; his dress, was "all jewels, from jasey to his diamond boots." It is to be expected, therefore, that his Christmasses were kept in splendour, regardless of expense; and this appears to have been the case even to the close of his short and unfortunate reign; as, in 1399, there was a royal Christmas at Westminster, with justings and running at the tilt throughout, and from twenty-six to twenty-eight oxen, with three hundred sheep, and fowls without number, were consumed every day. In the previous Christmas, at Lichfield where the Pope's nuncio and several foreign gentlemen were present, there were spent two hundred tuns of wine, and two thousand oxen, with their appurtenances. It is to be assumed that the pudding was in proportion to the beef; so these, in point of feasting, must have been royal Christmasses indeed.

In the midst of all this grandeur, there was a want of cleanliness and comfort in the rush-strewn floors and imperfectly furnished rooms and tables, that would have been very evident to a modern guest; and the manners at table, even in good society, would rather shock our present fastidious habits. Chaucer, not long previously, in describing the prioresse, who appears to have been a well-bred and educated person for the time, proves the usual slovenliness of the domestic habits, by showing what she avoided—

> "At mete was she wel ytaughte withalle;
> She lette no morsel from hire lippes falle,
> Ne wette hire fingres in hire sauce depe.
> Wel coude she carie a morsel, and wel kepe,
> Thatte no drope ne felle upon hire brest.
> In curtesie was sette ful moche hire lest.
> Hire over lippe wiped she so clene,
> That in hire cuppe was no ferthing sene,
> Of grese, whan she dronken hadde hire draught."

or, according to the Roman de la Rose, from whence Chaucer took this account,—

> "Et si doit si sagement boyre,
> Que sur soy n'en espande goutte."

It must be remembered, however, that there were no forks

in those days. The Boke of Curtasye of the same age, reprobates a practice that is even now scarcely obsolete, and may unexpectedly be seen in company, where it excites surprise, to say the least of it;—

> " Clense not thi tethe at mete sittande,
> With knyfe ne stre, styk ne wande."

Richard also had his pageants, or disguisings, but instead of looking to the brute or feathered creation for models, we find, on one occasion, there is a charge for twenty-one linen coifs for counterfeiting men of the law, in the king's play or diversion at Christmas, 1389. If the men of the law had been as plentiful as at present, there would have been no need of making any counterfeits, where a sufficient quantity of real ones might have been procured so cheap. The unfortunate Richard was murdered on Twelfth Day, 1400, a sad finish to all his Christmasses. At the same time, a plan was laid by the earls of Kent and Huntingdon (recently degraded from the dukedoms of Exeter and Surrey), with the earl of Salisbury and others, to gain access, under colour of a Christmas mumming, at Windsor, where Henry the Fourth and the princes were keeping the feast, and thus effect the restoration of Richard; but one of the conspirators, the earl of Rutland (degraded from duke of Aumarle), gave timely notice of it, in order, as it is said, to forestal his father, the duke of York, who had got some knowledge of the plot. Henry the Fourth kept his Christmas feasts in the usual style, and does not require any particular notice, which might tend to needless repetition.

CHAPTER III.

 HE wild course of Henry the Fifth, while Prince of Wales, and his brilliant but short career as king, are well known, and are immortalised by Shakespeare;—

" Never was such a sudden scholar made :
Never came reformation in a flood,
With such a heady current, scouring faults ;"

his historical plays have probably supplied many with their principal knowledge of the early annals of our country, from King Lear downwards; and we must not quarrel with the dramatic fate of Cordelia, although her real story was more prosperous, as we have, consequently, some of the most pathetic passages in the works of our immortal bard—that is, if such bard there ever was; for the overbearing mass of intellect, imagination, and beauty, presented to us under the name of Shakespeare, is such, that one almost considers the name a myth, and decides that, at least, the Seven Sages must have been engaged in its production. When his warlike avocations allowed him Henry the Fifth kept the feast with splendour; but his reign was nearly brought to a close at its outset, if we are to believe those historians who state that, when he was keeping the Christmas of 1413-14, at Eltham, there was a plot for seizing him and his three brothers, and the principal clergy, and killing them. As this plot was, however, attributed to the Lollards, some of whom were taken and executed, and rewards offered for Sir John Oldcastle, Lord Cobham, imputing thereby the attempts to him, the account must be taken with considerable allowance.

Even in the midst of the horrors of war Henry did not forget the Christian mercies of this tide; for during the siege of Rouen in his sixth year, and that city being in great extremity from hunger, he ceased hostilities on Christmas Day, and gave food to all his famishing enemies who would accept of it.

"Alle thay to have mete and drynke therto,
And, again, save condyte to come and to go."

Something like this occurred, in 1428, at the siege of Orleans, " where the solemnities and festivities of Christmas gave a short interval of repose: the English lords requested of the French commanders, that they might have a night of minstrelsy with trumpets and clarions. They borrowed these musicians and instruments from the French, and Dunois and Suffolk also exchanged gifts. In his eighth year, Henry, with his queen, the "most fair" Katherine, sojourned at Paris during the feast, and "kept such solemn estate, so plentiful a house, so princely pastime, and gave so many gifts, that from all parts of France, noblemen and others resorted to his palace, to see his estate, and do him honour." This was a stroke of policy to ingratiate himself with the French, and the French king at the same time kept his Christmas quietly.

Henry the Sixth, for the first few years of his troubled reign, was a mere child; though, in the tenth year of his reign, and the same of his age, having just previously received the homage of the French and Norman nobles at Paris, he celebrated the Feast with great solemnity at Rouen; a place where, not long after, some of those in high places of our country were to disgrace themselves by the cruel punishment of Joan of Arc. He seems afterwards to have kept his Christmas in the usual manner, until the disastrous wars of York and Lancaster, during which the fate of the monarch,—and, indeed, who, for the time being, was such monarch—depended on the predominance of the white or red rose.

There are several instances recorded of New Year's Gifts, or Christmas Boxes, given to and by him when a boy; amongst others, to his mother Queen Katherine; to Queen Jane, widow of Henry the Fourth; and, to the Cardinal of England; being tablets of gold, ornamented with precious stones. On one occasion he gave his mother a ruby, set in a ring of gold, that the duke of Bedford had given him at a previous Christmas. At another time he gave his mother a tablet of gold, with a crucifix garnished with sapphires and pearls, weighing about fourteen ounces of gold, which was bought of John Patteslee, goldsmith, for forty pounds. The usual payment to the heralds for their largess seems to have been a hundred shillings. A small quarto book, with rich illuminations, given to Henry by the abbot of Edmundsbury, is now in the British Museum. The kings of arms and heralds were accustomed, in preceding reigns, to have their livery out of the great wardrobe, at Christmas, like other squires of the court; but the practice having apparently got into disuse during the boyhood of Henry, they petitioned, in the eighteenth year of his reign, to have them again, which was granted, and they again were decorated as at present, like gilded court cards.

In 1428, a sum of four pounds was given to Jakke Travaill and companions, for making divers plays and interludes before the king, at Christmas.

Plays and interludes, with disguisings and mummings, were of very ancient date, and derived, like many other things, from the heathens. As early as 408 stage plays and spectacles were forbidden by the Concilium Africanum, on the Lord's day, and other solemn Christian festivals, and by several subsequent councils, whose orders seem to have been but little attended to, showing how deep-rooted was the attachment to these shows. The early secular plays, principally performed by strolling minstrels, were frequently of a comic nature, but of a gross character, and accompanied by music, dancing, and mimicry. About the twelfth century the ecclesiastics introduced miracle-plays and scripture-histories, to counteract the secular plays, and these became common in the time of Henry the Second; the miracle-play of St. Katherine was acted at Dunstaple early in the twelfth century. London became famous for them, and in some places different trade-guilds produced each their separate play or mystery, as we find in the case of the Chester and Coventry Mysteries, and others. It was found expedient in these to introduce some comic passages, to relieve the length of the performances, and attract the notice of the audience, who probably paid on the voluntary system, as each thought proper. Thus, in the 'Chester Mysteries,' about the fourteenth century, Noah's wife refuses to go into the ark, without her gossips, every one, and swears by Christ and by Saint John; and when she is at last forced in, she salutes Noah with a hearty box on the ear. In the Cornish Mystery of the 'Creation of the World,' by Jordan, which is, however, nearly three centuries later in date, the lady is much more civil, and is very careful to collect her property, like a thrifty housewife, because "they cost store of money." In the 'Secunda Pastorum' of the Towneley Mysteries, which are said to be about a century later than those of Chester, Mak, the buffoon of the piece, steals a sheep from the Shepherds, while they are asleep, and takes it home to his wife, who puts it into the cradle, endeavouring to make it pass for a child, and praying that if ever she beguiled the Shepherds, who have come in search of it, she may eat the child lying there. The trick, however, is discovered, one of the Shepherds, going to kiss the child, finds the long snout. A similar story is told of Archie Armstrong, the jester, in the seventeenth century, excepting that his fraud was not discovered. In the 'Slaughter of the Innocents,' a cowardly character, called Watkyn, requests Herod to knight him, that he may be properly qualified to assist; he is nevertheless well beaten by the women, and goes to complain accordingly.

These Mysteries abound in anachronisms: Pharaoh in his pursuit of the Israelites, when in fear of drowning, recommends his people to lift up their hearts to Mahownde, or Mahomet; Herod constantly swears by him, sometimes even calling him St. Mahomed, as the Sicilian peasants swear by *Santu Diavolu*, and promises to make one of his counsellors Pope, by way of reward; Noah's wife swears by Mary; Caiaphas sings mass; and the Shepherds are acquainted with the fools of Gotham; but as individuals of this class are of a very ancient, as well as lasting, breed, the statement may be correct, if applied to some Gotham in Palestine. In the 'Mactatio Abel,' of the same collection, Cain is made to speak in the rudest dialect of West York, using the vulgarest phrases, with gross buffoonery.

The pilgrims and crusaders, on their return from the East, introduced other subjects, and the frequent use of the name of Mahomed or Mahomet may have some connection with them. The Christmas play of St. George and the Dragon—

"St. George! that swindg'd the dragon, and e'er since
Sits on his horseback, at mine hostess' door,"—

with the King of Egypt, and fair Sabra, his daughter, still extant in some parts of the country, may have the same origin. It is evidently of great antiquity; and the fact of its being performed in similar manner in the extreme northern and western parts of the country, a considerable part indeed being nearly identical, tends to prove this. "St. George!" was the old battle cry of the English, or "Sand Jors!" as an old German poem, of the fourteenth century, on the battle of Poictiers, calls it.

After the introduction of miracle-plays and mysteries, if there was a deficiency at any time of ecclesiastical performers, the clergy took secular players to assist them; and besides the fraternities and guilds, as before mentioned, some of the public schools also claimed an exclusive privilege of performing plays at particular times and places; the scholar of Paul's School, indeed, applied to Richard the Second to prohibit inexperienced persons from presenting the 'History of the Old Testament,' which the clergy had been at great expense to represent publicly at Christmas. The parish-clerks were also famed for their representations, which seem frequently to have taken place at Clerkenwell, and occasionally lasted for several days. One is mentioned by Stow, in 1409, at Skinner's Well, near Clerkenwell, which lasted eight days, commencing from the Creation of the World; which was indeed the favourite beginning, if we may judge from the sets of mysteries still extant; the authors thinking that date sufficiently remote: unlike some pedigree hunters, who some way down their ornamented tree, place a note, stating that about this time the world began; or the Chinese picture of the Creation, which has, in a corner, a Chinese mandarin looking on through a telescope. About the middle of the fifteenth century, moralities, or morals, appear to have been introduced, consisting of allegorical personifications, and with them the Vice with his dagger of lath and fool's coat. The scripture-plays were not, however, immediately abandoned, and may be met with, though perhaps in the shape of a puppet-show, as late certainly as the time of Queen Anne, when at Heatley's Booth, at Bartholomew Fair, might be seen the old Creation of the World, newly revived, commencing with the Creation of Adam and Eve, and finishing with rich Dives in Hell, and Lazarus in Abraham's bosom. The French had representations similar to those of the English, at least as early in date; and, in 1313, Philippe-le-Bel exhibited, on the occasion of conferring knighthood on his children, the following spectacles:—'Adam et Eve;' 'Les Trois Rois;' 'Le Meurte des Innocens;' N.S. riant avec Sa Mère, et mangeant des pommes; Hérode et Caiphe en mitre, &c. In France, and in Spain, where they had their Autos Sacramentales, as they called these mysteries, from an equally early date, these performances have been continued to modern times among the country people, and most of their collections of carols contain two or three short mysteries. The plays exhibited at court, during the Christmas, were probably different from those of the clergy, and more in the nature of mummeries, or disguisings, with pageants, until the time of Queen Elizabeth, when the regular drama was performed before her, a practice which has been renewed in the elegant Christmas festivities of our present Queen.

After Edward the Fourth became the undisputed king of this country, he resumed the custom of keeping Christmas with pomp, wearing his crown, and keeping his estate, and making presents to his household; but the parliament nevertheless, in 1465, thought it necessary to pass one of those useless acts against excess in dress, forbidding cloth of gold, and shoes with pikes more than two inches long, to any under a lord. In 1461, also, all diceing, or playing at cards, was prohibited except at Christmas. Cards forming then, as since, an essential part, in many places, of the Christmas amusements. Among the Christmas gifts, during this reign, several were given to players and minstrels. Margery Paston, in a letter to her husband John Paston, 24th Dec., 1484, says that his eldest son had gone to Lady Morley to know how the Christmas next after her husband's death was kept, and that there were no disguisings, nor harping, nor luting, nor singing, nor loud disports; but playing at the tables, and chess, and cards.

Richard the Third's reign was too short and turbulent to give much opportunity for festivities, but he nevertheless kept two or three Christmasses in state, and particularly in 1484, at Westminster, when he wore his crown at a royal banquet on the Epiphany, clad in rich attire, of which he was fond; and it was observed that the princess Elizabeth was dressed in splendid robes of the same form and colour as those of the queen, whence inferences were drawn that he wished to get rid of the queen, either by death or divorce. Yet even now we hardly know the real character of Richard, and whether there were not some lights to relieve the dark shade: ambitious he was, and unscrupulous, but eloquent, and brave or bold; and perhaps, after all, his hump was only a high-shoulder. The old Countess of Desmond, who danced with him in her youth, describes him as a handsome man, somewhat dazzled probably by dancing with royalty. Shakespeare has rather treated him like a mad dog, and given him a bad name.

With Henry the Seventh commenced that series of splendid Christmasses which lasted, with little interruption, until the time of the civil wars, and were especially magnificent in the first half of the reign of Henry the Eighth, and of which historians have left us such particulars, that we can fancy ourselves present at them. In Christmas, 1489, however, the measles were prevalent, and proved fatal to several ladies and gentlewomen, and there were no disguisings, and but few plays, though there was an abbot of Misrule, who "made much sport and did right well his office;" the ambassadors of Spain dined at the king's board on Twelfth Day, and the officers of arms had their largess, as they were accustomed. In the following year, to make up for it, there was a goodly disguising on New Year's Night, and many plays during the Christmas. There are some household books of this king still extant at the Chapter-House, which contain many particulars of the payments for the Christmas diversions. Among these there are numerous gifts to different sets of players; dramatic performances, such as they were, being frequent in this reign; but the payments are somewhat of the smallest, varying from ten shillings to £2. 13s. 4d. for each set of players, excepting on occasions when some of the gentlemen of his chapel played before him, who received as much as £6. 13s. 4d. for their services, which sum appears also to have been the usual reward for the lord of Misrule. It is probable, however, that the players had rewards from other people besides the king, and that when the cap was handed round a handsome collection was frequently made. On one occasion no less than £12. was given to a little maiden that danced: now, considering how careful Henry was of his money, and comparing her reward to that of the players, we must presume her to have been the Taglioni of her day. The payments by the nobles were frequently small; in Lord Howard's account there is one of 3s. 4d. to four players.

Besides the plays, there were disguisings and banquets; and Walter Alwyn and Jakes Haute had, at different Christmasses, each £20 and upwards, for the disguisings or revels. In 1493, on Twelfth Night, there was a great banquet and wassail, and a pageant of Saint George with a castle; and twelve lords, knights, and esquires, with twelve ladies, danced after the wassail. Henry the Eighth at this time was but a fat-cheeked child, so could scarcely reckon his taste for this sort of amusement—in which he afterwards so much delighted—from so early a date, but had plenty of opportunities subsequently of maturing it. On Twelfth Day the king made the accustomed offerings of gold, myrrh, and frankincense: the dean of the chapel sent to the Archbishop of Canterbury the offering by a clerk or priest, who was to have the next benefice in the gift of the archbishop. The king was to wear his crown and his royal robes, kirtle, surcoat, furred hood, and mantle, with long train, and his sword before him; his armills of gold set with rich stones on his arms, and his sceptre in his right hand.

The wassail was introduced in the evening with great ceremony: the steward, treasurer, and comptroller of the household went for it with their staves of office; the king's and the queen's sewers, having fair towels round their necks, and dishes in their hands, such as the king and queen should eat of; the king's and queen's carvers following in like manner. Then came in the ushers of the chamber, with the pile of cups—the king's, the queen's, and the bishop's—with the butlers and wine, to the cupboard, or sideboard as we should now call it; and squires of the body to bear them. The gentlemen of the chapel stood at one end of the hall, and when the steward came in with the wassail, he was to cry out three times, "Wassail, wassail, wassail!" to which they answered with a good song—no doubt a wassail song or a carol, as they were prevalent at this time.

The terms wassail and wassailing are, as before mentioned, of very early date. Mr. Hunter, in his interesting essay on Robin Hood, notices a payment of a hundred shillings made, in the time of Edward the Second, to Isabelle del Holde and Alisoun Conand, damsels of the queen, for crying Noël and Wessel. They were not, however, absolutely confined to

Christmas, but were used to indicate any convivial and festive meetings :—

> "The king doth wake to-night, and takes his rouse,
> Keeps wassel."

The meetings indeed were themselves called after them—

> "He is wit's peddler, and retails his wares
> At wakes and wassels, meetings, markets, fairs."

One of the earliest wassail songs is that introduced by Dissimulation, disguised as a religious person, in Bale's old play of Kynge Johan, about the middle of the sixteenth century. He brings in the cup by which the king is poisoned, stating that it "passith malmesaye, capryck, tyre, or ypocras," and then sings—

> "Wassayle, wassayle out of the mylke payle,
> Wassayle, wassayle as white as my nayle,
> Wassayle, wassayle in snowe, froste, and hayle,
> Wassayle, wassayle with partriche and rayle,
> Wassayle, wassayle that muche doth avayle,
> Wassayle, wassayle that never wylle fayle."

In Caxton's Chronicle the account of the death of King John represents the cup to have been filled with good ale; and the monk bearing it, knelt down, saying, "Syr, wassayll for euer the dayes so all lyf dronke ye of so good a cuppe."

The loving-cup, at city and other feasts, may be considered as an offshoot of the wassail-bowl, drinc-heil being converted into drink-all. In after times the term became applied almost exclusively to Christmas, perhaps from wassailing being more common at that period, and there was a custom in many places of carrying the bowl round, generally by young women, from door to door, with an appropriate song, the bearer expecting a small gift in return. Selden, in his 'Table Talk,' alluding to this custom, says, "The Pope, in sending relics to princes, does as wenches do by their wassails at New Year's tide, they present you with a cup, and you must drink of a slabby stuff; but the meaning is, you must give them moneys ten times more than it is worth."

The days generally chosen for the wassail bowl were Christmas Eve, New Year's Eve or Twelfth Night, which in some places was called Wassail eve. Machyn, in his Diary, mentions his being at supper at Mrs. Lentall's, at Henley-on-Thames, on Twelfth Eve, 1556, when there came in "xij wessells with maydens syngyng with their wessells, and after cam the cheyff wyffes syngyng with their wessells; and the gentyll-woman had hordenyd a grett tabull of bankett, dyssys of spyssys and frut, as marmelad, gynbred, gele, comfett, suger plat, and dyver odur." Master Machyn is somewhat arbitrary in his spelling, even allowing for the eccentricities in this art at the time in which he wrote.

In the seventeenth century the wassail bowl was carried round to the houses of the gentry and others, the bearers expecting a gratuity:—

> "Good dame, here at your door
>   Our wassel we begin;
> We are all maidens poor,
>   We pray now let us in
>   With our wassel.
>
> Our wassel we do fill
>   With apples and with spice,
> Then grant us your good will
>   To taste here once or twice
>   Of our good wassel."

The custom is still partially extant. Many great houses had, and no doubt still have, wassail bowls of massive silver. Wassail, in Ben Jonson's mask of Christmas, is described as a neat sempster and songster; her page bearing a brown bowl, dressed with ribbons and rosemary, before her.

The practice of introducing the bowl is still retained in Christmas meetings, though the component parts are generally ale, sugar, nutmeg, and a toast, omitting the roasted apples, which are necessary to constitute genuine lamb's wool; "lay a crab in the fire to roast for lamb's wool;" in olden times indeed the apple was almost an inseparable ingredient.—

> " . . . . sometimes lurk I in a gossip's bowl,
> In very likeness of a roasted crab;
> And, when she drinks, against her lips I bob,
> And on her wither'd dew-lap pour the ale."

There are several old wassail songs still existing, as well as some that bear a more modern stamp. In Devonshire, and elsewhere, it is an old custom to wassail the apple and pear trees, by pouring out a libation at the foot, in order that they may bear the better.

> " Wassaile the trees, that they may beare
> You many a plumb, and many a peare;
> For more or less fruits they will bring,
> As you doe give them wassailing."

From what we read of the character of Henry the Seventh, we cannot fancy him entering into these amusements with unrestrained hilarity, but to have treated them as part of the state ceremonies, counting the necessary cost with reluctance. All the forms to be adopted for each day were laid down in exact manner, and no doubt the time and quantity of smiles and laughter were properly regulated. Even his jokes were somewhat of a severe practical kind; he once asked an astrologer if he knew where he, the astrologer, should pass his Christmas, and on his professing his ignorance, told him that he was then the most skilled of the two, as he knew the astrologer would pass it in the Tower, and sent him there accordingly, and then we may suppose ate his Christmas dinner with much self-satisfaction. The custom of giving Christmas-boxes and New Year's Gifts, seems now to have been organised into a regular system; there was a graduated scale for giving and receiving, according to the rank of the parties, and the amount was as well ascertained as the *quiddam honorarium* to a barrister or a physician.

At New Year's Day in the morning, an usher of the chamber came to the door of the king's chamber, and said, "There is a New Year's Gift come from the queen," to which the king answered, "Sir, let it come in;" the usher with the gift was then admitted, and afterwards the ushers with gifts from the nobles, according to their rank, and these messengers had rewards given them, from ten marks to the queen's messenger, if a knight, down to forty shillings to an earl and countess's servant. The queen received gifts in the same manner, though of less value. The king was on this day to wear his kirtle, his surcoat, and his pane of arms, with his hat of estate, and his sword borne before him. No doubt an accurate list was kept of those expected to give their New Year's Gifts, and as their messengers arrived they were marked off; or, if they failed in their duty, were looked on with suspicion and ill will. In one year he gave away as much as £120 in New Year's Gifts, but this was probably in return for presents of much larger amount, or in reward to those bringing gifts; the whole must have been a sadly formal proceeding, and more to the glorification of man than any other purpose.

On Christmas Day and the other feast days, the queen made her offerings, amounting generally to five shillings in each case, and also gave away money in alms, charges being made for sixty shillings for this purpose on New Year's Eve. She also gave numerous sums at Christmas, in gifts; as, to the grooms and pages of the household £20; to the lord of Misrule 20s.; to my lord privy seal's fool 3s. 4d.

Cards were much used, as in former times, and sums of a hundred shillings are charged for the queen's "disporte at cardes." The lord, or abbot, of Misrule, as he was indiscriminately called, was now an important officer, and an essential accompaniment to the Christmas revels; payments are frequently made to him, generally of ten marks or £6. 13s. 4d. Under these or some other similar names this personage existed from very early times, not only at court, but in the houses of the nobility, of the lord-mayor and sheriffs, in the Inns of Court, and at the different colleges; he is even mentioned in the original draft of statutes, of Trinity College, Cambridge, in 1546, soon after which time he appears to have reached the summit of his magnificence. Many of the nobility kept the feast with great splendour, and probably during the time of Henry the Seventh, exceeded even the court in this respect. They had their own players, minstrels, and waits, and officers of their household, in imitation of the royal establishment; having among their retainers many gentlemen and frequently some knights.

Edward Stafford, duke of Buckingham, gave some princely entertainments during this reign; on the Epiphany, 1508, he had 459, to dinner, of different degrees, including 134 gentry, with two minstrels, six trumpets, four waits, and four players. The supply of provisions was fully commensurate with the demand, but it would not afford much interest to give it in detail; as unusual dishes now, may be mentioned a salt sturgeon, three swans, two peacocks, two herons, four dog fish, and half a fresh conger; oysters were probably scarce, as only 200 are mentioned, valued at 4d.; the wines were Gascony, Malvoisy, Rhenish, and Ossey, besides 259 flaggons (gallons) and one quart of ale; there were also two gallons of furmity, a dish which has continued in use to the present time. On the previous Christmas Day, the guests being fewer in number, the consumption of ale was only 171 flaggons and one quart, of which seventeen flaggons and three quarts were for breakfast; but this was not far from the time when the maids of honour had a chet loaf, a manchet, a gallon of ale, and a chine of beef for breakfast,

Swans were standard dishes formerly at great houses at Christmas, and other great festivals; Chaucer's monk, no doubt a good judge,

"A fat swan loved he best of any rost."

In the Northumberland Household Book, five are directed for Christmas Day, three for New Year's Day, and four for Twelfth Day. Except in the state of a cygnet, and that rarely, the bird now is not met with at table.

The humbler classes of society also had their rejoicings at this tide, and were allowed certain privileges and facilities for the purpose, the restrictions under which artificers, labourers, and servants were placed as to not playing at cards and certain other games being suspended during Christmas, when there was, among other sports, playing at cards for counters, nails, and points, in every house; but, as Stow says, more for pastime than for gain. The holidays, according to this annalist, extended from All-Hallows Evening to the day after Candlemas Day, and there was a penalty attached to any householder allowing such games, except during this time. Dramatic performances were exhibited at the houses of the great and wealthy, where the tenants and peasantry were allowed access, and cheered with good Christmas hospitality; carol singing was encouraged, and it is not improbable that some of our modern carols may be connected with this age, though somewhat modified.

CHAPTER IV.

HEN Henry the Eighth came to the throne the festivities at Christmas, as well as those at other seasons, were kept with great splendour. He was then young, of manly address, and tall handsome person, skilled in martial exercises, of great bodily strength and activity, and accomplished; fond of exhibiting his prowess; and, though naturally overbearing, possessed some chivalrous qualities in the early part of his reign, until freed from the advice of Wolsey, and spoiled by flattery and adulation, and the unrestrained indulgence of his passions; for, as the cardinal said of him in his dying state, "he is a prince of most royal courage; rather than miss any part of his will, he

will endanger one half of his kingdom." Had he not been so unfortunate as to rule in what was then a despotic monarchy, he might have passed through life as an impetuous, convivial, somewhat overbearing person, rather keeping his family in fear, but not much worse than characters we all now and then meet with in society, who bully their wives, children, servants, and clerks, bluster at committee meetings, and are somewhat troublesome members of clubs. As the case was, however, he presents a memorable example of the effects of uncontrolled selfishness, pride, and passion.

Plays, masques, pageants, and similar diversions were frequent and splendid during this reign, or rather during the first half of it; for after Henry became interested in the reformed religion, and encumbered with the succession of his wives, and also grew unwieldy in shape, and unfitted for personally partaking in their amusements, they gradually fell off, both in magnificence and in frequency, till they nearly ceased altogether. In his younger days he was generally a performer, and a skilful one, in those pastimes; and numerous entries may be found of payments of every description connected with Christmas—such as for disguisings, lord of Misrule, New Year's gifts, Christmas-boxes, &c. In his first year he kept it at Richmond with great royalty, and although there had not been time to arrange such a pageant or masque as we shall find in after-times, yet the lord of Misrule, whose payment, in the time of Henry the Seventh, never exceeded £6 13s. 4d., was paid £8 6s. 8d., which was afterwards increased to £15 6s. 8d. The lord of Misrule, in the first and several of the following years, was William Wynnesberry, who also appears in his father's reign: other persons named in this office are, Richard Pole, Edmund Travore, and William Tolly.

Sir Walter Scott gives a humorous account (except to the sufferer) of the ill usage of an apparitor, or macer, of the see of St. Andrew, in 1547. He was sent with letters of excommunication against Lord Borthwick, and, unluckily for him, chose the time when the inmates of his castle were engaged in the revels of the Abbot of Unreason, as this festive ruler was called in Scotland. The unfortunate apparitor was of course looked on as an alien enemy, or an outlaw, or any other terrible thing, and was immediately seized and well ducked; after which he was compelled to eat the parchment letters of excommunication, which had been previously steeped in a bowl of wine, and then to drink off the wine. In the play of Sir John Oldcastle, a similar incident is introduced, but the sumner of the Bishop of Rochester, who is the sufferer there, and has to eat the waxen seal also, is told that "tough wax is the purest of the honey."

In 1545, Sir Thomas Cawarden, who died 1560, was appointed master of the revels. In the same year payments were made to Robert Amadas, for plate of gold stuff for the disguising, of £151 12s. 2d.; and to William Buttry, for silk for the same purpose, of £133 7s. 5d.; so that, taking the difference of value of money into account, Henry began his reign with a determination to spare no expense in his entertainments, and subsequently the charges were much increased. In his second year the Christmas was kept at Richmond, and on the Twelfth Day we have a specimen of the pageants afterwards so much in fashion, though rather wild perhaps for our present tastes. This was devised like a mountain, glittering, as if with gold, and set with stones, on the top of which was a tree of gold, spreading out on every side with roses and pomegranates; it was brought towards the king, when out came a lady, dressed in cloth of gold, and the henchmen, or children of honour, who were dressed in some disguise, and they danced a morris before the king; after which they re-entered the mountain, which was drawn back, and then the wassail or banquet was brought in, and so ended the Christmas. These pageants must have been managed something like the pantomime or melo-dramatic devices we see on our own stage, and produced perhaps as much effect, taking into account the increase of modern fancy and expectation in this respect.

In his third year, at Greenwich, there was a magnificent Christmas, with such abundance of viands for all comers of any honest behaviour, as had been seldom seen; and the invention of the devisers of pageants was taxed to the utmost, and dancing-masters were doubtless in request for the rehearsals; the clever Mr. Flexmore would have been invaluable. On New Year's Night, there was erected in the hall, a castle, with gates, towers, and dungeon, garnished with artillery, and other warlike weapons of the most approved form; and in the front of it was written its name, "*Le Fortresse dangerus*," that is evidently, dangerous from the ladies' eyes, and not from the warlike preparations. For in this castle were six fair ladies, no doubt selected for their grace and beauty, all clothed in russet satin, laid over with leaves of gold, and each hood knit with laces of blue silk and gold; and coifs and caps of gold on their heads. From the abundance of gold on these occasions, we could almost imagine that some "diggins" must have been known then. Well, after this castle, with the golden damsels in it, had been drawn about the hall, and the queen had seen it, (for Henry really was attached to her for the first few years of his reign,) in came the king with five select companions, dressed in coats,

of which half was of velvet satin, with spangles of gold, the other half of rich cloth of gold, having on their heads caps of russet satin, embroidered with fine gold bullion. These gallant knights vigorously assaulted the castle, and the ladies seeing them so courageous, capitulated with them, and yielded it up, after which they came down and danced together for some time, when the ladies in their turn became the conquerors, and took the knights into the castle, which suddenly vanished out of sight; by which we must assume, not that they all vanished into the air, but that they were drawn out of the hall as fast as the living, and probably concealed machinery used for the purpose, could make away with them. The sports of this Christmas, however, were not yet at an end; for on the night of the Epiphany, the king and eleven chosen companions were disguised after the manner of Italy, called a mask, a thing not before seen in England; they were dressed in long and broad garments, wrought with gold, and had visors and caps of gold; and after the banquet they came in with six gentlemen, disguised in silk, bearing staff torches, and desired the ladies to dance. Some of them were content to do so, but others that knew the fashion of it refused, because it was a thing not commonly seen, something like the hesitation shown when the waltz, the polka, and other strange matters, were first introduced here, the passion for which, after a little time, made up for the shyness with which they were at first admitted into good society.

These pageants must have been gorgeous affairs, as far as dress and decorations, but would hardly suit the present taste; the descriptions here given will enable any one inclined (if any) to imitate them.

In the following year the Christmas was again kept at

Greenwich, and on Twelfth Day a mount was introduced, ornamented with flowers of silk, and full of slips of broom, signifying Plantagenet; the branches being made of green satin, and the flowers of flat gold of Damascus. On the top was a goodly beacon giving light, round which sat the king and five others, dressed in coats and caps of crimson velvet, spangled and embroidered with gold. Four wodehouses (or wild men) drew the mount towards the queen, and then the king and his companions descended and danced; the mount then suddenly opened, and out came six ladies, dressed in crimson satin, embroidered with gold and pearls, and with French hoods on their heads, and they danced by themselves for a time; after which the lords and ladies danced together; the ladies then re-entered the mount, which was conveyed out of the hall, and then there was a very sumptuous banquet.

These French hoods were probably a new fashion, and as fashions travelled into the country but slow in those times, when there were neither electric telegraphs, railroads, stage-coaches, newspapers, magazines, nor penny, nor, indeed, any other postage, they do not seem to have got into Cornwall much before the year 1550; for the wife of one of the prisoners condemned to suffer for the riot at that time, intending to go to beg his life, took so long to adjust her new French hood to her taste, that her husband was hung before she arrived. It is to be hoped that she was not taking this course of revenging Henry's injuries to the sex.

In the fifth year of this reign, Sir Harry Guildford, master of the revels, immortalised his name by inventing an interlude, in which was a moresco dance of six persons and two ladies.

In the sixth year, there was another grand Christmas; and on Twelfth Night the pageant may be considered as a ballet of action, differing from some of modern times, simply in this: that in ours professing to mean something, the meaning cannot be discovered, while in these there was no meaning at all. On New Year's Night the king and the Duke of Suffolk, his chivalrous brother-in-law, with two others, dressed in mantles, hose, doublets, and coats of cloth of silver, lined with blue velvet, the silver being pounsed, so that the velvet might be seen through, led in four ladies in gowns, after the fashion of Savoy, of blue velvet, lined with cloth of gold; and mantles like tippets, knit together of silver; with bonnets of burnished gold. They were accompanied by four torch-bearers, in white and blue satin. The fanciful attire of the party pleased much, especially the queen, into whose chamber they went and danced, after which they put off their visors, and made themselves known, when the queen heartily thanked the king for her goodly pastime, and kissed him; finding it necessary, in these early times, probably to flatter his vanity, and keep him in good humour.

On Twelfth Night we have the ballet, though what we should call now of limited interest. The king and the queen came into the hall at Greenwich, where this Christmas was kept, when suddenly a tent of cloth of gold entered; before it stood four men-at-arms, armed at all points, with swords in their hands, then, at the sound of trumpets, four more came in, and a fierce, but bloodless, combat ensued, of four to four; but before the victory could be awarded to either party, suddenly (again) there came out of a place like a wood, eight wild men, with ugly weapons and terrible visages, dressed in green moss made of silk, green moss being the assumed substance of which wild men make their apparel. These attacked the knights, but after a terrific combat of eight to eight, were driven out of the hall by the knights, who followed them. After these warlike representations the tent opened, and six ladies and six lords, richly apparelled, came out and danced; after which they again entered the tent, which was conveyed out of the hall; and then the king and queen were served with a right sumptuous banquet, which, indeed, formed an essential part of every entertainment.

There were payments made this Christmas to Leonard Friscobald of £247 12s. 7d., for velvets and silks for the disguising; and to Richard Gybson, for certain apparel for the same, of £137 14s. 0½d.; and, in after years, we find other similar payments to this Gybson; so that trade benefited by these amusements, which is a natural consequence.

In his seventh year Henry kept his Christmas at Eltham; and in the fine old hall there, on Twelfth Night, a castle was introduced, having in it ladies and knights dressed in braids of gold, with moving spangles, silver and gilt, set in crimson satin, and not fastened; the ladies' heads and bodies being after the fashion of Amsterdam. This castle was attacked by certain vagrant knights, who were, however, repulsed after a severe struggle. Dancing then of course took place; and afterwards a banquet of 200 dishes, with great plenty to everybody.

In his eighth year, there was a grand Christmas at Greenwich; and on Twelfth Night, the Queen of Scots also being a visitor, an artificial garden was set up, called the Garden of Espérance. This had towers at each corner, and was surmounted with gilt rails, and the banks were all set with artificial flowers of silk and gold, the leaves being of green satin, "so that they seemed very flowers." In the middle was a pillar of antique work, all gold, and set with pearls and stones, and on the top an arch crowned with gold, within which stood a bush of red and white roses of silk and gold, and a bush of pomegranates of like materials. Of course there were knights and ladies, richly apparelled, walking in this garden; there were indeed six of each, who came down and danced, and were afterwards conveyed out of the hall in the garden, and the entertainments concluded as usual with a great banquet. Our friend Richard Gybson had £130 19s. 0½d. for divers things bought by him for this disguising.

In the following year, in consequence of the prevalence of the sweating sickness from July to December, there was no solemn Christmas kept at Court; but in several following years it was kept much as before, and it will be needless to multiply examples, especially as the pageants were in general of a less marked description.

As, in nearly every year, there were payments made to sets of players, the highest being in general £4 to the king's old players, who are distinguished from the king's players, whose fee was usually but £3 6s. 8d., it seems that during the Christmas, on what may be called the off-nights, there were some performances by them. The children also of the king's chapel gave their assistance, but their services were estimated higher, as there are several payments of £6 13s. 4d. to Mr. Cornish, for playing before the king with them.

In his tenth year, also, the gentlemen of the king's chapel had £13 6s. 8d. for their good attendance in Christmas, and there are similar charges in subsequent years.

In the eleventh year there was another mask, and Richard Gybson received £207 5s. 1½d. for the revels called "a maskelyn at New Hall, or Beaulieu, in Essex.

In the fourteenth year the Christmas was kept at Eltham, where the Cardinal made many reformations in the royal household, and all that had no masters were sent away; in modern phrase, no followers were allowed.

In the sixteenth year there were grand feats of arms, and an assault made on a strong artificial fort at Greenwich, where the king and the Duke of Suffolk distinguished themselves; the whole concluding with masks and dancing.

In his seventeenth year—in consequence of the prevalence of the plague according to historians, and partly perhaps because he was now maturing his plans for the possession of Ann Boleyn (who would not yield to him, as her sister Mary had done), and for the divorce of Queen Catherine, though not effected until long afterwards—the king kept his Christmas quietly at Eltham, whence it was called the still Christmas. Wolsey, however, would not follow his master's example, and kept a royal Christmas at Richmond, with plays and disguisings, which gave much offence to see him keep an open court, and the king a secret one.

In the following year, however, the king made up for this intermission of revels, by keeping a solemn Christmas at Greenwich, with revels, masks, disguisings, and banquets; and there were justs kept on the 30th of December, and also on the 3d of January, where 300 spears were broken. Afterwards the king and fifteen others, in masking apparel, took barge, and went to the Cardinal's place, where was a great company of lords and ladies at supper,—

> ".......... having heard by fame
> Of this so noble and so fair assembly,
> This night to meet here, they could do no less,
> Out of the great respect they bear to beauty."

The maskers danced, after which the ladies plucked away their visors, so that they were all known; and the sports were concluded with a great banquet. Previous to this time the Christmas festivities at the Inns of Court had become celebrated, and as we shall find, in subsequent reigns, surpassed those of the court in fancy, and wit, and real splendour; nor is this a matter of surprise when we consider the concentration of talent that must always exist in these communities, some fresh from the universities, embued with classic lore, though in the age of which we are now writing perhaps somewhat pedantic; others, fraught with the accumulated knowledge of years, sharpened by the continual collision with intellects as keen as their own; and few perhaps are better able to appreciate true wit and humour than those who seek it as a relief from deep and wearing mental labour, not that all hard and plodding students can appreciate them, many are but what we used to call at school, muzzes, *et præterea nihil.*

That the entertainments were somewhat stiff or pedantic was of the spirit of the times, and yet there was a freedom in dancing "round about the coal fire," which would scarcely suit the present day, though it would attract a considerable number of spectators to see the barristers, dressed in their best, singing and dancing, before the chancellor, judges, and benchers, and that on penalty of being disbarred; a threat absolutely held out, in the time of James the First, at Lincoln's Inn, because they did not dance on Candlemas Day, according to the ancient order of the Society, and some were indeed put out of commons by decimation. Imagine an unfortunate suitor inquiring about a favourite counsel, who had his case at his fingers' ends, and being told he was disbarred, because he had refused to dance the night before with his opponent's counsel; the benchers not having taken into consideration the difficulty of a little man, as he was, polk-ing with a fat barrister, gown, and wig, and all. Dugdale gives the following programme of the performances at a date somewhat later than that of which we are now speaking. " First, the solemn revells (after dinner and the play ended,) are begun by the whole house, judges, sergeants-at-law, benchers; the *utter and inner barr;* and they led by the *master of the revels;* and one of the gentlemen of the utter barr are chosen to sing a song to the judges, sergeants, or masters of the bench; which is usually performed; and in default thereof there may be an amerciament. Then the judges and benchers take their places, and sit down at the upper end of the hall. Which done, the *utter barristers* and *inner barristers* perform a second solemn revell before them. Which ended, the *utter barristers* take their places and sit down. Some of the gentlemen of the *inner barr* do present the house with dancing, which is called the *post revels*, and continue their dances till the judges or bench think meet to rise and depart." So that a barrister might be punished for not singing, as well as not dancing. Whether he was obliged to sing carols, or might choose his own song, such as, " Oh! brief is my joy," " Ye shall walk in silk attire, and siller ha' to spend," " Bid me discourse," &c., does not appear on record. Lincoln's Inn celebrated Christmas as early as the time of Henry the Sixth, but the Temple and Gray's Inn afterwards disputed the palm with it, and indeed the latter on some occasions seems to have surpassed the other Inns of Court.

The first particular account of any regulations for conducting one of these grand Christmasses, is in the ninth of Henry the Eighth, when, besides the King for Christmas Day, the marshal, and master of the revels, it is ordered that the King of the Cockneys on Christmas Day should sit and have due service, and that he and all his officers should use honest manner and good order, without any waste or destruction making in wines, brawn, chely, or other vitails; and also that he and his marshal, butler, and constable-marshal should have their lawful and honest commandments by delivery of the officers of Christmas; and that the said King of Cockneys nor none of his officers meddle neither in the buttery nor in the steward of Christmas his office, upon pain of forty shillings for every such meddling; and, lastly, "that Jack Straw and all his adherents should be thenceforth utterly banisht, and no more to be used in this house, upon pain to forfeit, for every time, five pounds, to be levied on every fellow hapning to offend against this rule."

Who this Jack Straw was, and what his offences were, does not appear, unless a kind of Wat Tyler against the peace and dignity of the King of Cockneys. One of the leaders of Wat Tyler's insurrection, indeed, according to some accounts, the next in command, assumed the name of Jack Straw, others being called Wyl Wawe, Jack Shepherd, Tom Miller, and Hob Carter; besides the celebrated priest, John Ball, who began one of his sermons on Blackheath with

"When Adam dolue and Evah span,
Who was then a gentle-man?"

But there was also a Jack Straw hung and quartered in the eighth of Henry the Sixth.

In the eighteenth year of Henry, the Society of Gray's Inn got into a worse difficulty than paying allegiance to Jack Straw, and that, too, in perfect innocence on their part; but they had a play or disguising, which had been in great part devised by Serjeant John Roe twenty years before. **The plot was, that Lord Governance was ruled by Dissipation and Negligence, by whose misgovernance and evil order, Lady Public-weal was put from Governance, which caused *Rumor populi*, Inward grudge, and Disdain of wanton sovreignetie to rise with a great multitude to expel Negligence and Dissipation, and restore Public-weal again to her estate.** It was set forth with rich and costly apparel, with masks and morescoes, and was highly praised. But the proud Wolsey, who was then busying himself about the intended divorce, fancied it reflected on him, and sent in a great fury for the unlucky serjeant, took his coif from him, and sent him to the Fleet prison, together with one of the actors, Thomas Moyle of Kent, who probably gained this unenviable distinction by having excelled in the performance of the character intrusted to him; all the actors were highly rebuked and threatened. After a time the matter was satisfactorily explained, and the captive revellers were liberated.

It was found prudent from time to time to make regulations in respect to these revels, in order to limit the expenses, and, if possible, to check the rivalry between the different societies, and they were not therefore performed every year

During the Christmas of 1529, Cardinal Wolsey, who had been disgraced a short time before, was dangerously ill, which produced a short return of favour with the selfish monarch, who became much worried with his state, and also the unsettled position of his own domestic arrangements; for although it was supposed that Ann Boleyn was in fact living with him as his queen, yet no divorce had taken place from Catherine, who had still a strong party in her favour, and excited much sympathy. However, for the king's recreation, a solemn

Christmas was kept at Greenwich, with justs, banquets, masks and disguisings, attended by the two legates and many of the nobility; but the queen gave them no manner of countenance, her mind being so troubled. In the two following years she kept the Christmas with him, and there were masks and interludes; but in his twenty-third year, at a solemn Christmas at Greenwich, there was no mirth, the queen and her ladies being absent—like Queen Vashti she refused to come, and no wonder, for in a very few days after her royal estate was given unto another, and Henry publicly married Anne Boleyn. After this time he does not appear himself to have mixed in the Christmas festivities, though yearly entries may be found of payments to players, for playing before him, and sometimes to the gentlemen of the chapel, and the children as before, with occasional notices of solemn Christmasses; but his temper grew worse, and his zest for these amusements gradually less, as his age and person increased.

In the Christmas of his twenty-ninth year, after the death of Queen Jane in the previous October, he appeared in mourning apparel, which was somewhat unnecessary, as he had made an offer, although an unsuccessful one, to the Duchess Dowager of Longueville, within a month after the death of his wife. His Twelfth Day, 1540, was rather unlucky for him; although great rejoicings were going forward, as he then married Anne of Cleves, from whom, as it is known, he was soon after divorced.

Card playing and other games were still continued, and different payments were made on this account; the king, one Christmas, having as much as £212 10s. for this purpose. Payments were made also to Princess Mary to disport her with at Christmas, generally £20, and in her own private accounts are payments at Christmas, varying from £1 to £4, to have in her purse and to play at cards. The Lady Anne Boleyn received as much as £100 at a time, towards her New Year's Gift. The Princess Mary, from her childhood, had an establishment of her own, and was accustomed to these festivities before she had completed her sixth year, having a lord of Misrule, John Thurgoode, one of the valets of her household about this time; but the sanction of the great cardinal was necessary even for her; and in 1525 there is an application by the Council of her household to him, to know whether they may appoint a lord of Misrule, and provide for interludes, disguisings, or plays, and a banquet; and whether the princess was to send New Year's Gifts to the king and queen, and the French queen, and of what value. The princess herself had received New Year's Gifts as early as her third year, when the cardinal gave her a cup of gold; the French queen, a pomander; Lady Mountjoy, two smocks; a favourite gift by the bye, as we shall hereafter see that Queen Elizabeth had many of these, handsomely decorated, given to her. In after years we find at different times gifts of the following nature given to the Princess Mary. Lady Dorset and others gave her wrought smocks and handkerchiefs; her brother the prince, a little tablet of gold; the Princess Elizabeth, a little chain, and a pair of hose, wrought in gold and silk; the Lady Margaret, a gown of carnation satin of the Venice fashion; Lady Butler, a pepperbox, silver-gilt; the Earl of Hertford, a diamond ring; three Venetians, a fair steel glass; Mr. Thomas Hobbs, yeoman of the robes, a pair of silver snuffers; Mrs. Whelar, a pen and inkhorn, silver-gilt; the Italian dancer, a partlet of gold, wrought; Lady Brown, a fuming-box of silver; and the king's master-cook, a marchpane; which was the usual present of this functionary. All the servants who brought these gifts had handsome presents in money in return, the king's messenger having as much as forty shillings given him. Besides money gifts to her own household, and to the king's minstrels and musicians, among whom the harper had 5s., she gave others of value in various Christmasses to distinguished persons; as, in 1543, a chair to the king, of which the covering and embroidery cost £21 6s. 8d.; also, to the lord admiral, a brooch of gold, of the history of Moses striking water out of the rock, and a balas set in the same; she herself having a brooch of the history of Noah's flood, set with little diamonds and rubies; the king, and the queen for the time being, and the Prince Edward, as we may imagine, also received gifts from his sisters; and on one occasion the Lady Elizabeth gave him a cambric shirt of her own working. In the present day it would probably have been a couvrette, or an embroidered smoking cap, though he was rather young for that. His times were innocent of this strange fashion, though they had quite sufficient eccentricities of their own to answer for. It is a pity that the recent act, compelling chimneys to consume their own smoke, does not extend to smokers; it is almost worth while mooting the point, whether it does or not.

The nobility kept the feast in manner similar to the court, making allowance for difference of station. They had their lord of Misrule, or master of the revels, and their minstrels, their players, with their interludes and disguisings; the chaplain being frequently the maker of the interludes; and most minute rules were laid down to regulate the different payments and gifts. The Earl of Northumberland, whose household book has been so often quoted in illustration of the manners and customs of this age, used to give, when he was at home, to those of his chapel, if they played the play of the Nativity on Christmas Day, 20s.; and to his master of the revels, 20s.; to the king's servant, bringing a New Year's gift, he gave £5, or if a special friend of his own, £6 13s. 4d.; to the queen's servant, £3 6s. 8d.; but to the servant (probably a domestic), bringing one from Lord Percy, only 12d.; to his three minstrels, on New Year's Day, for playing at the chamber doors of the different members of the family £1 3s. 4d.; to his six trumpets, 20s.; to his officer of arms, for crying largess, 20s.; to the grooms of his chamber, to put in their box, 20s.; to the abbot of Misrule, 20s.; to his chaplain for making an interlude, the price seems to be 13s. 4d., rather moderate when compared with the other gifts. Different presents also to various sets of players; also 20s. each to the barne-bishops (boy-bishops) of Beverley and York, showing that the custom still existed.

Traces of the boy-bishop may be found as far back as the Constantinopolitan synod in 867, and as early as Edward the First's reign, one of them was permitted to sing vespers before him at Heton, near Newcastle, in 1299, when on his way to Scotland, and received forty shillings for himself and the boys who sang with him. In the time of Edward the Second payments were made to this personage; and Dean Colet, in his regulations for St. Paul's School, 1512, directs the scholars to go every Childermas Day to St. Paul's to hear the child-bishop's sermon, and each to offer him a penny. Henry the Eighth, however, put down the custom, which was revived by Queen Mary, but finally abolished by Elizabeth.

The Earl of Northumberland's three henchmen presented him with gloves, and received 6s. 8d. in return; and his footmen also gave him gloves, and received 3s. 4d. in reward. My lord and lady were accustomed to make offerings at high mass on Christmas Day, New Year's Day, and Twelfth Day; but of rather small amount, his lordship's being 12d. and her ladyship's 8d. In lesser establishments there was, of course, less state and smaller payments; and in the household accounts of the Lestranges of Hunstanton, in the eleventh of Henry, is a payment of 4d. to the Lord of Christmas, at Kyngstede. Different sums also are charged for New Year's gifts.

The lower classes still continued the customs of their forefathers, but occasionally required some check, to prevent their revelries becoming of too gross a description, and to amend abuses. In the third of Henry the Eighth, people were forbidden to appear abroad like mummers, their faces covered with vizors, and in disguised apparel. But it was by no means the intention to debar them from proper recreations during this season; many indulgences being afforded them, and their landlords and masters assisted them with the means of enjoying their customary festivities, listening to their legendary tales round the Yule-log, and occasionally joining in their sports; a practice scarcely yet obsolete in some parts of the country, and pity it should become so.

> "A Christmas gambol oft' would cheer
> The poor man's heart through half the year."

In the thirty-third of Henry, when certain games were forbidden to artificers, husbandmen, apprentices, servants, and others of that class, they were still allowed to play at tables, tennis, dice, cards, bowls, clash, coyting, and logating, at Christmas; though there is a proclamation by the Sheriff of York, where the privilege is extended beyond our ideas of liberality, as all manner of whores and thieves, dice-players, carders, and all other unthrifty folk, were to be welcome in the town, whether they came late or early, at the reverence of the high feast of Yule, till the twelve days were passed. One fancies a spice of irony in this invitation. Heywood, the epigrammatist, at a little later date, used to say, that he did not like to play at king and queen, but at Christmas, according to the old order of England; and that few men played at cards, but at Christmas; and then almost all, men and boys. Heywood evidently had not been initiated into any of our whist clubs, or he would have found not a few who play at other times than Christmas. And as to that time, there are still many houses where cards are regularly produced on Christmas Day, a practice which, certainly, to those unaccustomed to it, even the old order of England will not qualify.

There is a story told of an ambitious shoemaker, whose Christmas coat was spoiled, in the reign of Henry, by his seeking to imitate his superiors; and this at a time when the distinction of apparel was marked, and not as at present, when simplicity of dress is frequently the best mark of a gentleman. Sir Philip Calthrop, having bought as much fine French tawney cloth as would make him a gown, gave it to a tailor, at Norwich, to make up, when John Drake, a shoemaker, passing by, and admiring it, ordered one of the same materials and fashion. Sir Philip, calling in on a subsequent day, and seeing a similar gown-piece, asked for whom it was made, when he was told it was for a shoemaker, and to be of the same fashion as his own: upon which, his pride being touched, he ordered the tailor to make his gown as full of cuts as his shears would make it. The tailor fulfilled his directions, and performed the same operation for the gown of the unfortunate shoemaker, who, by some accident, could not go to fetch it away until Christmas morning, intending, no doubt, to astonish his wife and dazzle his companions with his splendour. On seeing the havoc made in his intended state dress, he began to cry out vehemently, but was told it was made exactly like the knight's; upon which he exclaimed, " By my latchet, I will never wear gentleman's fashion again."

Payments were made by Henry the Eighth to waits, at Canterbury, as they were by Henry the Seventh, as well as at other places. These, however, were not at Christmas time, nor were they peculiar to Christmas, but formed part of the musical establishments of the court and the nobility. Originally, indeed, they do not seem of necessity to have been of a musical class; or, at any rate, there were some who were not so; as, in the time of Henry the Third, Simon le Wayte held a virgate of land at Rockingham, in Northamptonshire, on the tenure of being castle-wayte, or watch, and the same custom was observed in other places. This Simon le Wayte fled for theft, and was not the only suspected person of his craft: for, at the time the treasury exchequer was broken open and robbed, in the time of Edward the First, Gilbertus le Wayte, who was keeper of the watch, was very naturally taken up on suspicion, but it does not appear what was done with him. After this the wait seems to have been a musician, usually playing the pipe or hautboy, who kept watch at night, and made *bon guet* at the different chamber doors, particularly at Christmas time; and Edward the Fourth had one attached to his establishment for this purpose. In the old lay of Richard Cœur-de-Lion, there is notice of—

" A wayte ther com in a kernel (*battlement*),
And a pypyd a moot in a flagel" (*flageolet*).

Among the minstrels in the household of Edward the Third, there were three waits, who had 12*d*. a day in time of war, and only 20*s*. a year in time of peace. Henry the Sixth also had one in his household, and frequent mention is made of them from his time to the end of Henry the Eighth, and in subsequent reigns. In Charles the First's band, of fifty-eight, there were twenty-five for the waits; and, as is well known, they exist to the present time; the regular wait even exhibiting his regular appointment and badge, with the portcullis, although waking people at most irregular hours, and with most irregular tunes. The City of London had its waits, who attended the Lord Mayor on public occasions, such as Lord Mayor's day, and on public feasts, and great dinners. They are described as having blue gowns, red sleeves and caps, every one having his silver collar about his neck. Several other towns also had their own establishments of waits, and there are many entries of payments made to them by our kings, and other great personages; as, to the waits of Canterbury, before mentioned, those of Colchester—as far back as Edward the Fourth—Dover, Coventry, Northampton, Newcastle, &c.; and as they appear to have been on the watch to catch any great person that came in their way, they would seem to have handed down this part of their trade to the bell-ringers of the present age, part of whose occupation appears to be to get paid for not ringing. One of the old towers in Newcastle was formerly called the wait's tower, and was the place of their meeting. There is a tradition of their having played to Oliver Cromwell, on his route to or from Scotland.

CHAPTER V.

LTHOUGH in the short reign of Edward the Sixth, the splendour of the royal Christmasses was, in general, somewhat reduced, yet, in 1551-2, there was one of the most magnificent revellings on record; for the youthful king being much grieved at the condemnation of the Duke of Somerset, it was thought expedient to divert his mind, by additional pastimes, at the following Christmas. George Ferrers, of Lincoln's Inn, being a gentleman of some rank, was appointed lord of Misrule, or master of the king's pastimes, and acquitted himself so well as to afford great delight to many, and some to the king, but "not in proportion to his heaviness." George Ferrers seems

to have been well adapted for his responsible office; **not only** being a gentleman, **but a person of decision**, and determined to carry it through, with due spirit and display; and **to see that his officers, as well as himself, were well attended to.** He complained to the master of the revels, Sir Thomas Cawarden, that the apparel provided for his counsellors was not sufficient, or fit for the purpose, and no doubt had the defect remedied; as, from the account of the expenses, the dresses were handsome, and his own in particular may be called superb. He also stated he should require John Smyth, as his disard, or clown; besides jugglers, tumblers, and fools, &c.; and a new fool's coat, with a hood, was made for **Smyth**, what he had already not being fit for the purpose. The dress of this clown, who was probably a well-known court fool, from his being applied for by name, will show that no expense was spared, even about the officers of this gallant lord of Misrule. He had a long fool's coat, of yellow cloth of gold, all over fringed with white, red, and green velvet, containing 7½ yards, at £2 per yard, garded with plain yellow cloth of gold, four yards, at 33s. 4d. per yard; with a hood, and a pair of buskins, of the same figured gold, containing 2½ yards, at £5; and a girdle of yellow sarcenet, containing one quarter, 16d. The whole value being £26 14s. 8d., a goodly sum for the dress of a jester.

At the risk of being tedious, the various dresses of the lord of Misrule himself must be mentioned, to give some notion of the style in which this celebrated revelling was got up. On Christmas Day, and during that week, he wore a robe of white baudekyn (a rich stuff, made of silk, interwoven with golden thread), containing nine yards, at 16s. a yard, garded with embroidered cloth of gold, wrought in knots,

fourteen yards, at 11s. 1d. a yard; having a fur of red feathers, with a cape of camlet thrum. A coat of flat silver, fine with works, five yards at 50s., with an embroidered gard of leaves of gold, and silk, coloured, containing fifteen yards, at 20s. A cap of maintenance, of red feathers and camlet thrum, very rich, with a plume of feathers. A pair of hose, the breeches made of a gard of cloth of gold, embroidered in panes; nine yards of garding, at 13s. 4d., lined with silver sarcenet, one ell, at 8s. A pair of buskins, of white baudekyn, one yard, at 16s., besides making and other charges, 8s. more. A pair of pantacles, of Bruges satin, 3s. 4d.; a girdle of yellow sarcenet, containing a quarter of a yard, 16s. The whole cost being £52 8s. 8d., independent of the cap of maintenance.

For the remaining dresses, it is unnecessary to state the quantities and particular prices. He had, for New Year's Day, and that week, a robe of red baudekyn, with an embroidered gard of purple silver; a coat of the same materials, embroidered and garded in like manner; a pair of hose, slopwise; the breeches of cloth of gold figured with red and green velvet, with a cut gard of cloth of gold on it; and a pair of buskins of red baudekyn; the cost being £34 15s. A hunter's coat, of cloth of gold, figured with red and green velvet church-work, garded with a border of cloth of gold, embroidered, lined with under sleeves of white baudekyn; a hat of plain cloth of gold, garnished with leaves of green satin. The cost £19 11s. 1d. For Twelfth Day, and his progress in London, he wore a robe of wrought purple furred velvet, the inside white and black, like powdered ermine, with a coat, a head-piece, and a scapular, of the same; the garment welted above, with blue and yellow gold tinsel; the hat garnished with purple velvet, striped with threads of silver;

and an ell of white and blue taffeta, for laces for the same. A pair of hose, the breeches of purple cloth of silver, welted with purple tinsel and gold. A pair of buskins, striped purple velvet, with threads of silver, £33 12s.; the above sums being exclusive of workmanship, and other necessary materials. These dresses, which were supplied from the king's stores, must have satisfied the cravings of the most finished exquisite: and, taking into account that he was attended by the following attendants of his court, besides Venus, who formed part of the pageant, and that they were all handsomely or appropriately dressed, it was enough to turn any moderate man's head. His suite was composed of his heir apparent, who was John Smyth, before mentioned, three other sons, and two natural sons (the sons being represented in handsome fool's dresses), counsellors, pages of honour, gentlemen ushers, sergeant at arms, a provost marshal, under marshal, lieutenant of ordnance, heralds for himself, others for Venus, a trumpeter for himself, and another for Venus, an orator, interpreter, a jailor, footmen, a messenger, an Irishman, an Irishwoman, six hunters, jugglers, a fool for his lordship, and one for Venus.

On the 4th of January, he went by water, from Greenwich to London, and landed at the Tower wharf, attended by a number of young knights and gentlemen, with trumpets, bagpipes, and flutes, and a morris dance with a tabret. One strange part of the procession, also, was a cart, with the pillory, gibbet, and stocks. He then rode through Tower-street, where he was received by Sergeant Vawce, the lord of Misrule to John Mainard, one of the sheriffs of London, who conducted him to the house of Sir George Barne, the lord mayor, where there was a banquet: and, at his departure, the lord mayor gave him a standing cup, with a cover of silver-gilt, of the value of £10, for a reward. He also set a hogshead of wine and a barrel of beer at his gate, for the train that followed him.

The motto taken by Ferrers was, *semper ferians* (always keeping holiday), and his crest was the holm-bush, or evergreen holly. He had himself to incur considerable expenses, independent of the assistance he received from the king's stores; but the honour qualified this, and, of course, men of family and property were selected for the onerous office.

In the following year the revels were kept nearly in the same manner; and, on this occasion, the king's lord of Misrule was graciously pleased to knight the sheriff's lord of Misrule; and they had a great banquet at my lord Treasurer's.

Towards the end of the short reign of Edward, it was enacted, that the Eves of Christmas Day, the Circumcision, and the Epiphany, should be kept as fasts. But this was repealed very early in the reign of Mary, who, about the same time, issued a proclamation to prevent books, ballads, and interludes, from touching on points of doctrine in religion; and which, in effect, stopped all interludes and dramas, without special license. Her short reign was not very congenial to Christmas festivities, her own melancholy temperament, and domestic disappointments, interfering with them at court; but they were still kept up throughout the country, although much checked by the persecutions on account of religion. And what more fierce and rancorous than the persecution of man by his fellow-man, of Christian by his so-called fellow Christian, in the name of the All-merciful God; slaying and torturing by fire and sword, for difference in the worship of that Being, who abounds in pity and compassion for the erring sinner! Proud, cold, vindictive man! it will be an awful question to answer hereafter, "What hast thou done? The voice of thy brother's blood crieth unto me from the ground."

The Christmas masques were not, however, abandoned, and in the first Christmas after the marriage of Philip and Mary, there was one where the characters seem somewhat incongruous with the disposition of Mary, as there were six Venuses, or amorous ladies, with six cupids, and male and female Turks, &c.

Among the numerous miscellaneous New Year's gifts presented to Mary in 1556, were the fore part of a kyrtell, and a pair of sleeves, of cloth of silver, richly embroidered all over with Venice silver, and raised with silver and black silk, given by the princess Elizabeth; a table, painted of the queen's marriage, by Suete, painter; a smock, wrought all over with silk, and collar and ruffs of damask, gold, pearl, and silver, by the Duchess of Somerset; six sugar loaves, six tapnetts of figs, four barrels of suckets, and orange water, &c., by Lady Yorke, who, apparently, had a sweet tooth; two fat oxen, by Mr. Michael Wentworth—in the present time we should have taken them for granted, as prize oxen; two guinea-cocks, scalded by Gent; a marchpane, and two dishes of jelly, by Burrage, master cook; a fat goose and a capon, by Mrs. Preston; a cake of spice bread, by Kelley, plasterer; nutmegs and ginger, and a long stalk of cinnamon elect, in a box, by Smalwodde, grocer; a basket of pomegranates, cherries, apples, oranges, and lemons, by Harris, fruiterer; three rolls of songs, by Sheparde, of the chapel; a fair lute, edged with passamayne of gold and silk, by Browne, instrument maker.

The lord-mayor kept his state as usual, and in the end of January, 1557, the lord treasurer's lord of Misrule,—for this officer's power was frequently extended to Candlemas Day—came to the lord-mayor with his suite, and invited him to dinner.

In the following year there is a notice of the lord of Misrule, which would be rather strange if we did not know that going to the Poultry Compter in those days was not always a mark of disgrace or difficulty, as in recent times; but after all allowance made, some part of the account is suspicious; however, as we have not got the name of the master reveller, we may give the story, that on New Year's Eve a lord of Misrule, with his herald, trumpets, and drums, and several attendants, disguised in white, went to London, and was brought to the Poultry Compter, and divers of his men lay all night there, and they went astray home again, by four and six together, to Westminster, on horseback and on foot. It is to be hoped that those who came disguised in white did not go home disguised in liquor; but let us give them the benefit of the doubt.

Queen Elizabeth, who, to powerful intellect, joined much of the arbitrary temper of her father, possessed also great vanity and fondness of display. In her time, therefore, the festivities were renewed with great pomp and show; and theatrical entertainments were also particularly encouraged, and were frequently performed before the queen, especially at Christmas time. To restrain somewhat the great expenses of these entertainments, she directed, in her second year, estimates to be made of them previously; but this wholesome practice, judging from the cost of after years, did not exist very long. In 1559, which may be called her first Christmas, the play before her, on Christmas Night, unluckily contained some offensive or indecent matter, as the players were commanded to leave off, and the mask came in dancing. On the Twelfth Night following there was a play, and then a goodly mask, and afterwards a great banquet.

In 1561, a lord of Misrule, having with him a train of 100 horsemen, richly apparelled, rode through London to the Inner Temple, where there was great revelling throughout the Christmas; Lord Robert Dudley, afterwards Earl of Leicester, being the constable and marshal, under the name of Palaphilos; and Christopher Hatton, afterwards chancellor, was master of the game. A sort of parliament had been previously held on St. Thomas's Eve to decide whether the Society should keep Christmas; and if so, the oldest bencher delivered a speech on the occasion, the oldest butler was to publish the officers' names, and then, "in token of joy and good liking, the bench and company pass beneath the hearth, and sing a carol, and so to boyer." It was at this Temple Grand Christmas that Ferrex and Porrex, which may be considered as the first play assuming the character of the regular tragedy, was performed. The revels at these Grand Christmasses generally continued throughout the whole twelve days; Christmas Day, New Year's Day, and Twelfth Day, being more particularly distinguished. On this occasion, at the breakfast of Twelfth Day, were brawn, mustard, and malmsey; the dinner of two courses to be served in the hall, and after the first course came the master of the game, apparelled in green velvet, and the ranger of the forest in green satin, bearing a green bow with arrows, each of them having a hunting horn about his neck; after blowing three blasts of venery, they paced three times round the fire, which was then placed in the middle of the hall. The master of the game next made three courtesies and knelt down, and petitioned to be admitted into the service of the lord of the feast. This ceremony having been performed, a huntsman came into the hall with a fox, and a purse-net with a cat, both bound at the end of a staff, and nine or ten couple of hounds, the horns blowing. The fox and cat were then set upon by the hounds, and killed beneath the fire; a pleasant Christmas amusement. This sport being finished, the marshal ushered all in their proper places, and after the second course, the oldest of the masters of the revels sang a song, with the assistance of others present; after some repose and further revels, supper of two courses was served, and when that was finished, the marshal was borne in by four men, on a sort of scaffold or framework, and taken three times round the hearth, crying out, "A lord, a lord," &c.; after which he came down and went to dance. The lord of Misrule then addressed himself to the banquet,—the unfortunate fox and cat ought to have formed part—which ended with minstrelsy, mirth, and dancing; when they all departed to rest.

In 1573, there was some urgent expedition necessary in getting the revels ready in time; for a set of unfortunate plasterers were kept at work all night, and as they could not be spared, nor trusted, to go abroad to supper, they were allowed bread, and cheese, and beer, for that meal. The queen generally had masks of different kinds before her at Christmas time, of greater or less magnificence; but mention must not be omitted of the celebrated Christmas at Gray's Inn, in 1594, of which an account was published under the title of Gesta Grayorum. Mr. Henry Helmes, the Christmas Prince, took for his style, "The High and Mighty Prince; Henry, Prince of Purpoole; Arch-duke of Stapulia and

Bernardia; Duke of High and Nether Holborn; Marquis of St. Giles and Tottenham; Count Palatine of Bloomsbury and Clerkenwell; Great Lord of the Cantons of Islington, Kentish Town, Paddington, and Knightsbridge; Knight of the most heroical Order of the Helmet; and sovereign of the same." According to our views, the entertainments would be considered heavy and pedantic in their nature; but they were in the style of the age, and seem to have given much satisfaction. There was a cessation of sports from Twelfth Night till the 1st of February, the prince being supposed absent in Russia on public affairs. On that day he was received at Blackwall, as if on his return, and that and the following day were spent in revelling and feasting, which then ceased until Shrovetide, when a mask was performed before the queen, containing, as usual, some gross flattery, and she was so much pleased with the performance, that on the courtiers dancing a measure after it, she exclaimed, "What! shall we have bread and cheese after a banquet."

She was particularly partial to theatrical performances, and throughout her reign frequent mention is made of the plays performed during Christmas, at Court, and the rewards given to the players; the children of St. Paul's also, and the scholars on her new foundation in Westminster, often performed before her at this season.

In 1560 and several following years, Sebastian Westcott, master of the children of St. Paul's, received £6 13s. 4d., for their services, which seems to have been the usual price paid to regular players for a play, until the end of her reign, when it was increased to £10. Richard Farrant, the master of the children of Windsor, received for their services, in 1574, as much as £13 6s. 8d.

In 1560, Sir Thomas Benger was made master of the revels, succeeding Sir Thomas Cawarden; he dying in 1577, Mr. Thomas Blagrave, who had acted since 1573, held the office for a short time; but Mr. Edmund Tylney was appointed in 1579, and died in 1610.

The play performed on Twelfth Night, 1571, was called Narcissus, in which a live fox was let loose and chased by dogs; so that the introduction of live animals on the stage is not a modern invention. On New Year's Day 1574, the children of Westminster performed Truth, Faithfulness, and Mercy. The scholars on the foundation at Westminster, known as the queen's scholars, have continued the custom of acting plays to the present time, the performances having for very many years past been one of Terence's plays, of which four are taken in rotation, and excellent acting is in general exhibited to a select and talented audience; the concluding ceremony of the cap, however, reminds one of the usual termination of the country Christmas play of St. George. In the beginning of this reign there are references to the custom, then called an old one, of scholars being allowed, even by their foundation deed, to bar out their masters a week before Christmas and Easter.

At Christmas 1574, she had a company of Italian players, amongst others, one of them was a tumbler. On New Year's Night 1582, there were also sundry feats of tumbling by the servants of Lord Strange, besides plays during the Christmas, and a mask of ladies. In several following years a tumbler, called Symons, seems to have been famed for divers feats of activity, and the queen apparently took pleasure in such exhibitions. In 1600, a person, called Nycke, tumbled before her, and 14s. are charged for his silk hose. In her latter years we find Edward Allen, John Heming, and Thomas Pope, presenting plays before her. The rewards given to the players, vary from £6 13s. 4d. to £40. As the 'Merry Wives of Windsor,' written at the queen's request, and other of Shakespeare's plays, were performed at court, we may fairly presume that some of them were performed at Christmas, and that the great Bard himself may have acted before her.

In 1592, the vice-chancellor, and heads of colleges, at Cambridge, were directed to act a comedy before the queen, at Christmas; but these unfortunate victims of too much learning were obliged to memorialize the vice-chamberlain, stating their inability to act in English, and asking leave to perform in Latin. They must have been in their glory in the reign of Elizabeth's successor, the pedant James, whom, on one occasion, they addressed as Jacobissime Jacobe. Like her predecessors, the queen would play at dice at Christmas time, but she had dice set for her that threw the high numbers only, as fives and sixes; and, as she knew not the trick, she was kept in good humour by her success, as she, of course, won; and her courtiers probably thought it worth some sacrifice to avoid incurring the effects of the paternal temper existing in her.

Kemp, in his celebrated morris-dance, from London to Norwich, takes particular notice of the Norwich waits, saying that few cities have the like, and none better; who, besides their excellency in wind instruments, their rare cunning on the viol and violin, had admirable voices, every one of them being able to serve as a chorister in any cathedral church. One Richard Reede, a wait of Cambridge, is particularly mentioned, as having 20s. for his attendance at a gentleman's mansion, during the Christmas of 1574. Besides these,

Puttenham speaks of tavern minstrels, that gave a fit of mirth for a groat, much in the style of our present peripatetic street musicians; their matter being for the most part stories of old time, as the tale of Sir Topas, the exploits of Bevis of Southampton, Guy of Warwick, Adam Bell, and Clymm of the Clough, and such other old romances or historical rhymes, made purposely for recreation of the common people at Christmas dinners, and brideales, and in taverns, and alehouses, and such other places of base resort.

The nobility, as in former times, imitated the court in the manner of keeping Christmas, and the gentry followed in their steps; but they were allured to town by the superior festivities in the metropolis, to the neglect of their friends and dependents in the country, besides dissipating their means in London, and thus causing an inability to preserve proper hospitality and charity in their own neighbourhood. In order to check this practice, an order was made in 1589, directing the gentlemen of Norfolk and Suffolk to leave London before Christmas, and repair to their own countries, there to keep hospitality among their neighbours. Their presence also would not only enable them to increase the real enjoyment of their dependents, but would serve to controul any tendency to riot or debauch at the country alehouses, at this time the resort of many idle strollers, under the guise of minstrels, jugglers, revellers, &c., and would, if right-minded themselves, give a proper direction to the festivities.

"At Christmas be mery, and thanke god of all;
And feast thy pore neighbours, the great with the small."

In 1581, there was a book written by Thomas Lovell,

published by John Aldee, against the 'Use and Abuse of Dauncinge and Mynstralsye.' It is of a puritanical nature, being a supposed dialogue between Custom who defends them, and Verity who attacks them and is made victorious. Custom, however, pleads hard for dancing at Christmas time, showing that it had been a usage of long standing.

> "Christmas is a mery time,
>   good mirth therfore to make;
> Young men and maids together may
>   their legs in daunces shake;
> Wee se it with some gentlemen
>   a common use to be,
> At that time to provide to have
>   some pleasant minstrelsie."

Towards the end of the Queen's life, when she herself failed in health and spirit, there was in general a great abatement in Christmas festivities; the country taking the tone from the monarch. In 'Summer's Last Will and Testament,' written about this time, Autumn talks of Christmas, as—

> " . . . . . a pinch-back, cut-throat churl,
> That keeps no open house, as he should do,
> Delighteth in no game or fellowship,
> Loves no good deeds and hateth talk;
> But sitteth in a corner turning crabs,
> Or coughing o'er a warmed pot of ale;"

and in 'Father Hubbard's Tales,' by Middleton, the Ant's Tale, referring probably to the time about the end of this reign, and showing the nature of the amusements in vogue at Christmas, the writer says, "Do but imagine now what a sad Christmas we all kept in the country, without either carols, wassail-bowls, dancing of Sellenger's round in moonshine about maypoles, shoeing the mare, hoodman-blind, hot-cockles, or any of our old Christmas gambols; no, not so much as choosing king and queen on Twelfth Night."

With Elizabeth's fondness for luxury and dress, and her passion for adulation, it may well be imagined that her New Year's Gifts were rigidly expected, or exacted, from all classes connected with her; from Matthew Parker, Archbishop of Canterbury, down to Smyth the dustman; and they were of a most miscellaneous description. In the preceding reigns, when she was princess, she was in the habit of giving and receiving them, but in a comparatively quiet and unobtrusive manner, frequently consisting of presents of gilt plate, and the messengers with gifts to her always receiving rewards; but on one occasion she gave her brother, King Edward, a translation in Latin, in her own hand, of an Italian sermon of Occhini; her pride of scholarship even then showing itself. There are many instances of authors giving compositions of their own as New Year's Gifts, and of books being printed with that name, no doubt by way of attracting at this season. On New Year's Day, 1561, Nowell, Dean of St. Paul's, who preached before the queen on that day, got much blamed by her, for having laid on her cushion, as a New Year's Gift, a prayer-book richly bound, having several fine cuts and pictures of the stories of saints and martyrs; for she considered these as being contrary to the proclamation against images, pictures, and Romish relics in churches, and desired such mistake might never occur again. One can fancy the venerable Dean shrinking under the stern rebuke of the peremptory young lady on a point of ecclesiastical discipline. In return for the gifts presented to her, she generally gave articles of gilt plate, as cups, bowls, salts, &c., varying according to the rank of the person; from 400 ounces to Sir Christopher Hatton, to two ounces to Mrs. Tomysen, the dwarf; and also presents of money to the servants. It would be useless to insert a long list of these gifts, a few will show the variety, the value and taste of some, and the strangeness, according to our ideas, of others.

In 1560, she had a pair of silk stockings given her by Mrs. Montagu, her silk-woman, which by some are said to have been the first pair worn in England; however, they became common soon afterwards. It may be mentioned, as an act of kindness, that in this year she gave sixty French crowns, as a New Year's Gift, to —— Penne, widow, who had been formerly nurse to King Edward. In the following year she received presents in money from £40 by the Archbishop of Canterbury, in a red silk purse in demy sovereigns, to £4 by Lady Cheeke, in a russet silk purse; also various articles of dress, most of them richly wrought, among which were smocks worked in silk; and standing collars and partelets wrought with gold, silver, and silk; and miscellaneous articles, from handsome pieces of jewellery, down to one pye of quinces, by John Betts, servant of the pastry, who received two gilt spoons in return. In subsequent years the gifts are much of the same nature, and a few only need be particularised. Some may be considered as partaking of a professional character: her doctors generally giving a pot of orange blossoms and a pot of ginger, or something similar; and her apothecary a box of lozenges, or a pot of conserves; while her cook gave a marchpane, made into some kind of device; and her serjeant of the pastry, a quince pie, and sometimes a pie of quinces and wardens gilt.

In 1574, the favourite, Earl of Leicester, gave her a splendid fan, that ladies now might envy, being of white feathers, set in a handle of gold; one side of it garnished with two very fair emeralds, one of them especially fine, and garnished with diamonds and rubies; and the other side garnished with diamonds and rubies; and on each side a white bear and two pearls hanging, a lion rampant with a white muzzled bear at his foot. Handsomely wrought smocks are frequently mentioned. This article, as is well known, was different from that in present wear, the ornamental part could be safely exhibited, and gentlemen could present them without breach of decorum; though in our present fastidious days, a New Year's Gift to a lady of a chemisette, berthe, or gilêt, might be considered as a somewhat eccentric *gage d'amour*.

In 1578, Philip Sidney gave a cambric smock, which may be considered as quite in the florid or decorated style of workmanship; the sleeves and collar being wrought with black work, and edged with a small bone lace of gold and silver; and a suite of ruffs cutwork, flourished with gold and silver, and set with spangles. In the same year, Sir Gawen Carew gave one worked with Venice gold, and edged with a small bone lace of Venice gold; Smyth, the dustman, gave two bolts of cambric; her doctors and apothecary, pots of ginger and candy; and Mark Anthony, a violl.

In the following year, Morrys Watkins, whoever he might be, gave eighteen larks in a cage, and received 20*s*. in reward. In several years there are handsome gowns, petticoats, kirtles, doblets, and mantles, some embroidered with precious stones, bracelets, and other ornaments; so that it does not appear so very surprising that at her death, Elizabeth left a hoard of 2000 dresses behind her. It must be presumed, however, that she was not in the habit of giving away any of her apparel, or her ladies' maids would have had rich perquisites.

In 1582, Lady Howard gave her a jewel of gold, representing a cat and mice playing with her, garnished with small diamonds and pearls; typifying perhaps the queen and her maids; and she received from eight maskers a flower of gold, garnished with sparks of diamonds, rubies, and opals, with an agate of her majesty's "phisnamy," and a pearl pendant, with devices painted in it.

In 1589, she had a jewel of gold, like an alpha and omega, whatever that might be, garnished with sparks of diamonds. Sir Francis Drake also gave her a fan of white and red feathers, the handle of gold, enamelled with a half moon of mother of pearl, within that a half moon garnished with sparks of diamonds, and a few seed pearls on one side, having her majesty's picture within it, and on the other side a device with a crow over it. Lord North, in his Household Book, charges £10, as his New Year's Gift to the queen, and £16 10s. given at court at New Year's tide. It need scarcely be observed that the custom of New Year's Gifts was prevalent among all classes, and many examples might be given of payments on account of them in the domestic records of the age.

The customs in France about this time were very similar to ours. In Sully's 'Memoirs,' 1606, it is stated, " Les cérémonies du jour de l'an, des rois et jours suivans, se passèrent à l'accoustumée, en présens, festins, banquets, balets, mascarades, courses de bague, et autres réjouissances et magnificences, le roy, la reine, et la reine Marguerite vous ayant envoyé vos estrennes, et à madame vostre femme aussi."

CHAPTER VI.

LAYS and other Christmas festivities continued throughout the reign of James the First; and amongst others we find 'Measure for Measure,' and the 'Plaie of Errors,' by Shaxberd—a new reading as to the spelling of the name of our glorious bard—also 'King Lear,' and 'Love's Labour's Lost.' Many of Fletcher's plays likewise were first acted before the court at Christmas.

Masks were performed almost yearly; and in one of them, the 'Queen's Mask of Moors,' the queen with eleven ladies of honour took parts. Ben Jonson himself wrote several for the court, and Inigo Jones assisted in the scenery and decorations. James performed one good act, by inflicting a penalty of £10 on any one making use, in plays, shows, or pageants, jestingly or profanely, of the Holy Name of God, or of our Saviour, or of the Holy Ghost, or of the Trinity.

At the very commencement of this reign, John Hemynges and his company received £53 for performing six interludes or plays; and on the 8th of January, 1604, the queen and her ladies presented a mask, by Samuel Daniell, called the 'Vision of the Twelve Goddesses.' In the following year, Hemynges and his company received £60, for the same number of plays, and £10 a play seems to have been the usual reward. At the same time, the queen and her ladies performed Ben Jonson's mask of 'Blackness,' being the first in which he was employed. It was got up in a magnificent style, having cost the exchequer £3000. After the performance, there was a banquet in the great-chamber, which was so furiously assailed by the hungry guests, that the table and trestles went down before one bit was touched.

There are some strange stories of scenes of excessive conviviality in this reign, particularly during the visit of the Danish king, Christian the Fourth, in 1606, when, on one occasion, during the personation of the mask of 'Solomon, and the Queen of Sheba'—the King of Denmark being the Solomon of the night—the representative of the Queen of Sheba had imprudently imbibed too much of the nectar that she was to have offered to Solomon, and stumbling, distributed her classic offerings of wine, jelly, and cakes, over his dress. He in his turn, attempting to dance, found it necessary to fall, and cling to the floor, until taken off to bed.

" *Cassio.* Is your Englishman so exquisite in his drinking?
Iago. Why, he drinks you with facility, your Dane dead drunk."

Some ladies, representing Faith, Hope, Charity, Victory, and Peace, who were assumed to have been the attendants of the Queen of Sheba, on her celebrated visit, sympathised with their mistress, and were obliged, with proper assistance to guide their tottering limbs, to retire for a time in a state of maudlin sensibility.

From Gervase Markham's account, in his 'English Housewife,' of a moderate dinner of this time, we may somewhat judge of the prevalent profusion:—The first course should consist of "sixteen full dishes; that is, dishes of meat that are of substance, and not empty, or for show—as thus, for example; first, a shield of brawn, with mustard; secondly, a boyl'd capon; thirdly, a boyl'd piece of beef; fourthly, a chine of beef, rosted; fifthly, a neat's tongue, rosted; sixthly, a pig, rosted; seventhly, chewets baked; eighthly, a goose, rosted; ninthly, a swan, rosted; tenthly, a turkey, rosted; the eleventh, a haunch of venison, rosted; the twelfth, a pasty of venison; the thirteenth, a kid, with a pudding in the belly; the fourteenth, an olive-pye; the fifteenth, a couple of capons; the sixteenth, a custard, or dowsets. Now, to these full dishes may be added, sallets, fricases, quelque choses, and devised paste, as many dishes more, which make the full service no less than two and thirty dishes; which is as much as can conveniently stand on one table, and in one mess. And after this manner you may proportion both your second and third courses, holding fulness on one half of the dishes, and show in the other; which will be both frugal in the splendour, contentment to the guest, and much pleasure and delight to the beholder."

If this was a frugal—a sort of friendly—dinner, what must

have been a state one—of the Belgravian or East Indian class, for instance?

On Twelfth Night, 1606, the mask of 'Hymen,' by Ben Jonson, was performed, in honour of the unfortunate marriage of Robert, Earl of Essex, with Lady Frances, daughter of the Earl of Suffolk, afterwards so well known as the vicious wife of the equally vicious favourite, Somerset. In the following year was the mask of 'Beauty,' in which the queen and her ladies took part; but, though intended for Twelfth Night, it was not performed, for some reason, until Sunday, the 14th of January, Sunday being by no means an unusual day for these festivities. The following Christmas was dull and heavy, like the weather; still there were plays at court.

On the 1st of January, 1611, Prince Henry, accompanied by twelve other persons of rank, performed the mask of 'Oberon,' of which the expenses were £1092 6s. 10d., including £16 paid to Inigo Jones, for his labour; it being the joint production of him and Ben Jonson, and contained a variety of delicate music. It was performed in the new and beautiful banquetting-house, at Whitehall. There were, likewise, two other masks, by Ben Jonson and Inigo Jones, in the same Christmas, which cost the queen £600. In one of them, called, 'Love freed from Ignorance and Folly'—the name of the other being 'Love Restored'—there were twelve she-fools introduced, dressed in coloured taffeta, lined with fustian, who performed a dance, and received each £1 for her trouble. In November, 1612, Prince Henry died; a prince who, according to most accounts, was much loved, and from whose early promise much was expected. Whether his father much mourned him seems a doubtful question: it has been surmised that he was jealous of his popularity. At all events the following Christmas was kept with the usual festivities, and his daughter Elizabeth was affianced to the Palatine.

On the 26th of December, 1613, the favourite, Somerset, was married to the Countess of Essex, at Whitehall, in the presence of the King, Queen, and Prince Charles, and many of the nobility, and several entertainments were given in the course of the Christmas, to the well-matched pair. On the 4th of January, they went to a grand entertainment, at Merchant Tailors' Hall, and, after supper, were entertained with a wassail, two pleasant masks, and dancing. On Twelfth Day the gentlemen of Gray's Inn invited them to a mask—the 'Mask of Flowers'—but they did not consent willingly to this act, evidently considering it a degradation, their repugnance having been overcome by Lord Bacon. It appears to have been performed at the banquetting-house.

In 1616, Ben Jonson presented the well-known mask, called the 'Mask of Christmas,' the principal characters being Christmas and his children, Misrule, Carol, Minced-Pie, Gambol, Post and Pair, New Year's Gift, Mumming, Wassel, Offering, and Baby-Cake. Prince Charles performed, and obtained great applause in his mask, called 'The Vision of Delight, or Prince's Mask,' represented on Twelfth Night, 1618, when the Muscovy ambassadors were feasted at court, and a sum of £750 was issued for the occasion. A mask of ladies had been prepared for the same Christmas, and many rehearsals had taken place, but for some reason it was forbidden by the king and queen; to the great disappointment of the ladies, no doubt.

The Inns of Court continued their revels as in former reigns. Sir Simon D'Ewes complains of some great irregularities at the Temple, in 1620, and some subsequent years, arising from gambling and quarrelling. In Christmas, 1622-3, the Society of the Middle Temple incurred the displeasure of the king—who apparently cared little for any one but himself—by a demonstration in favour of his amiable and talented daughter, Elizabeth of Bohemia. The lieutenant of the Middle Temple had thirty of the best gentlemen of the society to sup with him; during the meal, he took a cup of wine in one hand, and his drawn sword in the other, and drank a health to the distressed Lady Elizabeth, after which he kissed his sword, and swore to live and die in her service, and then passed the cup and sword round.

On the Twelfth Day in the same Christmas, a ludicrous scene occurred, for at dead of night, the gentlemen of Gray's Inn, in order to make an end of their Christmas, shot off all the chambers they had borrowed from the Tower, which were as many as filled four carts. The king, who, as is well known, could not bear the sight of a naked sword, being awakened with the noise, started out of bed, crying out, "Treason! treason!" The city was in confusion, and the court in arms, the Earl of Arundel running to the king's bed-chamber, with his sword drawn, to rescue his sovereign.

In 1607, there was a celebrated exhibition of the Christmas Prince, at St. John's College, Oxford, conducted with more than usual pomp. A numerous court was appointed, and pageants and dramatic performances were from time to time exhibited; the "Prince," Mr. Thomas Tucker, continuing in his office until Shrove Tuesday. There were some disturbances, in consequence of the inability of many people to find room, but probably not more than occur now occasionally at the Commemoration. Sir John Finett, who was master of the ceremonies to **James the First** and **Charles the First**, and who seems to have considered the settlement of points of etiquette as the very essence of good government, in his quaint publication, called 'Philoxenis,' gives many curious particulars of disputes, in several years, both in this reign and the following one, between the royal ambassadors; and claims of precedence, and fanciful privileges on the part of themselves and their wives; and of his own skill and finesse in arranging them, so as in general to give satisfaction, and prevent the peace of Europe from being disturbed, which, from his statement, but for his diplomatic powers, would appear to have been inevitable, had one ambassador's wife got a back to her chair, while another only had an ottoman. On New Year's Night, for instance, the intended mask was obliged to be postponed, in consequence of some scruple on these formal matters, of the French ambassador, but Sir John happily overcame this before Twelfth Day, when the mask was proceeded with, and the French, Venetian, and Savoyard ambassadors were present. In the following year the prince was a principal actor in the mask, and the French ambassador took umbrage, because the Spanish ambassador was invited. This schism was beyond Sir John Finett's controul; a correspondence ensued, but the French ambassador was recalled before his time had expired. Many of the disputes remind one of the points of etiquette respecting the old French court privilege of the tabouret—as to wearing a cocked hat fore and aft, as it is called, or athwart the head—as to wearing a hat always in a club-room, or in the House of Commons, if a member—as to the number of yards to a peeress' train —as to the feather in the cap of a Highland chief or chieftain —as to the persons entitled to wear long-tailed wigs, or short-tailed wigs, or wigs with a curly tail—and many other equally important points. However, etiquette is probably necessary for the good rule of society, and high and low have their own regulations. We find, in the East, it is considered a highly aristocratic privilege, on ceremonial occasions, that the palanquin should be borne crossways, instead of lengthways, probably because it has a greater chance of being in the way; but it is thought of so much importance, that a few years since, Sri Sunkur Bharti, and Sidha Lingayah Charanti, whoever those grandees might have been, contested the point by appeal to the privy council.

The practice of giving New Year's Gifts and Christmas Boxes remained as before; the value of the gifts to the king having become quite a matter of regulation. An earl, for instance, was to buy a new purse of about 5s. price, and put in it twenty pieces of 20s. value each, and go to the presence chamber on New Year's Day, about eight in the morning, and give them to the lord chamberlain; then to go to the jewel house for a ticket to receive 18s. 6d. as a gift, and give 6d. there for a box for the ticket; then to go to Sir Wm. Veall's office, and receive the 18s. 6d.; then to the jewel house again, and choose a piece of plate of about thirty ounces weight, and mark it, and fetch it away in the afternoon, give the gentleman that delivered it to him 40s. in gold, and to the box 2s. and to the porter 6d.

On New Year's Day, 1604, the young prince, then in his tenth year, gave his father as his gift, a short Latin poem, in hexameter verse, which no doubt delighted the king. In 1610, he gave his sister, for his New Year's Gift, a cabinet of ivory, wrought with silver; five years before this, when she was eight years of age, she had received from the corporation of Coventry a pair of fat oxen, as their gift at this season; certainly a very substantial mark of respect, but a sort of *bon-bon* that would somewhat astonish the royal nursery at present.

The New Year's Gifts, given by the Prince Palatine in 1612, when he married the Princess Elizabeth, were of a sumptuous description, but may be considered more in the light of marriage presents than New Year's Gifts. The jewels, he gave to his mistress alone, were valued at £35,000, comprising a rich chain of diamonds, with pendant diamonds for the ears; and two pearls scarcely to be equalled for size and beauty. To each of her attendants he gave £100; and to her chief usher, £150; to Mrs. Dudley, a chain of pearls and diamonds, worth £500; to Lord and Lady Harrington, golden and gilt plate of the value of £2000; to the prince, a rapier and pair of spurs set with diamonds; and handsome presents to the king and queen. There was great splendour in dress at this wedding; the Lady Wotton had a gown that cost £50 a yard; and Lord Montacute spent £15,000 in apparel for his two daughters. Our ladies (independent of jewels) would have some difficulty to match this at present; but there was great extravagance of dress, in general, in the course of this reign. Even Archie Armstrong, the well-known court-jester, had, on the occasion of this marriage, a coat of crimson velvet and gold lace, yellow worsted hose, and crimson garters.

As specimens of the gifts presented in private life, we find Sir Francis Bacon sending to the lady and daughters of Sir M. Hicks some carnation stockings, with a request that they would wear them for his sake. This would be considered a strange sort of keepsake from a gentleman to a lady at present; but, as the Queen of Spain, in the former days of Spanish etiquette, was said to have no legs; so, from the long dresses now worn, it does not appear to signify much, except as a matter of personal convenience to themselves, whether our ladies have legs or not.

Turkeys and capons were Christmas presents during this age, as the former are still: Justice Greedy says,—

". . . . . . I remember thy wife brought me,
Last New Year's tide, a couple of fat turkeys."

The goose was the more ancient dish than the turkey, which was not introduced into England until the sixteenth century, and the goose is still the favourite bird in Paris and other parts of France, as it also is in the west and some other parts of England. Indeed the Norfolk people may fairly be suspected of having introduced the turkey as the Christmas bird, when we find that several tons weight of them are sent to London from that county annually at this season, some individual birds weighing at least a quarter of a hundred. In Spain patients used to present their medical attendants with turkeys; so that men in large practice had to establish a little trade in them. These turkeys were driven by gipseys from parts of Old Castile, chiefly from Salamanca; the march was about 400 miles, and lasted about half a year, so that the birds left the farmer in the state of chickenhood, but arrived almost at the maturity of turkeyhood on the journey.

There was a good deal of gambling at court during Christmas, in the course of this reign, no one being admitted that brought less than £300. In one night, Montgomery, who played the king's money, won for him £750, which he had for his trouble; Lord Monteagle lost for the queen £400, and Sir Robert Cary for the prince, £300. The following may give some notion of the manner of keeping Christmas, by an English gentleman, at this time, as mentioned in Armin's 'Nest of Ninnies.' "At a Christmas time, when good logs furnish the hall fire, when brawne is in season, and indeed all reveling is regarded, this gallant knight kept open house for all commers, where beefe, beere, and bread was no niggard. Amongst all the pleasures provided, a noyse of minstrells and a Lincolnshire bagpipe was prepared; the minstrells for the great chamber, the bagpipe for the hall; the minstrells to serve up the knight's meate, and the bagpipe for the common dauncing."

The Christmas-block or Yule-log, above referred to, is of very ancient date.

> "Heap on more wood—the wind is chill;
> But let it whistle as it will,
> We'll keep our Christmas merry still."

A massive piece of wood was selected, frequently the rugged root of a tree grotesquely marked, which was brought into the great hall or kitchen, with rejoicing and merriment. The old Christmas gambol of drawing Dun out of the mire—which is referred to as far back as the 'Towneley Mysteries,' "Bot if this draght be welle drawen Don is in the myre,"—was probably connected originally with drawing in the Christmas block.

> "If thou art Dun we'll draw thee from the mire,
> Of this (save reverence) love, wherein thou stick'st
> Up to the ears."

A log of wood is brought in, which is called Dun the cart-horse, and is supposed to stick in the mire. Some of the party then advance and try to extricate him, but they require more assistance; this continues till all are engaged, and Dun is at length drawn out, " I see I'm born still to draw Dun out o' th' mire for you." Much fun arises from the feigned awkwardness of the revellers, and contrivances to drop the log on each other's toes. Herrick says—

> " Come, bring with a noise,
> My merrie merrie boyes,
> The Christmas log to the firing;
> While my good dame, she
> Bids ye all be free,
> And drinke to your heart's desiring.
>
> With the last yeere's brand
> Light the new block, and
> For good success in his spending,
> On your psalteries play,
> That sweet luck may
> Come while the log is a teending,"

Formerly, each of the family sat down on the log in turn, sang a Yule song, and drank to a merry Christmas and happy New Year: after which they had, as part of their feast, Yule dough, or Yule cakes, on which were impressed the figure of the infant Jesus, and sometimes they were made in the shape of a little image, studded with currants and baked, and the bakers gave them as presents to their customers. Bowls of frumenty, made from wheat cakes or creed wheat, boiled in milk, with sugar and nutmeg, &c., also made part of the feast. Nor was the wassail bowl, or the tankard of spiced ale, omitted, but formed a prominent part of the entertainment; Christmas ale being generally of superlative merit.

Horace brings out his log and his best wine, as some of his winter comforts.

> " Dissolve frigus, ligna super foco
> Large reponens; atque benignius
> Deprome quadrimum Sabina,
> O Thaliarche merum diota,"

and in the same ode, refers to pastimes similar to some of ours at Christmas,—

> " Nunc et latentis proditor intimo
> Gratus puellæ risus ab angulo,
> Pignusque dereptum lacertis,
> Aut digito male pertinaci."

Christmas candles of large size, frequently presents from the chandlers, were at the same time used in some places; and, when tired of the sports, the party gathered round the log, and sang carols, or told legendary tales. The Essex logs appear to have been in repute, " We shall have some Essex logs yet to keep Christmas with," says a character in one of Middleton's plays; and there were sometimes services reserved to furnish these Christmas logs; as the cellarist of St. Edmundsbury, for instance, held Hardwick under the Abbey, and was bound annually to provide four Christmas stocks, each of eight feet in length. The strangest log on record, however, is that mentioned by Froissart, at a great feast held by the Count de Foix. After dinner he went up into a gallery, to which there was an ascent of twenty-four steps; it being cold, he complained that the fire was not large enough, on which a person named Ernauton d'Espaign, having seen below several asses laden with wood, went down and brought up-stairs on his back one of the largest, with his load of wood, and threw him on the fire, feet upwards, to the delight of the count and the astonishment of all; and of the poor ass, no doubt, more than all.

A small portion of the log was to be carefully preserved to light that of the following year; and on the last day of its being in use, which, in some places, was on Candlemas Day, a small piece having been kept on purpose, the custom was to—

> "Kindle the Christmas brand, and then
> Till sunne-set let it burne;
> Which quencht, then lay it up agen,
> Till Christmas next returne.
>
> Part must be kept, wherewith to teend
> The Christmas log next yeare;
> And where 'tis safely kept, the fiend
> Can do no mischiefe there."

The Souche de Noël, in some places on the Continent, was very similar to our log.

As to minstrels, the waits of Southwark, according to the Citizen in the 'Knight of the Burning Pestle,' were as rare fellows as any in England, and two shillings would bring them all o'er the water with a vengeance, as if they were mad. In the commencement of the following reign a character in a play by Shirley introduces the city waits in a speech that, with one slight alteration, is applicable to the present panic felt by many persons respecting the possibility of foreign invasion: "We will have the city waites down with us, and a noise of trumpets; we can have drums in the country, and the train-band, and then let the [French] come an they dare."

Burton, in his 'Anatomy of Melancholy,' mentions "The ordinary recreations which we have in winter, and in most solitary times busie our minds with, are *cardes, tables,* and *dice, shovelboard, chesse-play,* the philosopher's game, small trunkes, shuttle-cocke, billiards, musicke, masks, singing, dancing, ulegames, frolicks, jests, riddles, catches, purposes, questions and commands, merry tales of errant knights, queenes, lovers, lords, ladies, giants, dwarfes, theeves, cheaters, witches, fayries, goblins, friers," &c.

After the accession of Charles the First, Christmas was frequently observed with great splendour, and a variety of plays, masks, and pageants, in which the king and queen, with some of the courtiers, occasionally took part, until about the year 1641, when the civil disturbances interfered with all social enjoyments, and the spirit of fanaticism even endeavoured to abolish any commemoration of the Nativity of our Saviour. The king had his mask on Twelfth Day, and the queen hers on the Shrovetide following, and considerable sums were granted for the expenses, often exceeding £2000.

The Christmas of 1632-3 was dull; the queen, having some little infirmity, the bile or some such thing, kept in, and there was but one play and no dancing; the gambling however remained as before, the king carrying away £1850, of which the queen took half. On Twelfth Night however she feasted the king at Somerset House, and presented a pastoral, in which she herself took part, and which, with other masks, cost considerably more than £2000.

In the following year there were no masks, but 'Cymbeline' was acted before the court, and well liked. Prynne, in his 'Histriomastix,' having been supposed to reflect on the queen for her love of these diversions, was severely punished, as is well known.

In the Christmas of 1641-2 only one play was acted, being on Twelfth Day, at the cockpit in Whitehall; but the king and queen were in no mood to be present, as the king on the previous day had paid his eventful visit to the House of Commons to demand the five members: and after this time he had matter of too much moment to engage his attention to allow of any further indulgence in festivities or amusement, thenceforth, alas! unknown to him. The struggle then began on the part of the Puritans to abolish Christmas as a festival altogether. The first ordinances to suppress the performance of plays were issued in 1642, and doubt began to be expressed as to the proper manner of keeping this feast: in Christmas 1643, some in the city opened their shops, but they were shut again, people being afraid of any popish observance, as they called it, of the day. On one occasion, 1644, Christmas Day was kept as a fast, as it fell on the last Wednesday of the month, which was the day appointed by parliament for a monthly fast, and it was ordered that this should not be an exception.

Ministers were prohibited from preaching God's word on the Nativity, and were imprisoned if they attempted to do so; and in 1647 the parish officers of St. Margaret's, Westminster, were committed and fined for allowing some of them to preach on Christmas Day, and for adorning the Church with rosemary and bays.

On the 3d of June in that year, the parliament abolished the observance of Christmas and many other holidays, directing that, instead of them, all scholars, apprentices, and servants should, with leave of their masters, have a holiday on the second Tuesday in every month. On this being proclaimed at Canterbury, just previous to the ensuing Christmas, and the mayor directing a market to be kept on that day, a serious disturbance took place, wherein many were severely hurt.

On the 24th of December, 1652, the observance of Christmas Day was strongly prohibited, and several entries may be found in Evelyn's Memoirs, in that and subsequent years, to the effect that no service was allowed in the churches on that day, so that it was kept at home or privately by the right-minded, who occasionally got into difficulty in consequence. Evelyn with his wife and others, while taking the sacrament on Christmas Day, 1657, were taken into custody for breach of the ordinance of the parliament, but were let off. In a satirical list of supposed works called 'Bibliotheca Parliamenti,' 1653, is 'An Act for the speedy suppressing all Plays, the Fools being all turned Commanders or Parliament men.' Even in the midst of fanaticism, however, Christmas festivities could not be entirely abolished; and in the 'Vindication of Christmas,' old Father Christmas, complaining of his treatment for the last twelve years, says, "But welcome, or not welcome, I am come;" and says his best welcome was with some Devonshire farmers, thus describing his entertainment:—"After dinner we arose from the boord, and sate by the fire, where the harth was imbrodered all over with roasted apples, piping hot, expecting a bole of ale for a cooler, which immediately was transformed into warm lambwool. After which we discoursed merily, without either prophaness or obscenity; some went to cards: others sang carols and pleasant songs (suitable to the times); then the poor labouring hinds, and maidservants, with the plow-boys, went nimbly to dancing; the poor toyling wretches being glad of my company, because they had little or no sport at all till I came amongst them; and therefore they skipped and leaped for joy, singing a carol to the tune of hey,

> 'Let's dance and sing, and make good chear,
>   For Christmas comes but once a year;
> Draw hogsheads dry, let flagons fly,
>   For now the bells shall ring;
> Whilst we endeavour to make good
>   The title 'gainst a king.'

Thus, at active games and gambols of hot cockles, shoeing the wild mare, and the like harmless sports, some part of the tedious night was spent; and early in the morning, I took my leave of them, promising they should have my presence again the next 25th of December, 1653."

Herrick, in his 'New Year's Gift' sent to Sir Simeon Steward, sings—

> "Of Christmas sports, the wassel boule,
> That tost up after fox-i-th'-hole;
> Of blind-man-buffe, and of the care
> That young men have to shooe the mare;
> Of Twelf-tide cakes, of pease and beanes,
> Wherewith ye make those merry sceanes,
> When as ye chuse your king and queen,
> And cry out, 'Hey for our town green.'"

The noblemen and gentry were, in the early part of the reign, directed to return to their mansion-houses in the country, to keep up hospitality during the Christmas; and many of them lived like petty princes, their household establishments forming almost a mimic court. The Christmas feast was kept up, the poor man's heart was cheered by earthly comforts, and he was led to the contemplation of the eternal blessings bestowed on man at this tide. The great hall resounded with the mirth of the servants, and tenants, and other dependents, whose gambols amused the lord of the mansion, and his family, and friends; and their presence and participation in the festivities, together with the shows exhibited by them, of which the poorer class were frequently allowed to be the amused spectators, encouraged them, and mitigated the trials and privations of the winter.

A splendid Christmas, held by Richard Evelyn, Esq., High Sheriff of Surrey and Sussex, in 1634, at Wotton, may be taken as an example. A lord of Misrule was appointed; in this case, Owen Flood, gentleman, trumpeter to Mr. Evelyn, was chosen, and regulations were made to support his authority; amongst others, that if any man should kiss any maid, widow, or wife, except to bid welcome or farewell, without his lordship's consent, he should have punishment as his lordship should think convenient; it is to be presumed, however, that the misletoe bough was a privileged place, a sort of kissing sanctuary. The hall of the mansion being open on these occasions, many gifts were made to assist in provisioning the guests, and, at this time, the contributions were, two sides of venison, two half brawns, three pigs, ninety capons, five geese, six turkeys, four rabbits, eight partridges, two pullets, five sugar-loaves, half a pound of nutmegs, one basket of apples and eggs, three baskets of apples, and two baskets of pears.

The Christmas festivities, at some of the colleges, and at the Inns of Court, were continued in this reign. In 1627-8, there was a collision between Mr. Palmer, lord of Misrule of the Temple, and the lord-mayor and city authorities. The Temple lord chose to claim rents of 5$s.$ a piece from the houses in Ram Alley and Fleet Street, and broke open doors to enforce it, if not quietly opened. The lord-mayor went with his watch to meet him, and after some scuffle, Mr. Palmer was wounded and taken prisoner, and sent to the Compter, and, after two nights, was released, by the intercession of the attorney-general, on payment of all damages, and restoring the rents.

In the ninth of Charles, the Inns of Court spent £2400 about their Christmas celebration, and the king was so pleased with it, that he asked 120 of the members to a mask at Whitehall, on the following Shrove Tuesday.

There was also a splendid Christmas at the Middle Temple, in 1635, when Mr. Francis Vivian, of Cornwall, who had been fined in the Star Chamber, about three years before, in respect of a castle he held in that county, was the Christmas Prince, and expended £2000 out of his own pocket, beyond the allowance of the Society, in order to support his state with sufficient dignity. He had his lord keeper, lord treasurer, eight white staves, captain of pensioners and his guard, and two chaplains, who, when they preached before him, saluted him on ascending the pulpit with three low bows, as was then done to the king. The lord-mayor and sheriffs supplied him with wine, and Lord Holland, his justice in Eyre, with venison. These descriptions really make us regret the cessation of such festivities.

In December, 1641, Evelyn was elected one of the comptrollers of the Middle Temple revellers, the Christmas being kept with great solemnity; but he got excused from serving. The most magnificent entertainment, however, given by the Inns of Court, was on Candlemas Day, 1633—which day was frequently distinguished by a farewell Christmas entertainment, and the rule of the Christmas Prince extended to it—

when the two Temples, Lincoln's Inn and Gray's Inn, jointly presented Shirley's 'Triumph of Peace,' at an expense to the Societies of more than £20,000. The music, under the superintendence of William Lawes and Simon Ives, cost £1000, and the dresses of the horsemen were valued at £10,000. Whitelocke and Hyde were two of the principal managers, and the former wrote for it his celebrated 'Coranto.' The king was so much entertained, that he requested it to be performed again a few days afterwards at Merchant Tailors' Hall. Whether Gray's Inn was more or less inclined to play than the other Inns is not very material; but the following order, in the fourth of Charles, may be taken either way, "that all playing at dice, cards, or otherwise, in the hall, buttry, or butler's chamber, should be thenceforth barred, and forbidden at all times of the year, the twenty days in Christmas only excepted." The Inner Temple, not to be outdone in propriety, ordered, in 1632, that no play should be continued after twelve at night, not even on Christmas Eve.

New Year's Gifts were given as in former reigns; even little Jeffery Hudson gave the queen in 1638, 'The New Year's Gift,' written by Microphilus, meaning himself. The Duke of Buckingham, who was regardless of expense, appears to have given £20 to the celebrated Archie, the king's jester; and £13 6s. 8d. to the king's fool, meaning his other court fool, probably David Dromon. There is a story told of Archie, who having fooled many was fooled himself; and perhaps by this very nobleman. Archie went to him, or to the nobleman whoever he was, to bid him good morrow on New Year's Day, and received twenty pieces of gold as his New Year's Gift; but covetously desiring more, shook them in his hand, and said they were too light. The donor said,

" I prithee, Archie, let me see them again, for there is one among them I would be loth to part with." Archie unsuspectingly returned them, expecting them to be increased; but the nobleman put them in his pocket, with this remark, " I once gave money into a fool's hand, who had not the wit to keep it." The story of his having stolen a sheep, and hid it in a cradle, has been mentioned before, but is probably spurious.

This Archie, or Archibald Armstrong, may be considered as the last of the regular or official court fools; for Killigrew, in the succeeding reign, although a licensed wit, was of a higher class, both by birth and education; and Pepys's account of his having a fee for cap and bells was apparently meant as a joke. The last play, in which the regular fool was introduced, was probably, ' The Woman Captain,' by Shadwell, 1680. Tarleton, in the preceding century, was a celebrated performer in these characters.

A strange appendage this officer or attendant was to royal and noble establishments; known even in oriental courts; and continued from the time of the Anglo-Saxons, or perhaps of the ancient Britons, to the time of which we are now writing. They often became such favourites as to gain great influence with their royal and noble masters, and frequently possessed more wit and discretion than the so-called or self-called sages, who endeavoured to make them their laughing stock, but whose attempts frequently flew back, like the boomarang, on their own heads. They differed of course much in merit, from the fellow of infinite jest to the mere practical joker, or the half-witted butt for the gibes of others. Will Somers was a recognised favourite of the capricious Henry the Eighth, and appears to have been a man of good conduct; two or three portraits of him may be still seen among the royal pictures at Hampton Court. It would be out of place to give any anecdotes of these characters here, or we might begin with Goles, the domestic fool of William the Conqueror, when Duke of Normandy, who saved his master's life by giving timely notice of a conspiracy; then mentioning William Picolf, who held land from King John on performing fool's service; Martinot of Gascoigne, fool to Edward the First; Robert le Foll, to Edward the Second; Ward, to Richard the Second, who, having some personal resemblance to that king, was induced after his death to personate him, for the purpose of an insurrection; Peche, in the time of Henry the Seventh; Sexton, Somers, and Williams, in the time of Henry the Eighth, the latter having been fool to Cardinal Wolsey, and when recommended by him to the king, after his disgrace, the faithful servant was obliged to be moved from his old master almost by force; Chester, who seems to have been somewhat of an impertinent disposition, in the time of Queen Elizabeth; with others that might be named, down to Archie Armstrong, Davie Dromon, George Stone, and Dicky Pearce; with a few words for Jane the female fool to Queen Mary; female fools, however, being rare. There were also celebrated professional fools in continental courts, as Moret, Bagot, Chichot, who was a man of courage, and accompanied his master to the wars; Triboulet, fool to Francis the First; and Mathurine, a female fool, who was with Henry the Fourth of France when he was stabbed by Jean Chastel, and was the means of the criminal being discovered.

Will Somers's notion of cramming himself with salt beef, when on a voyage, may be submitted to travellers for consideration. When he was crossing to Boulogne with his master, Henry, the weather was rough, and he was observed to eat salt beef greedily, and on the king asking him the reason why he preferred salt meat when there was plenty of fresh, he replied, "Don't blame me for filling my stomach with salt meat, because, if we are cast away, I know what a quantity of water I shall have to drink after it." These personages, however, did not always enjoy their privileges without drawbacks, and were liable to punishment, even to whipping. George Stone, in the time of James the First, had a sound flogging for saying, when the Earl of Nottingham went ambassador to Spain, that there went sixty fools into Spain, besides my lord admiral and his two sons. Archie Armstrong, as is well known, was sentenced to have his coat pulled over his head, discharged the king's service, and banished the court, for abuse of Archbishop Laud, having given "great praise to God, but little *laud* to the devil." It was not, however, of much consequence to him, for he was a careful man, and by this time—

> "Archee, by kings and princes grac'd of late,
> Jested himself into a fair estate."

CHAPTER VII.

E have observed that the churchwardens of St. Margaret's, Westminster, were fined in 1617 for decorating their church at Christmas. The practice, as before referred to, existed from the earliest times; and in the churchwardens' accounts of various parishes in the fifteenth and following centuries, entries may be found of payments for holme, holly, and ivy; and even during the Commonwealth the practice was not extinct, although the puritans tried to abolish it; for in 'Festorum Metropolis,' 1652, the author, who supports the cause of Christmas, then endeavoured to be suppressed by the puritans, mentions the trimming of churches and houses with bays,

rosemary, holly, ivy, box, and privet, and answers the objections made to the practice. Coles also, in his 'Art of Simpling,' 1656, says, that in some places setting up holly, ivy, rosemary, bays, &c. in churches at Christmas, was still in use. Aubrey mentions it as the custom in many parts of Oxfordshire for the maid-servant to ask one of the men for ivy to dress the house, and if he refused or neglected it, she was to steal a pair of his breeches, and nail them up to the gate in the yard or highway. Poor Robin, whose Almanac contains many allusions to Christmas customs, in a Christmas song of 1695, sings,

" With holly and ivy
So green and so gay,
We deck up our houses
As fresh as the day;
With bays and rosemary,
And laurel compleate,
And every one now
Is a king in conceite."

The practice has continued to the present time, when the addition of the chrysanthemum, satin flower, and other everlastings, mingling with the red berry of the holly and the waxen one of the mystic misletoe, together with occasionally the myrtle and laurustinum, have a very pleasing and cheerful effect. In most places these greens and flowers are taken down after Twelfth Day, except in churches, where they are frequently kept till Lent; but, according to Herrick, they should remain in houses until Candlemas Day, and then

" Down with the rosemary and so
Down with the baies and misletoe;
Down with the holly, ivie, all
Wherewith ye drest the Christmas hall;

> That so the superstitious find
> No one least branch there left behind,
> For look, how many leaves there be
> Neglected there, maids, trust to me,
> So many goblins you shall see."

After the Restoration, the festive as well as the sacred observance of Christmas was immediately resumed, and on the very first Christmas Day, Evelyn says, Dr. Rainbow preached before the king, when the service was performed with music, voices, &c., as formerly. The court revels, however, never recovered their former splendour; plays, masks, and pageants were nearly abandoned, and the festivities gradually assumed the form of a mere state party, until in the time of our present gifted queen, the plays at court have been resumed with the utmost taste and talent. The manners of the country in general had been much changed during the ascendancy of the puritan party and the troubles occasioned by the civil wars; and the habits of Charles the Second were of too indolent and sensual a nature to care much for any trouble in the court pageants, though gambling at the groom-porter's was prevalent—Charles generally opening there the Christmas revels, if they may be so called; the play was deep, of which many instances are given, the ladies joining in it. A pastoral, however, by Crowne, called 'Calisto,' was at one time acted by the daughters of the Duke of York (afterwards James the Second) and the young nobility; and Lady Anne, afterwards queen, about the same time acted the part of Semandra, in Lee's 'Mithridates.' Betterton and his wife instructed the performers; in remembrance of which, when Anne came to the throne, she gave the latter a pension of £100 a year.

The Inns of Court continued their revels; and in January, 1662, Pepys mentions that while he was at Faithorne's, the celebrated engraver's, he saw the king's life-guards, he being gone to Lincoln's Inn, where, according to old custom, there was a prince and all his nobles, and other matters of sport and charge. Evelyn, who was present at these revels, speaks somewhat disdainfully of them, calling them "the solemn foolerie of the Prince de la Grange, where came the king, duke," &c. It began with a grand mask, and a formal pleading before the mock princes, grandees, nobles, and knights of the sun. He had his lord chancellor, chamberlain, treasurer, and other royal officers, gloriously clad and attended; and ended in a magnificent banquet; one Mr. Lort being the "young spark" who maintained the pageantry.

In January, 1688, Evelyn went, after the meeting of the Royal Society, to see the revels at the Middle Temple, which he calls an old, but riotous, custom, and had no relation to virtue or policy. He did not know that the most eager in these sports are frequently among the wisest of their class, and that the philosopher can sometimes wear the garb of folly gracefully.

Towards the end of the seventeenth century, however, these revels ceased, having gradually fallen off, and the dignity of master of the revels, instead of being eagerly sought for, as in former times, required a bribe or premium to induce any member to take it upon him. We find, for instance, in the records of Gray's Inn, on the 3d of November, 1682, that Mr. Richard Gipps, on his promise to perform the office of master of the revels that and the next term, should be called to the bar, of grace, that is, without payment of the usual fees.

The amusing gossip Pepys was a much more agreeable

Christmas companion apparently than Evelyn. How one would like to have joined such a party as he describes on the 4th of January, 1667, when having had company to dinner, at night, the last thing they had was a flagon of ale and apples drunk out of a wood cup as a Christmas draught, which made all merry! This was keeping up the old custom of the wassail bowl (was Knipp of this sociable party?); and no doubt Pepys entered heartily into all the old customs, and certainly was liberal as to his gifts; for, on December 28th, 1668, he says that drums, trumpets, and boxes cost him much money that Christmas. On the previous Christmas Day he had been quiet, though probably in expectation of some approaching party, having dined at home with his wife, who sat undressed all day until ten at night, altering and lacing of a "noble petticoat." So, ladies we see, even in those times, contrived and worked a little to vary and ornament that apparel which adds so much grace to their charms; and though "when unadorned, adorned the most," is frequently quoted with approbation, yet it probably is often misunderstood, and simplicity with taste in ornament is always an object of admiration. Pepys gives an amusing account of Sir George Downing, a man of thrift, who asked some poor people (poor relations probably) to dine with him at Christmas, and gave them nothing but beef, porridge, pudding, and pork; there was nothing said during the dinner, except his mother would remark, "It's good broth, son." "Yes, it is good broth," he would answer. "Confirm all," says the lady, and say, "Yes, very good broth." By and bye, she would say, "Good pork;" to which the son would respond, "Yes, very good pork." And so throughout the scanty bill of fare, the humble guests saying nothing, as they went not out of love or esteem, but for the purpose of getting a good dinner, a rare occurrence perhaps to some of them.

The Rev. Henry Teonge, chaplain of one of our ships of war, gives the following description of a Christmas Day of quite another sort, in 1675, "Crismas Day wee keepe thus: At four in the morning our trumpeters all doe flatt their trumpetts, and begin at our captain's cabin, and thence to all the officers' and gentlemen's cabins; playing a levite at each cabine door, and bidding good morrow, wishing a merry Crismas. After they goe to their station, viz. on the poope, and sound three levitts in honour of the morning. At ten we goe to prayers and sermon; text, Zacc. ix, 9. Our captaine had all his officers and gentlemen to dinner with him, where wee had excellent good fayre: a ribb of beefe, plumb-puddings, minct pyes, &c., and plenty of good wines of severall sorts; dranke healths to the king, to our wives and friends, and ended the day with much civill myrth." Teonge and his companions seem to have been a merry, pleasant set, and he thus describes their ensuing Twelfth Day. "Very ruff weather all the last night, and all this day. Wee are now past Zante; had wee beene there this day, wee had scene a greate solemnity; for this day being 12 day, the Greeke Bishop of Zante doth (as they call it) baptise the sea, with a great deale of ceremonie, sprinkling their gallys and fishing-tackle with holy water. But wee had much myrth on board, for wee had a greate kake made, in which was put a beane for the king, a pease for the queen, a cloave for the knave, a forked stick for the cuckold, a ragg for the slutt. The kake was cut into severall pieces in the great cabin, and all put into a napkin, out of which every one took his piece, as out of a lottery; then each piece is broaken to see what was in it, which caused much laughter, to see our leiuetenant prove the coockold, and more to see us tumble one over the other in the cabin, by reason of the ruff weather." The celebrated Lord Peterborough, then a youth, was one of the party on board this ship, as Lord Mordaunt.

Poor Robin's almanack, for 1675, gives some notion of the bill of fare for Christmas at this time among the middle classes.

" Now the season of the year
Bids thee to provide good cheer,
For to feast thy needy neighbours,
Who do live by their hard labours;
Then thy coyn freely bestow
For raisins, sun, and maligo;
No currans, prunes, nor sugar lack,
Pepper, both the white and black,
Nutmegs, ginger, cloves, and mace,
Rice for porridge i' th' first place;
Pork and mutton, veal and beef,
For hungry stomachs good relief;
Pig, goose, turkey, capon, coney,
What may be had for thy money;
Plum-pudding, and furmity,
Mutton pasties, Christmas pye;
Nappy ale, a full carouse
To the master of the house;
And instead of tobacco pipes,
The fidler up an old dance strikes."

In following years there are descriptions somewhat similar.

New Year's Gifts were continued; and at court they seem to have been arranged according to rule, and were generally in money. The aggregate amount presented was about £3000, sent in purses, worth 30s. or 40s. each, the donors receiving gifts of gilt plate in return. Pepys mentions his going to the jewell office, on the 4th of January, 1661, to choose a piece of plate for Earl Sandwich, who had given twenty pieces of gold in a purse. His account will suffice to show the perfect matter of routine then existing, as well as the amount of recognised official peculation. He chose a gilt tankard, weighing thirty-one ounces and a half, but this was an ounce and a half more than the Earl, or the value of the Earl's gift, was entitled to, this limit being thirty ounces; so Pepys was obliged to pay 12s. for the extra ounce and a half, so much was it a matter of calculation. He adds, " Strange it was for me to see what a company of small fees I was called upon by a great many to pay there, which, I perceive, is the manner that courtiers do get their estates."

The spirit of Christmas, however, had received a check in the time of the Commonwealth, which it struggled in vain to overcome entirely. The hospitality and festivities in private houses recovered, and were prevalent in the eighteenth century, and exist in many parts, and to a certain extent, even in the present utilitarian age; but the pageants and masks, in the royal household, and at the Inns of Court, had received a death-blow; although they were not actually abolished until the latter end of the century. Evelyn mentions a riotous and revelling Christmas at the Inner Temple, according to custom, as late as 1697, and says that his brother, who appears to have been a worthy, as well as a wealthy, squire, in the previous year *more veterum*, kept a Christmas at Wotton, in which they had not fewer than 300 bumpkins every holyday.

In 1702, Poor Robin makes complaints of the falling off of Christmas festivities.

> " But now landlords and tenants too
> In making feasts are very slow ;
> One in an age, or near so far,
> Or one perhaps each blazing star ;
> The cook now and the butler too,
> Have little or nothing for to do ;
> And fidlers who used to get scraps,
> Now cannot fill their hungry chaps ;
> Yet some true English blood still lives,
> Who gifts to the poor at *Christmas* gives,
> And to their neighbours make a feast,
> I wish their number were increast,
> And that their stock may never decay,
> *Christmas* may come again in play,
> And poor man keep it holyday."

Many of the popular ballads, in the latter part of the seventeenth century, refer to the same falling off in Christmas feasting, complaining of the degeneracy of the times. Poets and ballad writers, however, from the earliest times, certainly as far back as Homer, have been noted for this species of grumbling. Praising the bygone times, in order to conceal the annoyance at having had so many of our would-be-original good things said by our ancestors before us.

Nedham in his 'History of the Rebellion,' 1661, alluding to the times before the Commonwealth, says—

> " Gone are those golden days of yore,
>   When Christmas was a high day ;
> Whose sports we now shall see no more,
>   'Tis turn'd into Good Friday."

In 'The Old and Young Courtier,' printed in 1670, we have comparisons between the times of Elizabeth and the then modern times, including the following lines as to Christmas,—

> "With a good old fashion, when Christmasse was come,
> To call in all his old neighbours with bagpipe and drum,
> With good chear enough to furnish every old roome,
> And old liquor, able to make a cat speak, and man dumb.
>   Like an old courtier of the queen's,
>   And the queen's old courtier."

then comes the contrast,—

> "With a new fashion, when Christmas is drawing on,
> On a new journey to London, straight we all must begone,
> And leave none to keep house, but our new porter, John,
> Who relieves the poor with a thump on the back with a stone.
>   Like a young courtier of the king's,
>   And the king's young courtier."

In "'Time's Alteration; or, the Old Man's Rehearsal,' what brave dayes he knew a great while agone, when his old cap was new," there is much in the same strain,—

> "Black jacks to every man
> Were fill'd with wine and beer;
> No pewter pot nor can
> In those days did appear:
>
> Good cheer in a nobleman's house
> Was counted a seemly show;
> We wanted no brawn nor souse,
> When this old cap was new."

But, 'Old Christmas Returned,' probably written at the

time of the Restoration and prior to the last-named ballads, gives a more favourable view, and welcomes the return of Christmas.

> "All you that to feasting and mirth are inclin'd,
> Come here is good news for to pleasure your mind;
> Old Christmas is come for to keep open house,
> He scorns to be guilty of starving a mouse;
> Then come, boys, and welcome for diet the chief,
> Plum-pudding, goose, capon, minc'd pies and roast beef.
>
> A long time together he hath been forgot,
> They scarce could afford for to hang on the pot;
> Such miserly sneaking in England hath been,
> As by our forefathers ne'er us'd to be seen;
> But now he's returned you shall have in brief,
> Plum-pudding, goose, capon, minc'd pies and roast beef."

The last line forms the burden of every stanza. A few years later, in 1695, Poor Robin welcomes Christmas much in the same terms,—

> "Now, thrice welcome, Christmas,
> Which brings us good cheer,
> Minc'd pies and plumb-porridge,
> Good ale and strong beer;
> With pig, goose, and capon,
> The best that may be,
> So well doth the weather
> And our stomachs agree."

Really, one may say with Terence, "jamdudum animus est in patinis," and eating seems to be a happy invention, occupying a valuable portion of our existence. Old Tusser, long before, had recommended somewhat similar dishes for Christmas,—

> "Brawn, pudding, and souse, and good mustard withal,
> Beef, mutton, and pork, shred pies of the best,
> Pig, veal, goose, and capon, and turkey well dressed;
> Cheese, apples, and nuts, jolly carols to hear
> As then in the country is counted good cheer."

This was hearty and hospitable fare, fit for the fine old gentry of England; but Massinger talks of something more luxurious, hardly to be surpassed in our scientific days.

> "Men may talk of country Christmasses,
> Their thirty pound butter'd eggs, their pies of carps' tongues,
> Their pheasants drench'd with ambergris, the carcases
> Of three fat wethers bruised for gravy to
> Make sauce for a single peacock."

The well-known minced or Christmas pie is of considerable antiquity, and many references are made to it in early writers. It is customary, in London, to introduce them at the lord-mayor's feast, on the 9th of November, where many hundreds of them appear; but this is an irregularity that some archæological lord-mayor will, no doubt, by and bye, correct; at any rate they should be eaten under protest, or without prejudice, as lawyers say. They ought to be confined to the season of Christmas, and the practice of using up the remnant of the mince meat, even up to Easter, should be put a stop to by some of our ecclesiastical reformers. So much were they considered as connected with Christmas, that the puritans treated their use as a superstitious observance, and after the Restoration they almost served as a test of religious opinions. Bunyan, when in confinement and in distress for a comfortable meal, for some time refused to injure his morals by eating them when he might have done so. Misson, in the beginning of the last century, says they were made of neats' tongues, chicken, eggs, sugar, currants, lemon and orange peel, with various spices.

The modern receipts are similar, and the less meat they contain the better. The following is a well-tried and much approved one, and has been handed down in the same family for generations: "A pound of beef suet, chopped fine; a pound of raisins, do. stoned; a pound of currants, cleaned dry; a pound of apples, chopped fine; two or three eggs; allspice beat very fine, and sugar to your taste; a little salt, and as much brandy and wine as you like:" a small piece of citron in each pie is an improvement, and the cover or case should be oblong, in imitation of the crache or manger where our Saviour was laid, the ingredients themselves having been said to have some reference to the offering of the wise men.

James the First's dislike to the look of a naked sword took its rise from about the time of his birth; but Lord Feesimple, a cowardly character, in 'Amends for Ladies,' one of Field's plays, attributes his lack of courage to an incident during that extensive chopping season, the necessary precursor of minced pies. " I being in the kitchen, in my lord my father's house, the cook was making mine'd pies; so, sir, I standing by the dresser, there lay a heap of plums; here was he mincing; what did me? I, sir, being a notable little witty coxcomb, but popp'd my hand just under his chopping-knife, to snatch some raisins, and so was cut o'er the hand; and never since could I endure the sight of any edge tool." There is a superstition that in as many different houses as you eat minced pies during Christmas, so many happy months will you have in the ensuing year; you have only therefore to go to a different house each day in the Christmas to ensure a happy twelvemonth, a simple receipt, if effectual. Something like this is mentioned in 'Dives and Pauper,' by W. de Worde, 1496, where the custom is reprobated of judging of the weather of the coming year by that of the days of Christmas. This was also prognosticated by the day of the week on which Christmas Day fell, and there are some old Christmas songs referring to it. In the 'Golden Legend,' of the same printer, is a more laudable prejudice, "That what persone, beynge in clene lyfe, desyre on thys daye a boone of God; as ferre as it is ryghtfull and good for hym; our lorde at reuerēce of thys blessid and hye feste of his Natiuite wol graūt it to hym."

The north of England is celebrated for its Christmas pies of a different description, composed of turkeys, geese, game, and various small birds, weighing sometimes half a hundred weight and upwards, and calculated to meet the attacks of a large Christmas party throughout the festival. Plum-pudding, of which the old name is said to have been *hackin*, until the time of Charles the Second, is another valuable dish; though, fortunately for its admirers, not confined to Christmas time. Plum-porridge seems to be something like the French edition of plum-pudding brought up to our ambassador many years since, which had been boiled without the cloth; it is, however, mentioned by Misson, and not very many years since the custom existed of serving up a tureen of it at the table of the royal chaplains at St. James's Palace.

An amusing little book, called 'Round about our coal-fire, or Christmas Entertainments,' gives an account of the manner of observing this festival, by the middling classes, about the middle of the seventeenth century, and as the writer, in the spirit of grumbling, refers to former times, he may be supposed to carry back his reference to old times for a century earlier. "The manner of celebrating this great course of holydays," he says, "is vastly different now to what it was in former days: there was once upon a time hospitality in the land; an *English* gentleman, at the opening of the great day, had all his tenants and neighbours enter'd his hall by day-break, the strong beer was broach'd, and the black-jacks went plentifully about with toast, sugar, nutmeg, and good Cheshire cheese; the rooms were embower'd with holly, ivy, cypress, bays, laurel, and misleto, and a bouncing *Christmas* log in the chimney, glowing like the cheeks of a country milk-maid; there was the pewter as bright as *Clarinda*, and every bit of brass as polished as the most refined gentleman; the servants were then running here and there, with merry hearts and jolly countenances; every one was busy in welcoming of guests, and look'd as snug as new-lick'd puppies; the lasses were as blithe and buxom as the maids in good Queen *Bess's* days, when they eat sirloins of roast beef for breakfast; *Peg* would scuttle about to make a toast for *John*, while *Tom* run *harum scarum* to draw a jug of ale for *Margery*." "In these times all the spits were sparkling, the *hackin* (pudding) must be boil'd by day-break, or else two young men took the maiden by the arms, and run her round the market-place, till she was ashamed of her laziness." "This great festival was, in former times, kept with so much freedom and openness of heart, that every one in the country where a gentleman resided, possessed at least a day of pleasure in the *Christmas* holydays; the tables were all spread, from the first to the last, with the sirloyns of beef, the minc'd pies, the plumb-porridge, the capons, turkeys, geese, and plumb-puddings, were all brought upon the board; and all those who had sharp stomacks and sharp knives, eat heartily and were welcome, which gave rise to the proverb, *Merry in the hall, where beards wag all.* There were then turnspits employed, who, by the time dinner was over, would look as black and as greasy as a Welsh porridge-pot, but the jacks have since turned them all out of doors. The geese, who used to be fatted for the honest neighbours, have been of late sent to *London*, and the quills made into pens, to convey away the landlord's estate; the sheep are drove away, to raise money to answer the loss at a game at dice or cards, and their skins made into parchment for deeds and indentures; nay, even the poor innocent bee, who was used to pay its tribute to the lord once a year at least in good metheglin, for the entertainment of the guests, and its wax converted into beneficial plaisters for sick neighbours, is now used for the sealing of deeds to his disadvantage." He adds, however, "the spirit of hospitality has not quite forsaken us; several of the gentry are gone down to their respective seats in the country, in order to keep their *Christmas* in the old way, and entertain their tenants and tradesfolks as their ancestors used to do; and I wish them a merry *Christmas* accordingly."

He gives a ridiculous example of the influence of the squire in former times; that if he asked a neighbour what it was o'clock, the answer would be with a low scrape, "It is what your worship pleases." Dr. Arbuthnot, however, is reported to have given a similar answer to Queen Anne, "Whatever time it pleases your majesty."

Among the amusements mentioned are mumming or masquerading, when the squire's wardrobe was ransacked for

dresses, and burnt corks were in requisition; blind-man's buff, puss in the corner, questions and commands, hoop and hide, story-telling, and dancing. In some places it seems to have been the custom to dance in the country churches, after prayers, crying out, " Yole, yole, yole!" &c.

Previous to the time of Queen Anne, it had been the custom for the officers of his court and for the suitors to present gifts to the chancellor; the officers also exacting gifts from the suitors to reimburse themselves. The chancery bar breakfasted with the chancellor on the 1st of January, and gave him pecuniary New Year's Gifts to gain his good graces according to their means and liberality. The practice also was common to the other courts; and the marshal of the King's Bench used to present the judges with a piece of plate, a gift which Sir Matthew Hale wished to decline, but fearing he might injure his successors, he received the value in money, and distributed it among the poor prisoners. Sir Thomas More always returned the gifts, and being presented on one occasion, by one Mrs. Goaker, with a pair of gloves containing forty angels, he said to her, " Mistresse, since it were against good manners to refuse your New-year's gift, I am content to take your gloves, but as for the *lining* I utterly refuse it." When Lord Cowper, however, became lord keeper, in 1705, he determined to abolish the practice, and mentioned the subject to Godolphin, the prime minister, that he might not injure his patronage in the value of the place, but he was desired, in effect, to act as he thought proper. He incurred much obloquy at first from the other courts and public offices where the practice likewise existed, but he persevered, and his example was followed, though slowly, by them.

There is an old custom in the north of England, according to Brockett's 'North Country Glossary,' that the first person who enters the house on New Year's Day is called First-Foot, who is considered to influence the fate of the family, especially the female part, for the whole of the year. Need we doubt that the fair damsels of the household take good care that some favoured swain shall be this influential First-Foot, hoping perhaps that ere the next season he may have a dwelling of his own to receive such characters, instead of enacting it himself; of course he comes provided with an acceptable New Year's Gift.

CHAPTER VIII.

HE masks and pageants at court appear to have been gradually abandoned from the time of the Restoration, as before mentioned. They were succeeded by grand feasts and entertainments, which also fell gradually into disuse, and latterly even that relic, the Christmas tureen of plum-porridge, served up at the royal chaplains' table, was omitted, and the crown-pieces under their plates for New Year's Gifts soon followed. The poet-laureat has long since been relieved from that tax on his imagination, the New Year's Ode; and the only remaining ceremony is, I believe, the offering on Twelfth Day. George the First and

Second were in the habit of playing at hazard in public at the groom-porter's, where several of the nobility, and even some of the princesses, staked considerable sums; but in the time of George the Third the practice was abolished, and a handsome gratuity given to the groom-porter by way of compensation.

It will be understood that the remarks as to the abatement in Christmas festivities, apply more particularly to what may be considered as state or public observances; for Christmas feasting and revelry were still kept up throughout the last century in many parts, according as the spirit of hospitality prevailed, accompanied, but too frequently, by that excess for which those times have gained an unenviable celebrity, and where the motto appears to have been—

"Fill up the bowl, then, fill it high,
Fill all the glasses then, for why
Should every creature drink but I?
Why, man of morals, tell me why?"

Hals, in that very scarce book, his 'History of Cornwall,' reprinted, with some omissions, a few years since, by the late Davies Gilbert, P.R.S., mentions the hospitality existing in that county in the beginning of the eighteenth century, referring particularly to the establishment of John Carminow, who kept open house for all comers and goers, drinkers, minstrels, dancers, and what not, during the Christmas time; his usual allowance of provisions for that season being twelve fat bullocks, twenty Cornish bushels of wheat (about sixty of usual measure), thirty-six sheep, with hogs, lambs, and fowls, of all sorts, and drink made of wheat and oat malt proportionable; barley-malt being then little known in those parts. Genuine hospitality was indeed to be met with in most of the provinces; but still the general effect was a falling off in the observance of Christmas. Garrick, in returning thanks to his friend Bunbury (the caricaturist) for some Norfolk game, at Christmas, says,—

> " Few presents now to friends are sent,
> Few hours in merry-making spent;
> Old-fashioned folks there are indeed,
> Whose hogs and pigs at Christmas bleed;
> Whose honest hearts no modes refine,
> They send their puddings and their chine."

Even down to the present time—although the spirit has sadly abated, and been modified, and is still abating under the influence of the genius of the age, which requires work and not play—the festivities are yet kept up in many parts in a genial feeling of kindness and hospitality, not only in the dwellings of the humbler classes, who encroach upon their hard-gained earnings for the exigencies of the season, and of those of higher grade, where the luxuries mingle with the comforts of life; but also in the mansions of the opulent, and in the baronial hall, where still remain the better privileges of feudal state; and especially in the palace of our sovereign, who wisely considers the state of royalty not incompatible with the blessings of domestic enjoyment, and has shown how the dignity of a reigning queen is perfectly consistent with the exemplary performance of the duties of a wife and mother.

And surely a cheerful observance of this festival is quite allowable with the requirements for mental exertion of the present times; and hospitality and innocent revelry may be used as safety valves for our high pressure educational power,—

> " Kind hearts can make December blithe as May,
> And in each morrow find a New Year's Day."

In some parts the wassail-bowl may yet be found, though most commonly in the guise of toast and ale, without the roasted apples.

In juvenile parties, snap-dragon, throwing its mysterious and witch-like hue over the faces of the bystanders, is sometimes yet permitted. Not Poins's, who swallowed down candle-ends for flap-dragons; but the veritable Malaga fruit, carolling away in the frolicsome spirit, burning the fingers but rejoicing the palate of the adventurous youth, and half frightened little maiden reveller. The custom is old, but not quite so old as stated in the curious play of 'Lingua;' by the performance of one character, wherein—Tactus—Oliver Cromwell is said to have had his first dream of ambition.

"*Memory.* O, I remember this dish well; it was first invented by Pluto, to entertain Proserpina withal.

Phantastes. I think not so, Memory; for when Hercules had kill'd the flaming dragon of Hesperia, with the apples of that orchard he made this fiery meat; in memory whereof he named it snapdragon."

There is still a species of flapdragon in the west, among the peasantry, by means of a cup of ale or cyder with a lighted candle standing in it: the difficulty being for a man to drink the liquor, without having his face singed, while his companions are singing some doggrel verses about Tom Toddy.

The waits still remain, as we know from auricular experience, though their performances are of a most heterodox nature, generally comprising a polka or galope, with some of the latest opera airs, instead of the genuine old carol tunes; and indeed the street carol singer himself is almost extinct, and when met with, his stock is confined to three or four different carols, with one tune, while the broadside carols themselves are much limited, in variety, even to what they were a few years back, my own collection, which is large, having been commenced long since. Christmas-boxes still prevail; self-interest will endeavour to keep these alive, and most housekeepers have a list of regular applicants, besides a few speculators, who think it worth while to ask. The principal wait claims his privilege, under a regular appointment, by warrant and admission, with all the ancient forms of the city and liberty of Westminster, having a silver badge and chain, with the arms of that city. The constant dustmen, who have "no connection with the scavengers," in order to warn against base pretenders, leave printed applications, sometimes of a classical nature, as, for instance, requesting "you will not bestow your bounty on any persons who cannot produce a medal, having on one side a bust of Julius Cæsar's wife, surrounded with the superscription, '*Pompeia, Jul. Cæs. Uxor.*'" One hardly sees the connection between "Julius Cæsar's wife" and the dustman's Christmas-box, and it gives a curious sort of fame to be so selected; and, by parity of reasoning, it may be assumed that the dustmen of Rome would have carried round a medal with Nimrod's wife. These Christmas boxes, like New Year's gifts, are probably of pagan origin, but seem to differ, inasmuch as they are more commonly given to dependents, while the latter are frequently reciprocal, and if given by an inferior, as an offering to a superior, meet generally with some return. Some have derived the Christmas box from the practice of the monks to offer masses for the safety of all vessels that went long voyages, in each of which a box, under the controul of the priest, was kept for offerings; this was opened at Christmas, whence the name arose: but this does not seem a probable derivation. Apprentices, journeymen, and servants, even of the higher class, such as butlers of the Inns of Court, had their boxes. John Taylor, the water poet, without due reverence of the law, compared Westminster Hall to a butler's box, at Christmas, amongst gamesters; for whosoever loseth the box will be sure to be a winner. Some of these were earthen boxes, with a slit to receive money, and was broken after the collection was made; similar boxes of wood may still be seen. Many entries may be found in old accounts of payments made in the nature of Christmas boxes, and the kings of France indeed used to give presents to their soldiers at this time. In the countries where the disgraceful practice of slavery yet remains, a young slave child would appear to be considered as a desirable present, and advertisements to the following effect may be occasionally seen, outraging the feelings, and showing an utter indifference to the common ties of humanity. "To be sold, a little mulatto, two years of age, very pretty, and well adapted for a *festival present.*" It is to be presumed this "very pretty" child had a mother. Poor creature! When will this abomination of man selling his fellow-man cease on the earth? How would the slave-holders like to give the blacks their turn? We may remember that about the time of Julius Cæsar's wife, we have lately mentioned, and long before America was known, white slaves from Britain were imported into Rome, as valuable articles for the sports of the amphitheatres. However, we must leave slavery to the lash of 'Uncle Tom's Cabin;' but in describing a festival peculiarly commemorative of peace, good will, and freedom to man, one could not help raising a voice, however feeble, against such an evil.

In our younger days—addressing now of course those

whose younger days are past—the magic-lantern, even the common Dutch toy of the class, and especially the 'Galanti show,' used to afford great amusement; and when the phantasmagoria was introduced it seemed inexplicable. The dissolving views, and the great advances made in exhibitions of this class have placed the old lantern much in the back ground, and even the old-fashioned conjuring tricks are now known to nearly every school-boy, without taking into account the penetrating eyes of clever little ladies fixed on you, to find you out.

In recent times the Christmas tree has been introduced from the continent, and is productive of much amusement to old and young, and much taste can be displayed and expense also incurred in preparing its glittering and attractive fruit. It is delightful to watch the animated expectation and enjoyment of the children as the treasures are displayed and distributed; the parents equally participating in the pleasure, and enjoying the sports of their childhood over again. And where can the weary world-worn man find greater relief from his anxious toil and many cares, and haply his many sorrows, than in contemplating the amusements of artless children, and assisting as far as he is able; for it is not every one has tact for this purpose, and our young friends soon detect this, and discover the right "Simon Pure."

In the younger days of many of us the Christmas Pantomime was looked forward to as a source of the highest gratification, and the promise was in general realized; for who that ever saw *the* Grimaldi can ever forget the genuine pleasure afforded by his inimitable humour, laughable simplicity, and irresistible fun? Surely he never could belong to private or domestic life, but must have been always the same—stealing tarts from his own baker, and legs of mutton from his own butcher, and filling his pockets with his wife's dresses and bed-furniture. When, in after life, we were introduced to him, in private, and found a quiet, respectable gentleman, in plain clothes, and no red half-moon cheeks, talking as rationally as other people, we could hardly believe but that we had been imposed upon. Peace to thy memory, Grimaldi! for many a joyous hour hast thou given the young, and of many a weary hour hast thou relieved the old.

It is not our province to argue here whether the modern pantomime is derived from the ancient Greek, harlequin being Mereury; columbine, Psyche; pantaloon, Charon; and the clown, Momus—still retaining, in his painted face and wide mouth, the resemblance of the ancient masks. It is more probable that they were introduced into Italy, as Sismondi says, with other characters of the same class, in the sixteenth century, by the wandering comedians of the time.

The harlequin and searamouch in early times were, however, speaking characters, and often celebrated wits. Constantini, Tiberio Fiurilli (the inventor of the character of scaramouch), Cecchini, Sacchi, and Nicholas Barbieri, were all highly patronised by royalty; and the reputation of Domenic, who was occasionally admitted to the table of Louis the Fourteenth, is well known. The harlequinade or pantomime, as it is popularly called, was introduced here in 1717, by Mr. Rich, who was a celebrated harlequin himself, and acted under the name of Lun. This pantomime was called 'Harlequin Executed,' and was performed at the theatre in Lincoln's Inn Fields. Between 1717 and 1761, when he retired, he composed several harlequinades, which were all successful. The present handsome though somewhat bizarre dress of harlequin, is

said to have been introduced by Mr. Byrne, a celebrated performer, who was never excelled in this character, at Christmas, 1799, in 'Harlequin Amulet,' and at the same time he introduced new steps and leaps. Before this time the dress was a loose jacket and trousers, but the party-coloured jacket, though of inferior quality, was worn by merry-andrews at least a century before this time, and may have been modified from the motley of the fool. The wand of harlequin would seem to be somewhat akin to the dagger of lath of the old vice, but used for a different purpose, and the cap is an article of mystery, as, when placed on his head, he is rendered invisible to the other characters.

The pantaloon was taken from the Venetians, and his former dress, a gown over a red waistcoat, was that of a Venetian citizen. Pulcinello, or Punch, as I am informed by an Italian friend, of considerable literary acquirements—the Chevalier Mortara—is derived from one Paolo or Paol Cinello, who was an attendant or buffoon at an inn at Acerras, about the year 1600, and so famous for his humour, that Silvio Fiorillo, the comedian, persuaded him to join his troop, whence his fame soon spread.

In some parts, particularly in the west and north of the kingdom, the old Christmas play is still kept up, and a specimen is hereafter given. The subject of these plays, which agree in general effect, although varying in detail, is 'St. George and the Dragon, with the King of Egypt, and Fair Sabra, his daughter;' usually accompanied by 'Father Christmas and the Doctor,' and sometimes by very incongruous characters; as the great and exemplary man, whose loss the nation is now lamenting, as that of the first character in its history, the Duke of Wellington; and General Wolfe, who fights

St. George, and then sings a song about his own death, beginning—

> "Bold General Wolfe to his men did say,
> Come, come, ye lads, come follow me,
> To yonder mountain, which is so high;
> Ye lads of honour, all for your honour,
> Gain the victory or die."

Occasionally burlesque characters are introduced, who have nothing to do with the piece, as Hub-Bub, Old Squire, &c., and they generally announce themselves, as one mentioned about 1760, by Jackson, in his 'History of the Scottish Stage.'

> "My name it is Captain Calf-tail, Calf-tail,
> And on my back it is plain to be seen;
> Although I am simple and wear a fool's-cap,
> I am dearly beloved of a queen."

The buffoon of the piece used formerly to wear a calf-skin, "I'll go put on my devilish robes, I mean my Christmas calf's-skin suit, and then walk to the woods," says Robin Goodfellow, in the time of James the First. "I'll put me on my great carnation nose, and wrap me in a rousing calf-skin suit, and come like some hobgoblin." The performers, who are usually young persons in humble life, are attired, including St. George and the Dragon, much in the same manner, having white trousers and waistcoats, showing their shirt-sleeves, and decorated with ribbons and handkerchiefs; each carrying a drawn sword or cudgel in his hand: as one of the Somersetshire mummers says, "Here comes I liddle man Jan wi' my sword in my han!" They wear high caps of pasteboard, covered with fancy paper, and ornamented with beads, small pieces of looking-glass, bugles, &c., and generally have long strips of pith hanging down from the top, with shreds of different coloured cloth strung on them, the whole having a fanciful and smart effect. The Turk sometimes has a turban; Father Christmas is represented as a grotesque old man, with a large mask and comic wig, and a huge club in his hand; the Doctor has a three-cornered hat, and painted face, with some ludicrous dress, being the comic character of the piece; the lady is generally in the dress of last century, when it can be got up; and the hobby-horse, when introduced, which is rarely, has a representation of a horse's hide. Wellington and Wolfe, when they appear, are dressed in any sort of uniform that can be procured for the nonce, and no doubt will now be found as militia men of the county where the play is represented.

These plays are of very remote origin, and founded probably on the old mysteries before mentioned, the subject of St. George being introduced at the time of the crusades. A play was performed before Henry the Fifth at Windsor, in 1416, when the Emperor Sigismund was with him, founded on the incidents of the life of St. George, and "his ridyng and fighting with the dragon, with his speer in his hand."

It is curious to observe how near, in many cases, the style of the early drama approaches to the homeliness of our present country Christmas plays; so that one may suppose that not only their structure is derived from the ancient representations, but that even some of the speeches have been carried down with some little modification. When St. George struts in, saying, "Here am I, St. George," he is but repeating the introduction of characters sometimes used of old. Johnson, who wrote the favourite romance of the 'Seven Champions of Christendome,' about the time of

Elizabeth, took his subject from early metrical romances, and particularly from the story of St. George and the fair Sabra, in the old poetical legend of Sir Bevis of Hampton, which is older than Chaucer.

The Cornish had their Guary or Miracle Play from a very early date, and amphitheatres are still existing where they used to be performed.

The 'Creation of the World,' by William Jordan, of Helstone, in 1611, has been published by the late Davies Gilbert, as also two other Cornish mysteries, of much earlier date, 'The Passion of our Lord,' and the 'Resurrection.' Carew, in his 'Survey of the County,' gives an amusing anecdote of the stupidity, feigned or real, of one of the performers. It having come to his turn, the ordinary or manager, said "Goe forthe, man, and shew thy selfe." The actor stepped forward, and gravely repeated, "Goe forthe man, and shew thy selfe." The ordinary, in dismay, whispered to him, "Oh, you marre all the play." The actor, with very emphatic gesture, repeated aloud, "Oh, you marre all the play." The prompter, then losing his patience, reviled the actor with all the bitter terms he could think of, which the actor repeated with a serious countenance, as if part of the play. The ordinary was at last obliged to give over, the assembly having received a great deal more sport than twenty such guaries could have afforded.

The play of 'Alexander the Great,' acted in the north, and printed at Newcastle, in 1788, is very similar to the Cornish St. George; and others, all showing from their likeness a common origin, may be found in Scotland, Lancashire, Yorkshire, Gloucestershire, Dorsetshire, and other parts. In Yorkshire and Northumberland, and other places in the north, they had the sword or rapier dance, where the performers were dressed in frocks, or white shirts, with paper or pasteboard helmets,—calling themselves Hector, Paris, Guy of Warwick, and other great names, and performing many evolutions with their swords, accompanied by a fiddler or doctor, and a character called Bessy.

Cards, dancing, and music, are still resorted to; but the brawl, the pavan, the minuet, the gavot, the saraband, and even the country dance, excepting in the exhilirating form of Sir Roger de Coverley, have given place to the quadrille, the polka, and the galope; and if we look at the figures of some of the old dances, our drawing-room coryphees will not be sorry to be spared the task of learning them. Take the account of the brawl in one of our old plays, which one of the characters says she has forgotten: "Why! 'tis but two singles on the left, two on the right, three doubles, a traverse of six round; do this twice, curranto pace; a figure of eight, three singles broken down, come up, meet two doubles, fall back, and then honour." But if we have not gained much in the exhibition of this accomplishment, it is amply made up in the quality of our domestic musical acquirements, where, instead of a ditty or lesson, or sonata, droned out on the virginals or harpsichord, our ladies now treat us not only with the elegant compositions of the talented Osborne, and other able modern writers, but with the classical works of Beethoven, Mozart, and other masters of the noble science. Many of our male amateurs also, both vocal and instrumental, have acquired considerable skill; but as they in general are pretty well aware of their own merits, it will not be necessary to remind them here. Singing, however, is more particularly in quest at Christmas time, but the old carol is rarely now to be met with, though several of them possess much pleasing harmony. One of the great gratifications, however, of these Christmas meetings, where they can take place, is the re-union, even though for a short space, of relations and friends, renewing, as it were, the bonds of love and friendship; casting off for a time the cares of the world; joining, if not audibly, yet mentally, in the praise of that Creator, who has given us so much "richly to enjoy;" and, if it be His will that loved and familiar faces, one by one, drop off, yet are we not left comfortless; for though they cannot return to us, we, through faith in Him, whose Nativity we now commemorate, shall join them, in that blessed region, where the cares and trials of our weary pilgrimage here will be forgotten, as a dream that is past; and hope shall be fulfilled, when "the desire cometh," that "is a tree of life."

Our pagan ancestors observed their sacred festival at this season, in honour of their unknown gods, and of a mystic mythology, founded on the attributes of the Deity; but corrupted in the course of ages into a mass of fables and idolatry: but we keep it in commemoration of Him, who, as at this time, mercifully revealed Himself to us; who is omniscient and omnipresent, and of whom my lamented and learned friend, Dr. Macculloch, has emphatically said, referring to the true Christian, "Not an object will occur to him, in which he will not see the hand of God, and feel that he is under the eye of God; and if he but turn to contemplate the vacancy of the chamber around him, it is to feel that he is in the presence of his Maker; surrounded, even to contact, by Him who fills all space. Feeling this, can he dare to be evil?"

CHAPTER IX.

 H E subjects of the offerings at the Epiphany, with the accompanying legend of the Three Kings or Magi, and that of carol singing, require so much space that it has been thought preferable to devote particular chapters to them, rather than interrupt the narrative of Christmas festivities.

The offerings on the day of the Epiphany were in remembrance of the Manifestation of our Saviour to the Gentiles, and of the gifts made to Him by the Magi, or Wise Men of the East; when "the kings of Tarshish and of the isles brought presents; the kings of Sheba and Saba offered gifts," or, as the 'Bee Hive,' of the Romish Church, states it, "Kings came out of the Moor's land to worship Christ."

The king of the bean was the forerunner of our Twelfth-Day King; in the Saturnalia a king was elected, and as some say by beans, by way of lot, and he was invested with full power over the guests, and from him the lord of Misrule, under his various names, may take his origin; but the king of the bean and Twelfth-Day king were strictly confined to Twelfth Day, and ephemeral in their rule.

At the time of our Saviour's birth, there was an expectation of his appearance among many of the heathen nations; it is said even that the initiated in the religious mysteries of the Persians, possessed as a secret handed down from the time of Zoroaster, that a divine prophet should be born of a virgin, whose birth should be proclaimed by the appearance of a bright star. The celebrated prophecy of Balaam, also made an impression on the surrounding nations; "I shall see him, but not now; I shall behold him, but not nigh; there shall come a star out of Jacob, and a sceptre shall rise out of Israel, and shall smite the corners of Moab, and destroy all the children of Sheth." When the star eventually appeared, the Magi, or Three Kings, as they are commonly called, eagerly followed it to the cradle of our Saviour to pay their adorations,—

"See how from far upon the eastern road,
  The star-led wizards haste with odours sweet."

According to old legends, which are always fond of embellishment, this star was an eagle flying and beating the air with his wings, and had within it the form and likeness of a young child, and above him the sign of a cross. D'Israeli mentions some rays of this star, in a collection of relics.

There are numerous histories of the magi or kings themselves, all agreeing as to their number having been three, but some of them differing entirely in name. We may, however, consider Melchior, Jasper, and Balthasar, to be the genuine ones, and certainly more euphonious than Galagalath, Magalath, and Tharath; but even the legends that agree in the names, differ in the description of their persons, or in the appropriation of the presents given by them; but as Bede, in the seventh century, was the first writer in this country who has given a description of them, which he, no doubt, took from some earlier account, we may adopt, in the main, his history. According to this, Melchior was old, with gray hair and long beard, and offered gold to our Saviour in acknowledgment of his sovereignty; Jasper was young, without any beard, and offered frankincense in recognition of the divinity; and Balthasar was of a dark complexion, as a Moor, with a large spreading beard, and offered myrrh to our Saviour's humanity; or as one of my family, Sandys the traveller, translates the description from 'Festa Anglo-Romana,'—

"Three kings the King of kings three gifts did bring,
Myrrh, incense, gold, as to man, God, a king.
Three holy gifts be likewise given by thee
To Christ, even such as acceptable be
For myrrha tears; for frankincense impart
Submissive prayers; for pure gold a pure heart."

Many of the ancient ecclesiastical writers endeavoured to find out mystical meanings in every sacred subject, in which, however, they have followers in the present day; so that the variety in appearance of the Three Kings may be supposed to have some reference to the three races of man, where, according to the Armenian tradition, Shem had the region of the tawny, Japhet that of the ruddy, and Ham that of the blacks.

The early heralds, who considered that none could be ennobled, or good, or great, without the aid of their science, little anticipating that, in after times, any one might have "arms found" for him, with crest and motto, according to order and price, and having some vague notions of the early origin of the same, emblazoned coats of arms for all the great characters in the Bible, commencing with Adam—giving one even to our Saviour. It may, therefore, be readily supposed that the Three Kings had theirs. Their journey lasted twelve days, during which they required no refreshment, it seeming to them as one day. After they had presented their gifts, the Virgin Mary gave them in return one of our Saviour's swaddling clothes, which they took as a most noble gift. In after days they were baptised by St. Thomas, and some time subsequent to their deaths, their bodies were taken by the Empress Helena, in the fourth century, to Constantinople; from thence they were moved to Milan; and when this city was taken by the Emperor Frederick, in 1164, he gave these relics to Reinaldus, Archbishop of Cologne, whence they are commonly called the Three Kings of Cologne. There is some story of Louis the Eleventh having moved some of the bones from Cologne, as they were considered to be of sovereign virtue in royal ailments. Their names even were thought of great efficacy in falling-sickness and madness, if written on parchment, and hung about the patient's neck, with the sign of the cross; and, as it is to be presumed in all these cases, with a good deal of faith. Another charm is rather more extensive in its benefits:—

"Sancti Tres Reges
Gaspar, Melchior, Belthazar,
Orate pro nobis, nunc et en hora
Mortis nostræ.

"Ces billets ont touché aux trois têtes de S.S. Rois à Cologne.

Ils sont pour des voyageurs, contre les malheurs de chemins, maux de tête, mal caduque, fièvres, sorcellerie, toute sorte de malefice, et mort subite."

It was found in the purse of Jackson, a celebrated smuggler, convicted of murder, in 1749, but did not prove efficacious with him, as he died, struck with horror, just after being measured for his irons. Another charm is to write their names in virgin wax, with a cross against each, and place it under the head of one who has had any thing stolen from him, and he will dream of what has become of the stolen article. If he does not remember his dream, it must be his own fault, of course. The names of the Three Kings, together with those of the four shepherds, who went to our Lord in Bethlehem—Misael, Achael, Cyrianus, and Stephanus—(in the Chester mysteries they have the more humble names of Harvey, Tudd, and Haneken), form a charm against the bite of serpents, and other venomous reptiles and beasts. One John Aprilius, when he was hung, having implored their assistance, was more successful than Jackson; for, after having been suspended for three days, he was found to be alive, and being taken down, he went to Cologne, half naked, with the halter about his neck, to return thanks, and, probably, to request that next time he might be taken down a little sooner. One Roprecht, a robber, was hung for certain crimes against society, but his body disappeared from the gibbet, whether by the intervention of the Three Kings or not, was unknown.

In a short time, however, it was found hanging again, with the addition of a pair of boots and spurs. As he was now really dead, and could tell no tales, this freak of his absconding for a short time, for the purpose, apparently, of being hung over again in boots and spurs, could not be explained by the people; but the fact was, that some passer-by had, in the first instance, found him still living, and compassionately maintained him for some time; but, like the warmed viper, he returned to his old knavish practices, and stole his benefactor's horse, when, being pursued and taken, he was, after some trouble, replaced in his old noose, and left to his fate.

According to Picart, the Feast of the Epiphany was established in the fourth century, though Brady says it was first made a separate feast in 813. It became, however, one of the most popular of the Christmas festivals, and some of the most splendid entertainments were given on this day; and in our times it is probably the most popular day throughout the Christmas, thanks to the Twelfth Cake, and drawing for characters, with other amusements. It was a very early custom to choose a Twelfth day king, or king of the bean, as he was formerly called; and this was originally a case of election, although afterwards, as at present, taken by lot; but, at the same time, the practice of election was also continued, even to recent times; the French court choosing one of the courtiers for king, who was then waited on by the other nobles, as late as the time of the revolution, when, amongst other vagaries, the ruling citizens, for the time being, changed " La fête de Rois," to " La fête de Sans-culottes." The students and citizens in the various cities and universities in Germany, also, used to choose one of their companions for king; and this practice would appear preferable to our practice of drawing for characters, and would probably ensure the election of the person best calculated to promote the wit and enjoyment of the evening, instead of taking the chance of the least adapted, or who may be called the "slowest" of the party drawing the lucky card. Even now, however, occasionally an election is made, and the fortunate elect then chooses his court for the evening.

In the last century, the Twelfth Night cards represented ministers, maids of honour, and other attendants of a court, and the characters were to be supported throughout the night. At present they are in general grotesque, and seldom possess much wit or humour. Many early notices may be met with of the antiquity of the custom. In "Les Cricries de Paris," of the thirteenth century, the "Gastel à fève orroiz" is mentioned, which is described as a cake, with a bean for the "Fête de Rois," and we shall find a present given to the court minstrels on the Epiphany, in the name of the king of the bean, in the time of Edward the Third. Down to the time of the civil wars, the feast was observed with great splendour, not only at court, but at the Inns of Court, and the universities (where it was an old custom to choose the king by the bean in a cake), and in private mansions and houses.

The lord mayor and aldermen, and the crafts of London also, used to go to St. Paul's on Twelfth Day, to hear a sermon, which is mentioned as an old custom, in the early part of Elizabeth's reign.

The usual course, of choosing by the bean, was to insert it in the cake, though sometimes a piece of money was put in instead. The cake was then cut up, and the person to whom the piece with the bean fell was the king for the evening. Sometimes pieces were allotted to our Saviour, and the Virgin

Mary, and the Three Kings, which were given to the poor; and if the bean should be in either of these portions, the king was chosen by pulling straws. Baby-cake, in the mask of 'Christmas,' was attended by an usher, bearing a great cake, with a bean and pea. The king elect chose his queen, or occasionally a pea was inserted in the cake for the purpose, and they chose their officers; and in France, when either of them drank, the company were to cry out, on pain of forfeit, "Le Roi (ou la Reine) boit."

Louis the Fourteenth, on one occasion, in his youth, was king of the bean, but would not undertake the office, handing it over to his governor, De Souvre.

Herrick, in the seventeenth century, refers to the practice of choosing by the bean and pea:—

"Now, now the mirth comes,
  With the cake full of plums,
Where beane's the king of the sport here;
  Beside we must know,
  The pea also
Must revell as queene in the court here.

  Begin then to chuse,
  This night as ye use,
Who shall for the present delight here;
  Be a king by the lot,
  And who shall not
Be Twelfth-Day queene for the night heere."

The French twelfth-cake is still plain in appearance, containing a bean: it was composed, about 250 years since, of flour, honey, ginger and pepper; what it is made of now, Monsieur Verey can no doubt tell, if he will; they are however far exceeded in appearance by the rich frosted, almond-pasted, festooned, bedizened, and carefully-ornamented cakes of the English pattern, gladdening the eyes of joyful holiday young people, and through them the hearts of their parents. The eager grouping of passers-by, to see the shop-windows crowded with these elegant productions of confectionary science, causes stoppages in our highways and thoroughfares, with reiterated "Move-ons" from our policemen. About twenty-five years ago there was one exhibited, said to weigh one ton, but it might have weighed any given number, being simply several large wedges of cake, all plastered together, at the top and sides, with one uniform coat of sugar-frost. Speaking from memory, and with a taste somewhat blunted to these enjoyments, the flavour was somewhat below the average, and curiosity was rewarded by ascertaining—to use a bad pun, which it is hoped may be excused—that it really was μεγα 'κακον (mega cakon).

The adoration of the Magi was a favourite subject in the early mysteries. The celebrated Marguerite de Valois, Queen of Navarre, wrote one on it as well as on the Nativity, the Massacre of the Innocents, and the Flight into Egypt, which were all published in 1547, in the collection of her works, called 'Marguerites de la Marguerite des princesses, très-illustre Reyne de Navarre.'

There are said indeed to have been representations in the French churches of the Three Magi as early as the fifth century; and there are French mysteries relating to them in the eleventh century, and also a Latin one mentioned by Lebeuf, wherein Virgil accompanies the kings on their journey; and at the end of the Adoration joins them very piously in the benedicamus.

The first feast of the Three Kings was celebrated at Milan in 1336, by the friar preachers, and was called the Feast of the Star. A golden star was exhibited, as if in the sky, preceding them; the Three Kings appeared on horseback, crowned and richly clad, with a large retinue, and bearing golden cups filled with myrrh, frankincense, and gold. They asked Herod where Christ should be born, and having been answered in Bethlehem, proceeded to the church of St. Eustorgius, preceded by trumpets, horns, apes, baboons, &c. In the church, on one side of the altar, was the representation of a manger, with an ox and an ass; and the infant Saviour in the arms of his mother, to whom the kings then made their offerings. It forms a favourite subject in our early English Mysteries, which were suppressed early in the time of James the First; but it was introduced as a puppet-show at Bartholomew fair as late as the time of Queen Anne. In 'Dives and Pauper,' 1496, it is stated, " For to represente in playnge at Crystmasse Herodes and the Thre Kynges and other processes of the gospelles both than and at Ester, and other times also, it is lefull and comendable."

Several provincial French collections of Carols, published within these few years, contain a Mystery or Scripture play of the Adoration. The Feast of the Star, just mentioned, was retained to some extent in Germany up to the end of the last century; and Hoffman, in his 'Horæ Belgicæ,' contains the Star-song used on the occasion, as old perhaps as the fifteenth century, of which a nearly literal translation is given hereafter. The history of these kings was a favourite subject for tapestry and illuminations for books, of which numerous examples might be given; also for paintings on church and monastic walls, as Barclay, in his Egloges, says,

> ". . the Thre Kinges, with all their company,
> Their crownes glistning bright and oriently,
> With their presentes and giftes misticall.
> All this behelde I in picture on the wall."

The offerings by our sovereigns of gold, frankincense, and myrrh, continued down to the present time, is referred to elsewhere in this work. Melchior was said to have presented a golden apple, formerly belonging to Alexander the Great,—made from the tribute of the world—and thirty pieces of gold.

The history of these pieces of gold is curious, showing how ingeniously these legends were dovetailed together. They were first coined by Terah, the father of Abraham, and taken by the latter, when he left the land of the Chaldees. They were by him paid away to Ephron as part of the purchase money for the field and cave of Machpelah. The Ismaelites then, according to one account, paid them back as the price of Joseph to his brethren; and as, according to our version of the Scriptures, the price of Joseph was but twenty pieces, we may imagine the remainder were given for some other purpose; though Adam Davie, who wrote in 1312, referring to this event, says—" Ffor thritti pens thei sold that childe." The money was afterwards paid to Joseph by his brethren during the time of scarcity; and on the death of Jacob, his son paid them to the royal treasury of Sheba for spices to embalm him. The celebrated Queen of Sheba, on her visit to Solomon, presented them to him with many other gifts. In the time of his son Rehoboam, when the King of Egypt spoiled the temple, the King of Arabia, who accompanied him, received these pieces of money in his share of the plunder, and in his kingdom they remained until the time of

Melchior, who presented them to our Saviour. On the flight into Egypt, the holy family were closely pursued by Herod's soldiers, and coming to a field where a man was sowing asked the way: when they had passed on, the corn miraculously sprang up; just afterwards Herod's soldiers arrived and inquired of the sower if he had seen our Saviour and his parents, but he told them that no one had passed since his corn was sown, on which the soldiers turned back and gave up the pursuit.

This legend is mentioned in the carol of the Carnal and the Crane. In the hurry of the flight the Virgin Mary dropped these pieces of money and the other gifts. They were found by a shepherd, who kept them by him, and in after years, being afflicted by some disease incurable by mortal aid, applied to our Saviour, who healed him, and he then offered these gifts at the high altar. They were subsequently paid to Judas by the priests as the reward of his perfidy. There are two reasons given for his requiring thirty pieces of money: one that he considered he had lost thirty pieces by the box of precious ointment not having been sold for 300 pence, of which he would have purloined the tenth part; and the other, that having been sent by our Saviour, on Holy Thursday, with this amount of money, to provide for the last supper, he fell asleep in the way and was robbed. In the midst of his distress the rich *Jew*, Pilate, met him, and he then agreed to betray his master for the amount he had lost.

In one of our ancient chronicles there is a legend of the life of Judas, before he became an apostle, very similar, in many respects, to the well-known history of Œdipus, which need not be repeated here. When, smitten by remorse, he returned the money to the priests, and destroyed himself;

they applied half in purchase of the potter's field, and with the other half bribed the soldiers who guarded the sepulchre to say that the disciples came by night and stole the body of our Saviour. After this, having performed their mission, they were dispersed, and all traces of them lost. They were made of the purest gold, the term pieces of silver used in some parts of our translation with reference to them, being, according to the history, merely a common or generic name for money, like *argent* in French; on one side was a king's head crowned, and on the other some unintelligible Chaldaic characters, and they were said to have been worth three florins each.

There are many old manuscript histories of these kings in existence, at the Museum and elsewhere, one of which resolves the whole story into alchemy; and early printed histories, as by Güldenschaiff, in 1477, and Wynkyn de Worde, in the beginning of the sixteenth century. Some account of particularly splendid feasts on Twelfth Day have been mentioned in the foregoing pages.

Their names were occasionally used as a term of adjuration, which, in former times, whatever may be case now, was a mark of respect. Diccon, in that quaint production 'Gammer Gurton's Needle,' of which the plot and catastrophe would rather astonish a modern audience, says to Dame Chat,—

"There I will have you swear by oure dere lady of Bullaine,
Saint Dunstone and Saint Donnyke, with the Three Kings of Kallain,
That ye shall keep it secret."

I will now conclude this chapter with the 'Star Song,' before referred to—

" We come walking with our staves
    Wreathed with laurel,
  We seek the Lord Jesus, and would wish
    To put laurel on his knees ;
    Are the children of Charles the King,
    Pater bonne Franselyn, Jeremie.

We did come before Herod's door, &c.
Herod, the king, came himself before, &c.

Herod then spake with a false man's heart, &c.
Why is the youngest of three so swart ? &c.

Altho' he is swart, he is well be known, &c.
In orient land he has a throne, &c.

We all came over the lofty hill, &c.
And there saw we the Star stand still, &c.

Oh, Star ! you must not stand still so, &c.
But must with us to Bethlehem go, &c.

To Bethlehem, the lovely town, &c.
Where Mary and her child sit down, &c.

How small the child, and how great the good, &c.
A blessed New Year that gives us God, &c.

CHAPTER X.

 HE term carol, appears originally to have signified a song, joined with a dance, a union frequently found in early religious ceremonies; and it is used in this sense by Chaucer, Boccacio, Spenser, and others. By some it has been derived from *cantare*, to sing, and *rola*, an interjection of joy. It was, however, applied to joyous singing, and thus to festive songs; and as these became more frequent at Christmas, it has for a long time past, though not exclusively yet more particularly, designated those sung at this feast. But strictly, it should be applied only to those of a cheerful character, and not to the Christmas hymn, which is of a more

solemn cast; many of them, indeed, being more suitable for Passion Week than for Christmas; and a large and appropriate collection might be readily selected for that season, and an interesting work made to illustrate them. In practice, however, the word carol is applied indiscriminately to both classes, whether cheerful or solemn.

In the earlier times, music, both instrumental and vocal, was introduced into religious ceremonies, and was a necessary accompaniment to all the sacred feasts and games. Jubal's harp or organ, whatever that instrument may have been, was doubtless, like the harp of David, used on such occasions, and the science of music was a necessary part of the education of many of the priesthood. In the records and sculptures of the Hebrews, Greeks, Romans, Egyptians, and other great nations of antiquity, and in the recent discoveries at ancient Nineveh, we find descriptions and representations connected with it.

The Hebrews, as we know, had numerous psalms and hymns, one of the earliest on record being that of Miriam and her companions, on the overthrow of the Egyptians, when they celebrated the downfall of the horse and his rider, with timbrels and with dances. The Druids had recourse to music, and the Anglo-Saxons and Gothic nations made great use of hymns in their public worship. Some early specimens of the primitive music have been handed down to us, but do not impress us with much respect for the powers of harmony of our forefathers, and their neumes, and other obscure and imperfect methods of notation, must have cramped them. Certain of the old chants have a pleasing solemnity, and it has of late been much the custom to revive or to imitate them, commencing even with the old Ambrosian chant; though, as our ancestors considered the introduction of the Gregorian chant to have been a great improvement on it, we may very safely be of the same opinion, as this is really fine, and we need not here trouble ourselves with the Lydian, Phrygian, or Dorian modes. With respect to the merits of ancient music, our taste and skill have been so gradually improving, that we can scarcely be judges of what—though flat, insipid, and meaningless to us—might have given much gratification to the less educated ears of former times. Even within the last few years, a great advance has been made in our own musical knowledge: pieces and composers, popular in the early part of this century, are now scarcely known; and recollected, perhaps (if at all), with amazement at their having ever been listened to; while works of the great masters, then thought impracticable, and containing difficulties not understood, or considered insuperable, are played and appreciated in most good musical meetings. More might be said on this subject, but want of space, and not of materials, compels a postponement, till some future opportunity. It may be mentioned, that much curious information, respecting our ancient national airs, with the tunes themselves, will be found in the very interesting work on the subject, by my friend, Mr. William Chappell, who, it is to be hoped, will, at no distant time, increase our obligation to him, by further publication from the large store in his possession, still unedited. Many of these airs are very pleasing, yet simple in construction, and still remain popular after the lapse of centuries; they are, however, much more recent than the ancient music before referred to.

The Romans had their hymns on the calends of January, and the practice was adopted by the early Christians, especially on their Sabbath-days and festivals, and on the vigils of their saints. St. Paul and St. James both refer to this custom, and Pliny the younger, in a letter to Trajan, mentioning the Christians, says, "They were wont to meet together on a certain day, before it was light, and sing among themselves, alternately, a hymn to Christ, as to God." Bishop Taylor observes, that the well-known "Gloria in Excelsis," sung by the angels to the shepherds, on the night of the Nativity, is the earliest Christmas carol. We have many carols now existing, that are founded on the appearance of the angels to the shepherds; and the subject is represented in several of the ancient mysteries, and occasionally in a very familiar and homely manner.

In the Chester mysteries, for instance, the three shepherds, with their man Trowle, who is the buffoon of the piece (though the greater part of the play of the shepherds is of a humorous nature, comprising the homely dialogue of rustic labourers), having eaten their supper of sheep's head, soused in ale, with onions, garlic, and leeks, and other viands of like quality, and plenty of ale, are having a bout at wrestling, where Trowle throws his masters. In the midst of their sport the star appears, and afterwards the angels' song is heard. They then proceed reverently, though "rude in speech," to Bethlehem, and make their offerings; the first shepherd, addressing our Saviour,—

> "Heale, Kinge of heaven, so hie,
> Borne in a crebe,
> Mankinde unto Thee
> Thou haste made fullye.
> Heale, kinge! borne in a mayden's bower,
> Profittes did tell thou shouldest be our succore,
> Thus clarkes doth saye.

> Lor, I bringe thee a bell;
> I praie Thee save me from hell,
> So that I may with Thee dwell,
> And serve thee for aye."

The second Shepherd presents a flagon with a spoon, and the third a cap, but finishes his speech with some degree of pathos.

> " This gueifte, Sonne, I bringe Thee is but small,
> And though I come the hyndmoste of all,
> When Thou shall them to Thy blesse call,
> Good Lorde, yet thinke on me."

Well may we say, seeing how small our gifts are, "Good Lord, yet think on me."

In the second century, Telesphorus refers to the Christians celebrating public worship, on the night of the Nativity, and then solemnly singing the angels' hymn, because in the same night, Christ was declared to the Shepherds by an angel; and in the early times of Christianity the bishops were accustomed to sing hymns on Christmas Day among their clergy. Aurelius Prudentius, towards the end of the fourth century, wrote a divine hymn or carol in Latin, which is still extant; but, besides that it consists of twenty-nine stanzas, it is not of sufficient general interest to be printed here.

The Bretons were very similar in manners and language to the inhabitants of Britain, many of them having had the same origin, and being, in fact, a colony from our island. The Cornouaille of Bretagne, however, must not be confounded with our province of that name by the well-wishers of the latter, because the romance writers do not speak in such terms of some of their knights as their friends might have desired.

There is a Breton song, said to be as old as the fifth century, arranged as a dialogue between a Druid and a scholar, which is similar in idea and construction to the carol beginning, "In those twelve days," and to that called 'Man's Duty,' though the twelve subjects given are quite different from those in the carols, and refer to some druidical superstitions. It is called 'Ar Rannou,' or 'Les Series,' and is in the "dialecte de Cornouaille." The early missionaries engrafted on this a poem or song of the same construction, where the twelve subjects were connected with the Christian religion, and agree much with those in the carols, which there is fair reason to suppose may have been taken from this early poem. These subjects are,—one God; two Testaments; three Patriarchs; four Evangelists; five books of Moses; six water-vessels at Cana of Galilee; seven Sacraments; eight Beatitudes; nine degrees of Angels; ten Commandments; eleven stars that appeared to Joseph; twelve Apostles. The hymn itself is in Latin, and at the end of each verse all the previous subjects are repeated in the style of the 'House that Jack built,' an example to which I refer simply from its being so well known, the style itself being of great antiquity, and taken originally from an old Hebrew hymn, of which some particulars, with a translation, may be found in Halliwell's 'Nursery Rhymes of England;' but the butcher, the ox, the dog, and the cat, with the other characters mentioned there, have all a mystical meaning. The last verse of the old Latin hymn may be given as a specimen:—

".... Dic mihi quid duodecim?
.... Duodecim Apostoli;
Undecim stellæ
A Josepho visæ:

Decem mandate Dei,
Novem angelorum chori,
Octo beatitudines ;
Septem sacramenta ;
Sex hydriæ positæ
In Cana Galileæ ;
Quinque libri Moysis,
Quatuor Evangelistæ,
Tres Patriarchæ,
Duo testamenta ;
Unus est Deus,
Qui regnat in Cœlis."

In the fourth century, St. Ambrose introduced the chant known by his name, at Milan, of which he was the bishop, and some reformation took place in church music; and when the Gregorian chant was composed, about two centuries later, a still greater advance was made. The Anglo-Saxons, after their conversion, preserved their fondness for religious music, it being a common practice in their guilds that each member should sing two psalms daily, one for the dead, and the other for the living members. Particular hymns were appropriated to particular feasts; the Nativity, therefore, especially had its own. When the Anglo-Normans obtained the government, they equally encouraged music, and introduced greater pomp into their ceremonies.

In the twelfth century, or sooner, the monks composed legends in verse, of the lives of the saints, &c., for the proper holidays; and religious pieces suited to the time, with appropriate hymns, were recited at Christmas; some Latin hymns of this description of the twelfth and thirteenth centuries, being still extant.

King John, in 1201, gave 25s. to the clerks who chanted "Christus vincit" before him on Christmas Day; and these spiritual songs were gradually introduced into the palace, and private houses, together with others for the same purpose, of a lighter description, which were found acceptable, and thus the carol had its origin.

The theatrical exhibitions at this season, of which the subjects were originally taken from the Holy Scriptures, as they gradually ripened into maturity, also occasionally had songs incidental to them. The angels' song to the Shepherds, in the Towneley mysteries, may be taken as a carol.

> "Herkyn, hyrdes, awake, gyf lovyng ye shalle,
> He is borne for youre sake, Lorde perpetualle;
> He is comen to take and rawnson you alle,
> Youre sorowe to slake, Kyng imperialle,
>   He behestys;
> That chyld is borne
> At Bethlehem this morne,
> Ye shalle fynde Hym beforne
>   Betwix two bestys."

In the Coventry pageant of the Shearmen and Tailors, towards the beginning of the fifteenth century, there are three songs which are in the nature of carols. One, by the women, is a lullaby song, on our infant Saviour, beginning, "Lully lulla, thou littell tine' child," and referring to Herod's wrath. One by the Shepherds is short, and may serve as an example.

> "As I out rode this endenes (last) night,
> Of thre ioli sheppardes I saw a sight,
> And all a bowte there fold a star shone bright,
> They sange terli terlow,
> So mereli the sheppards ther pipes can blow."

In the same pageant one of the prophets says—

"Novellis, novellis of wondrfull mrvellys,
Were 'hy and defuce vnto the heryng,
Asse scripture tellis these strange novellis to you I bryng."

One of the earliest known carols, however, in our island, is the Anglo-Norman one, of the thirteenth century, first printed in Douce's 'Illustrations of Shakespeare,' with a free translation, which is not only of a cheerful, but of a festive nature, giving the

".... host's command,
And Christmas joins him hand in hand,
To drain the brimming bowl."

It is in effect a Christmas drinking song.

Edward the Fourth had regulations for the singing of songs before him at Christmas, by the clerks and children of his chapel, and the custom of singing songs had now become general. In some of the early ones, scraps of Latin were introduced, probably from the Christmas hymns, which they were intended in a great measure to supersede; as, for example, from additional MS., 5665, British Museum, about the time of Henry the Eighth, which contains several others.

"Now make us ioye in this feste,
In quo xpūs natus est,
A patre unigenitus,
iij zong maydens cam till us,
Syng we to hym and say well come,
Veni Redemptor gentium.

Agnoscnt omne seculum,
A bryzth sterre iij kyngs made come,
A solis ortus cardine,
So myzthi a lord ys non as he,
Veni Redemptor omniu gentium."

Others, again, were in a simple, familiar style, adapted to

the hearths of our unsophisticated ancestors; a style, by the by, we may soon expect to see again, if the taste for mediævalism and præ-Raphaelism extends much more, and we shall have a modern ode to parliament, beginning—

"Sit you merry gentlemen,
Let nothing you dismay."

In the fifteenth century, the Low Countries had their carols, similar to the English; in some cases, even the subjects being the same, and equally adapted to the simplicity of their hearers. Several examples of these are given by Hoffman, in the second part of his Horæ Belgicæ; and I must here express my thanks to Mr. Thoms, who will, *no doubt*, convey them safely to the editor of that very useful publication, 'Notes and Queries,' for the kind loan of this book.

There is a story on record, of a terrible plague at Goldsberg, in 1553, which carried off above 2500 persons, leaving not more than twenty-five housekeepers alive in the place. The plague having abated, one of the few survivors went, on Christmas Eve, to the lower ring, and sang a carol, according to old custom; he was gradually joined by others, to excite each other to thanksgiving; and thence arose a custom for the people to assemble in large numbers, at the upper and lower ring, on Christmas morning, to sing carols, beginning with, "Unto us this day a child is born."

In the time of Henry the Seventh, after the introduction of the wassail, a good song, that is, no doubt, a carol, was to be given in answer to the steward's cry of wassail, by those belonging to the chapel; and when the king held his state on other occasions, at Christmas, the carol was introduced. The reward given to the children of the chapel, for singing "Gloria in excelsis," appears to have been usually 10s.; and, in the seventh year of his reign, there is a payment of £1 to Newark, for making of a song, probably a carol. In the 'Northumberland Household Book,' the reward to the singers varies from 6s. 8d. to 20s. On Christmas Day, 1521, the Princess Mary gave 10s. to John Sentone, and other clerks, of the college of Windsor, singing before her. William Cornyshe, a musician of those days, was paid 13s. 4d. for setting a carol; but scanty reward, even if he was only arranging any well-known tune; but the price of a collection was low in proportion, for at St. Mary-at-Hill, in 1537, Sir Mark had only 3s. 4d. for 'Carolls for Christmas,' being five square books. One would gladly multiply this small fee by a good round figure, to get hold of these five square books now.

Few of the oldest song tunes had much melody, and there are probably none extant beyond the fifteenth century; but here I must again refer to Mr. Chappell's valuable collection of English airs.

Church music was cultivated in the sixteenth century, by clergy and laity, and secular music was also in request. The pious puritans, both in England and Scotland, used to unite their rhapsodies to popular song tunes (as has been done in modern times), frequently preserving a few lines at the commencement. Luther himself composed some appropriate hymns of thanksgiving for Christmas.

There are some collections of old carols and songs, with the music, of the early part of the sixteenth century, or somewhat earlier, in the British Museum, but not of a popular description, or of interest, except to the musical antiquary; and some of the old psalm tunes, as the Bristol, Salisbury, and Kenchester, have a similarity to the graver style of old carol tunes. Tusser, who prescribes jolly carols for Christmas, mentions one to be sung to the tune of King Solomon. Several of the existing carol tunes are very pleasing, and are of considerable antiquity; one or two of them, according to repute, having been known in Cornwall for three hundred years and upwards; and some of the northern tunes are, probably, equally old, though the age may be a little overstated. The natives of Cornwall have been famous for their carols from an early date. Seawen says, they had them at several times, especially at Christmas, which they solemnly sang, and sometimes used in their churches after prayers, the burthen of them being "Nowell, nowell, good news, good news, of the gospel."

Henry the Eighth, and his children, being skilled in music, and keeping also the Christmas feast with great magnificence, carol singing flourished; and Latin hymns being abolished at the time of the Reformation, the carols became still more in vogue, and were sung throughout the kingdom. At the grand Christmasses, at the Inns of Court, the master of the revels was, after dinner and supper, to sing a carol or song, and command other gentlemen to sing with him; but it is to be assumed that he selected such "other gentlemen" as could respond properly to his call. The Roman Catholics observed the custom equally with the Reformed church.

"And carols sing in prayse of Christ, and for to help them heare,
The organs answere every verse with sweete and solemne cheare."

The carols at this time seem to have been of two descriptions: one of a serious sort, sung commonly in churches, and through the streets, and from house to house, as they were in Shakespeare's time, ushering in the Christmas morning; and the other of a more convivial nature, and adapted to feasting. The festive carols were sung by the company, or by itinerant minstrels, that went round for the purpose, to the houses of the wealthy: some of them were called wassail songs. Those of the religious or grave style were getting out of use in private houses, until the time of the puritans, who, when they began to strive for the mastery, tried to bring them back, in substitution of the lighter ones, and subsequently endeavoured to abolish the latter altogether. As early as 1596, one of them says, that superstition and idolatry were entertained, which appeared in keeping of festival days, bonfires, pilgrimages, singing of carols at Yule.

The carol, beginning,

"All you that are to mirth inclined,"

was written by the well-known Thomas Deloney, at the end of the sixteenth century. In the former part of the seventeenth century, carols continued in great repute, and were introduced at all the feasts, even those of the higher ranks; and Bishop Andrews, in a sermon on the Nativity, in 1619, celebrates it as glorious in all places, as well at home with carols, as in the church with anthems.

At the celebrated feast of the 'Christmas Prince,' at St. John's College, Oxford, in 1607, the boar's head was ushered in with a peculiar carol, of which there were several connected with this important dish, and all the company joined in it by way of chorus. There is an amusing anecdote of carol singers of this date, in 'Pasquil's Jests,' 1609, which may as well be given in the words of the original.

"*A Tale of a Merry Christmas Carroll, sung by women.*

"There was sometime an old knight, who being disposed to make himselfe merry in a Christmas time, sent for many of his tenants, and poore neighbors, with their wives, to dinner; when, having made meat to be set on the table, would suffer no man to drinke, till he that was master ouer his wife should sing a carroll, to excuse all the company. Great nicenesse there was, who should bee the musician, now the cuckow time was so farre off. Yet, with much adoe, looking one upon another, after a dry hemme or two, a dreaming companion drew out as much as hee durst, towards an ill-fashioned ditty. When, having made an end, to the great comfort of the beholders, at last it came to the woman's table, where, likewise, commandment was given, that there should no drinke be touched till she that was master ouer her husband had sung a Christmas carroll; whereupon they fell all to such a singing, that there was never heard such a catterwalling peece of musicke; whereat the knight laughed heartely, that it did him halfe as muche good as a corner of his Christmas pie."

This jolly old knight might have been a descendant of the squire of Gamwell Hall, in the time of Robin Hood (who Mr. Hunter has lately brought down a little from his supposed aristocratic birth, and cleared from the mist of poetic legend) —for he is made to say,

> " . . . . Not a man here shall taste my *March* beer,
> Till a Christmas carol he does sing;
> Then all clapt their hands, and they shouted and sung,
> Till the hall and the parlour did ring."

Sir Thomas Overbury, who died in 1613, in his description of a Franklin, says, he kept the " wakefull ketches " on Christmas Eve, with other observances, yet held them no relics of popery; other writers of the same age also refer to them. As the rule of the puritans advanced, and the time of the

Commonwealth approached, endeavours were made, as stated in a former page, to suppress all observances of Christmas; and carol singing would naturally share the same fate, and join therefore in the struggle to avoid absolute destruction. In 'Festorum Metropolis,' 1652, it is stated, "As for our songs and carrols, brethren, they are collected and composed out of the Scriptures, containe matter of instruction and edification, they implant the history and benefits of Christ's birth in the minds of poor ignorant people; and oftentimes he is taken by a song that will flye a sermon." They were still preserved in private, and in remote places, and old Christmas, in his visit to Devonshire, before mentioned, names the carols and pleasant songs as part of the amusements of the evening. Warmstry, also, in his 'Vindication of Christmas,' in answer to an objection, whether the feast might not be a remnant of the Saturnalia, and whether the carols might not arise from the hymn to Ceres, during that feast called ιουλος, says "*Christmasse Kariles*, if they be such as are fit for the time, and of holy and sober composures, and used with Christian sobriety and piety, they are not unlawfull, and may be profitable, if they be sung with grace in the heart." An observation that may well be remembered in the present times, in answer to any objectors.

Warton mentions two celebrated itinerant ballad, and therefore doubtless carol, singers, about the middle of this century, called Outroaringe Dick and Wat Wimbars, who occasionally made 20s. a day, by attending fairs and meetings; but they must have been of earlier date, as they are mentioned also in 'Kind Hart's Dreame,' by Henry Chettle, in 1592; their gains, therefore, taking into account the difference of value in money, were large, and such as would tempt many a modern carol-singer, as well as some members of a recently reformed learned profession, anxiously looking for any respectable life-boat to save them from sinking.

After the Restoration, the people gladly returned to their amusements without restraint, and from the reaction, in many instances perhaps, went into the opposite extreme and indulged in too much conviviality. Carol singing was renewed with increased zeal.

> "Carols and not minc'd meat make Christmas pies,
> 'Tis mirth, not dishes, sets a table off;
> Brutes and phanaticks eat and never laugh."

It so continued down to the present century, when it apparently began to abate; but it will be unnecessary to give any references to prove the continuance of such a custom, when, to a certain extent, it exists at present, though this and other observances are much shorn of their honours. Many of us will recollect when at Christmas time every street of any note had its carol singers, with their bundle of various carols, whereas now scarcely one vagrant minstrel can be found throughout the town, brass bands having blown them out; but there is still some demand for the carols, and specimens of broadside carols may be procured from the printers of this class of literature, in St. Andrew's Street, Monmouth Court, Long Lane, and elsewhere.

In Birmingham also, and other large manufacturing towns, and other neighbourhoods where the practice of carol singing is retained, popular editions of the style called chap-books, as well as broadsides may be found; several of them of considerable antiquity, handed down for many generations, and frequently illustrated by woodcuts of the most grotesque nature in point of execution and design. Many of us will also recollect when carols were sung in the country, not only in the farm-houses, in mansions, and baronial halls, but likewise in churches—as Heath says, was the custom, in Scilly, in the middle of last century—and this with much propriety and right feeling.

> "If unmelodious was the song,
> It was a hearty note and strong."

Each succeeding year shows a falling-off in the number of houses where the practice is now admitted; and in many parts the carols are scarcely heard at all, people getting too refined, or—too good (?); the extreme west and north, and some of the manufacturing districts, being the most likely places to hear them, as they were, in former times, among the yeomanry of our land. The custom exists also in Ireland and Wales, there being many carols in the Welch language, some of which are of ancient date, and others recent; one David Jones, of Rhuddlan, having died about twenty years since, who for fifty-three successive years, sang at the church there, a new carol of his own composing every Christmas; a worthy poet laureat of his parish.

The practice of singing carols on the Continent is of ancient date. Crysostom, the unfortunate youth in Don Quixote, "was such a great man at composing couplets, that he made carols for Christmas Eve, and plays for the Lord's Day, which were represented by the young men in our village; and every body said they were tip-top."

The Spaniards, before their country got into so much confusion, used, in most respectable families, to set up a *nacimiento*, which was a rude imitation of rocks, with baby houses, &c., and clay figures, representing the Nativity, the Shepherds, the ox, and ass, kneeling to the Holy Infant, with Joseph and Mary in a ruinous stable. They had numerous collections of carols, and parties used to meet, dancing, reciting speeches, and singing carols to the sound of the zambomba, an instrument formed by stretching a piece of parchment, slightly covered with wax, over the mouth of an earthen jar, with a slender reed fixed in the centre, from which a sound was produced something like the tambourine, when rubbed by the finger. The only refreshments were Christmas cakes, called *oxaldres*, and sweet wines, and home-made liquors.

In France, the custom of carol singing was of very early date, and there are many collections of them, including several in the *patois*, or provincial dialect. They are called noël, or nouel, and sometimes nuel, derived evidently from the same source, as novell or nowell, used in some of our old carols, and references to Christmas, as in Chaucer, for instance.

> " Janus sit by the fuyr with double berd,
> And drynketh of his bugle horn the wyn;
> Biforn him stont the braun of toskid swyn,
> And nowel crieth every lusty man."

The term is, however, sometimes used in the sense of news or tidings. Some writers have derived it from natalis, as signifying a cry of joy at Christmas, but this seems a doubtful etymology. It may have the same origin as yule, or gule, but it was not absolutely confined to Christmas time, though it was probably borrowed from its use then. It was frequently used as a sort of burden to carols. In a carol, or hymn, by Herrade de Landsberg, Abbess of Hohenbourg, as early as the twelfth century, saluting the holy " crêche," or manger, she sings,

> " Leto leta concio
> Cinoël resonat tripudio,
> Cinoël hoc in natalitio,
> Cinoël, cinoël,
> Noël, noël, noël,
> Noël, noël, noël, noël, &c."

In Normandy it is called nuel. In Burgundy the people pronounce noé for noël. A priest at Dijon, wishing to avoid this error, fell into the opposite extreme, and in one of his discourses repeated three or four times, "l'Arche de noël, et le patriarche Noé." The Poitevins write nau; and in la vielle Bible des noëls, is found "chanter no." Rabelais talks of "les beaulx et joyeulx noelz, en langaige poitevin," and quotes the two last lines of the following commencement of one sung in Poitou, within the last twenty years, if not still.

> " Au sainct nau,
> Chanteray sans point m'y feindre,
> Je n'en daignerois rien craindre,
> Car le jour est ferian,
> Nau, nau, nau."

Many early instances occur of its use as a cry of joy; as at the baptism of Charles the Sixth, of France, in December, 1368; the entry of Philip, Duke of Burgundy, with his sister, into Paris, in 1429; and the entry into Paris of Charles the Seventh, in 1437, where the people proclaimed their delight with loud shouts of noël.

> " Ce jour vint le Roy à Verneuil,
> Où il fut receu à grand joye
> Du peuple joyeux à merveil,
> En criant Noël par la voye."

On the entry of Henry the Fifth into Rouen, in January,

1419, though this was about Christmas time, and on his return to London, he was received with cries of "Nowell! nowell!" and so afterwards, when the English Regent went through Paris in state, in 1428, "on crioit haultement nouel!" and again on the proclamation of Henry the Sixth.

The ancient French customs were in many respects similar to those of England, having a common origin; and Christmas was considered, in like manner, a great time for feasting and rejoicing. In the old poem, of the date of 1400, or thereabouts, called the "Bataille de Karesme et de charnage," Karesme has on his side all the fishes, both sea and fresh-water—being a decided advocate of temperance—vegetables, cheese, milk, &c.; Charnage has the animals, birds, &c. The battle is fierce, and the issue doubtful, when night separates the combatants; but Karesme, hearing that Noël was approaching, with considerable succour to his enemy, makes peace on certain terms, by advice of his council.

The practice of singing carols in France, in the language of the country, is of very early date, and had its origin, probably, as early as the time when the people ceased to understand or to use Latin, the Christmas hymns previously having been in that language. In "Les crieries de Paris," of the end of the thirteenth century, par Guillaume de la Villeneuve, appears, "Noël, noël, à moult granz cris;" meaning collections of noëls, of which it is said, that the Duc de la Vallière had a valuable manuscript collection of the fourteenth century. The editor of 'Noël Burguignon,' in 1720, mentions a volume that had come to his hands, containing three collections of old noëls, printed at Paris, in Gothic letters, of which the first two were without date; the first containing the noël mentioned by Rabelais; the third was dated 1520, composed by "*feu Maître Lucas le Moigne, en son vivant Curé de S. George de Pui-la-Garde, au diocese de Poitou.*" He also mentions an old noël in the time of Louis the Twelfth, to the tune of "*A vous point vu la Perronelle?*" Brunet gives the title of a collection printed at Lyon, about 1520, containing one in the patois of that province, which would appear to be different from that by Lucas le Moigne.

About 1540, Clement Marot made his celebrated version of the psalms into French rhyme, which were sung to popular tunes, and adopted by the French court; and some were probably introduced at Christmas, as well as the noëls. About the same time, Calvin introduced the psalms into his congregation at Geneva, and Sternhold and Hopkins brought out their version in England, "with apt notes to sing them withall."

In the same century was a collection of "Noëls vieux et nouveaux." Pasquier, in his work on France, published in 1643, says, "En ma ieunesse c'estoit une coustume que l'on ausit tournée en cérémonie, de chanter tous les soirs presque en chaque famille des noüels, qui estoient chansons spirituelles faites en l'honneur de nostre Seignor. Lesquelles on chante encores en plusieurs Eglises pendant que l'on célèbre la grand messe le iour de noüel, lors que le prestre reçoit les offrandes. Or cette allegresse manifesta encores hors les Eglises; parce que le peuple n'auoit moyen plus ouvert pour denoter sa ioye, que de crier en lieu public noüel, quand il vouloit congratuler à un Prince." In 1610, appeared 'Melanges de la musique de Eustaché du Caurroy, maistre de la musique de la Chappelle du Roy,' which contains some noëls, of one of which Burney has given the music; and it is said that the greater part of the noëls sung in France are gavots and other airs, which

Du Caurroy composed for Charles the Ninth. The well-known air, 'Charmante Gabrielle,' was also a Christmas hymn. In 'Recueil de Poètes Gascons, première partie, contenant les œuvres de Pierre Goudelin de Toulouse,' Amsterdam, 1700, are some carols. There are upwards of twenty different collections in the patois. In 1699, was a collection by Le Sieur Nicolas Saboly. In 1701, one was published at Dijon, in the dialect of the province, which at first gave some offence, from the freedom of the compositions; but the naïveté of the patois, which also prevented their being perfectly understood, saved them. There were subsequent editions of these. In 1720, the fourth edition of 'Noël Bourgignon de Gui Barôzai,' was published, containing thirty-four noëls, and two chansons, with the music to each, and an ample glossary; and there was a subsequent edition in 1736. There is also a recent edition by Fertiault, at Paris, in 1842. Many of these are written in a vein of burlesque humour, quite out of character with the subject, and in a very free and irreverent style. In the seventh noël, the salutation of the Virgin by the angel, is quite in the manner of a *petit maître*.

"Po lai fenétre el antri,
Et peù de queique distance,
Ai li fi lai reverance,
Car el étó bén épri.
Dei vo gar, mai chére aimie,
Dit-i d' ene douce voi, &c."

The effect of the salutation reminds one of the old lines,

"Gaude Virgo, Mater Christi,
Quæ per aurem concepisti."

and of a similar conceit in Molière's 'Ecole des Maris.'

There is some buffoonery introduced into the fourteenth of the Coventry plays, as gross as this, but which was adapted to the rude audiences of its time; and the language of the buffoons of the piece, Primus and Secundus Detractator, forms an exception to its general gravity and seriousness. The fifth noël, amongst other things, introduces the adoration and offering of the Three Kings, in the following manner.

" Ai lai Nativitati,
Chanton, je vo suplie,
Troi Roi d' autre coutai,
Moitre au estrôlôgie,
De l' anfan nôvea nai
Saivein lai prôfecie.

Ai lai Nativitai,
Chanton, je vo suplie,
De l'etoile guidai
Tô troi de compagnie,
Patire sans menai,
Gran seûte, ni meignie.

A lai Nativitai,
Chanton, je vo suplie,
L'un pris soin d'epotai,
De lai myére candie,
L'autre d'or efeignai,
E'ne bonne poignie.

Ai lai Nativitai,
Chanton, je vo suplie,
Le tier pu macherai,
Qu' ein Roi d'Etiôpie,
Prezanti po son plai
De l' ançan d' Airaibir."

The thirteenth is a dialogue between a shepherd and his wife, and begins in the following quaint way.

> "Fanne, coraige,
> Le Diale á mor,
> Aipre l'ornige,
> J'on le beá jor."

The glossary contains, incidentally, some curious particulars. It is stated to be the custom in the provinces, for the master of the family, with his wife and children, to sing noëls; "une très grosse buche," called *lai suche de noei*, was put on the fire, and the younger children were sent into the corner of the room, to pray that the *suche* might produce bon-bons; and on their return, packets of sugar-plums, &c., were found near the *suche*, to whom the children implicitly attributed the power of producing them.

There was a collection of Noëls Bourguignons, by De la Monnoye, of which a translation into the common language of the country was published in 1735. De la Monnoye was denounced by the priests at Dijon, for his carols; but the translation, though it might have taken off the sting, probably lessened the humour also.

In 1738 was published, at Troyes, 'La Grande Bible Renouvelles de Noëls Nouveaux,' in four parts, containing ninety noëls, many of them of a rude and humble description. In 1750, at Avignon, 'Nouveaux Cantiques Spirituels Provençaux,' with the music; it contains some noëls, though not exclusively confined to them. In 1785, at Paris, 'Noëls Nouveaux sur les Chants des Noëls anciens, notez pour en faciliter le chant,' par M. l'Abbé Pellegrin. In 1791, at Avignon, Recueil de Noëls Provençaux,' par le Sieur Peirol,

Menuisier d'Avignon, nouvelle édition. This contains forty-two noëls, besides five pieces of a different description. They are mostly of a light and joyous nature, and the subjects are very similar to those in our carols. In 1805, there was a collection of noëls published at St. Malo, and another edition in 1819, containing twenty-one noëls; and at the commencement of the work are three pastorals, or dramatic pieces, in the style of our old mysteries; one on the Birth of our Saviour; another on the Adoration of the Three Kings; and the third on the Massacre of the Innocents, where Herod orders all children under the age of *seven* to be killed, which gives his own son, who is one of the sufferers, an opportunity for making a speech; to this is added the regrets of Herod for the massacre, in the form of a dialogue between himself and the Innocents. I have also a collection of "Noëls Vieux et Nouveaux," of which the title-page and first two or three leaves are torn out. In 1807, there was a collection, at Avignon, of Noëls Provençaux, by Le Sieur Nicolas Saboly, a new edition, containing ninety. The tunes of some of the more favourite noëls may occasionally be found in collections of popular French airs; and among the chap books of the day are small collections of noëls at small prices, and collections of Spanish and German carols may be met with.

There are some curious burdens or refrains to some of the French noëls; one will be seen in the selection given, "Turelurelu, patapatan;" but these words are intended to represent the sounds of the flute and tambour. They often introduce in their old songs " Lurelure," or something similar; indeed " Leire la, Leire lauleire," is very ancient, as also is " Dondon," another refrain. " Mironton," " Biribi," and " Turlututu," are other terms, of which the explanation must be left to wordy antiquaries. The English refrains, however, seem equally as inexplicable as the French; unless we suppose, with some learned expositor, that the well-known " Down derry down " has reference to the oak, and is derived from the Druid, " Hob y deri danno;" but then how are we to account for " Hey troly loly lo," and " Dumble dum deary," &c.? In the Elizabethan age, " Hey, nonny, nonny " was somewhat a favourite, though there were some strange burdens also at this time, that would make us fancy that the celebrated Tarleton and Kemp must occasionally have improvised any clinking nonsense that entered their heads, which was afterwards printed with the songs.

CHAPTER XI.

EVERAL of the circumstances referred to in the carols, may also be found in the early mysteries, and are probably handed down from them, or from some legend common to both. Some, indeed, may have been derived from the Apocryphal New Testament, as from the birth of Mary, the Protevangelion, and the infancy. The tradition, for instance, of Joseph being an old man, is derived from both sources; in the Coventry Mysteries he complains of his age in many passages.

" . . . . I am so agyd and so olde,
  Yt both my leggys gyn to folde,
  I am ny almost lame."

In the cherry-tree carol, and in the Dutch date-tree carol, he is described as an old man, and weary. This cherry-tree carol, of which there are two or three varieties, one of which is printed in the following collection, appears to have been of the fifteenth century, if not older; as, in Hoffman's specimens of Dutch carols of that age, there is one very similar, merely substituting a date for a cherry tree, the date perhaps having been considered more oriental. The following is the translation given in 'Notes and Queries.'

"Joseph he led the ass,
　The bridle held he;
What found they by the way,
　But a date tree?
Oh! ass's foal, thou must stand still,
To gather dates it is our will,
　So weary are we.
The date tree bowed to the earth,
　To Mary's knee;
Mary would fill her lap
　From the date tree.
Joseph was an old man,
　And wearied was he.
Mary, let the date tree bide,
We have yet forty miles to ride,
　And late it will be.
Let us pray this Blessed Child
　Grant us mercie."

The tradition is also introduced in the early mysteries, and the following is the manner in which it is treated in the fifteenth of the Coventry plays, that may serve as a specimen of these performances, somewhat quaint and rude to our modern ears; and it would puzzle a practised Shakesperian reader, even a well-skilled relation of my own in this art, to give one of these ancient dramas with any effect.—Mary says,

> A my swete husbond, wolde ye telle to me
> What tre is yon standynge upon yon hylle?

Joseph. Forsoothe, Mary, it is clepyd a chery tre,
In tyme of yer ye myght fede yow yon yō fylle.

Maria. Turne ageyn, husbond, and beholde yon tre,
How yt it blomyght now so swetly.

Joseph. Cum on, Mary, yt we worn at yon cyte,
Or ellys we may be blamyd I telle yow lythly.

Maria. Now, my spouse, I pray yow to be hold
How ye cheryes growyn upon yon tre,
For to have yr of ryght fayn I wold,
And it plesyd yow to labor so mech for me.

Joseph. Yor desyr to fulfylle I shall assay sekyrly,
Ow to plucke yow of these cherries it is a werk wylde,
For ye tre is so hyg' it wol not be lyghtly,
Yr for lete hy pluk yow cheryes begatt yow wt childe.

Maria. Now, good Lord, I pray the, graunt me yis boun,
To have of yese cheries, and it be yor wylle,
Now I thank it God, yis tre bowyth to me down,
I may now gadery anowe and etyn my fylle.

Joseph. Ow, I know weyl I have offendyd my God i trinyte,
Spekyn to my spowse these unkynde wordys.
For now I beleve wel it may non other be,
But yt my spowse beryght ye kyngys son of blys,
He help us now at oure nede!"

In the French mystery, or Pastoral, as it is called, of the Naissance, on the first appearance of Joseph and Mary, in their humble condition, the host resists all the entreaties of his wife to let them in—she, with the compassion of a woman (found, as Mungo Park relates, even in the uncivilised interior of Africa) being moved with the apparent helpless condition of the Virgin—the surly host, however, says,

> "Fermez, fermez la porte,
> Nous ne logerons point des gens de cette sorte."

Thus repulsed, they then take shelter in the stable.

The legend of the roasted cock coming to life, in proof of our Saviour's birth, which is mentioned in the carol of the 'Carnal and the Crane,' may also be found in an old carol for St. Stephen's Day, of the time of Henry the Sixth; but in this, instead of crowing three times, as in the more modern carol, the bird, which in the older version is called a capon, crows, "Christus natus est." The legend of the husbandman, in the same carol, whose seed sprang up before Herod and his train arrived, has been already referred to, as forming part of one of the old mysteries.

The curious fancy, in the carol of 'I saw three ships,' is old; one of the ancient Dutch carols given by Hoffman, beginning

> "There comes a vessel laden,
> And on its highest gunwale,
> Mary holds the rudder,
> The angel steers it on."

And in an after verse,

> "In one unbroken course
> There comes that ship to land,
> It brings to us rich gifts,
> Forgiveness is sent to us."

Ritson also mentions the following lines, as sung at Christmas time, about the middle of the sixteenth century.

> "There comes a ship far sailing then,
> Saint Michel was the stieres-man;
> Saint John sate in the horn.
> Our Lord harped, our Lady sang,
> And all the bells of heaven they rang,
> On Christ's Sonday at morn."

A modern broadside carol, called 'The Sunny Bank,' gives these lines thus.

> "O he did whistle, and she did sing,
> And all the bells on earth did ring,
> For joy that our Saviour he was born
> On Christmas Day in the morning."

Hone, in his Mysteries, mentions a carol printed by J. Bradford, Little Britain, 1701, having a large woodcut, representing the stable at Bethlehem; our Saviour in the crib, watched by the Virgin and Joseph; shepherds kneeling, and angels attending; a man playing on the bagpipes; a woman with a basket of fruit on her head; a sheep bleating, and an ox lowing on the ground; a raven croaking, and a crow cawing on the hay-rack; a cock crowing above them; and angels singing in the sky. The animals and birds have labels, which are thus explained. The cock croweth, *Christus natus est*, Christ is born. The raven asked, *Quando?* When? The cow replied, *Hac nocte*, this night. The ox cryeth out, *Ubi? Ubi?* Where? where? The sheep bleated out, *Bethlehem*, Bethlehem. Voice from heaven sounded, *Gloria in Excelsis*, Glory be on high. There is an old French mystery of the Nativity, referred to in "Noei Borguignon de Gui Barôzai," where four animals are introduced, much in the same manner; the ox and ass of the manger, the cock of the passion, and the lamb of St. John the Baptist. The cock exclaims, with a piercing voice, *Christus natus est*. The ox, with a lengthened bellowing, demands *Ubi?* pronouncing it oubi. The lamb answers *Bethleem*, lengthening the first syllable; and the ass concludes, with *hinhamus, hinhamus*, signifying *eamus*.

Several carols refer to the crucifixion and resurrection, and, as formerly observed, are more adapted to Easter than Christmas; but there are also regular Christmas carols, which carry our Saviour's history down to the time of his death. It may be readily supposed, that the cross itself has a legend attached to it, and its origin indeed dates from the death of Adam. When he was at the point of death, he directed his son Seth to apply to the angel of Paradise, for some of the oil of mercy, and obtained from him three kernels from an apple of the tree of life, which he was instructed to plant after Adam's death; one in his mouth, and one in each nostril. From the tree which sprang from these kernels, the rod of Moses, with which he worked his miracles, was taken, and also the wood with which he cured the bitter water, and the pole whereon the brazen serpent was raised. At the time of building Solomon's temple, the tree was cut down for use, but it was in every case found too long or too short, or with some other defect, and was thrown aside as unserviceable for the temple, and applied as a foot-bridge; but the Queen of Sheba, during her visit to King Solomon, refused to pass over it, stating it would prove the ruin of the Jews. It was then used as a seat, but the Sybil would not sit on it, predicting that the Redeemer would die triumphantly on it, for the salvation of mankind. It afterwards remained in the pool of Bethesda until the time of the crucifixon, when some difficulty arising in procuring proper wood for the cross, some of the Jews thought of this tree, which they found perfectly adapted for the purpose.

One of the versions of the legend states, that a smith being applied to, to make three nails to fasten our Saviour to the cross, he refused to do so, and feigned sickness, upon which his wife came forward and made them. After the crucifixion, the cross, with its nails, became buried in rubbish, and was lost sight of, until Helena, the mother of Constantine the Great, went to Jerusalem, in 326, and after diligent search found it, together with the crosses of the two thieves, Titus (the penitent) and Dumachus, the former of whom had prevented the latter from robbing Joseph and Mary, on their flight to Egypt, and the child Jesus had then foretold that they would be crucified with Him, thirty years afterwards, and that Titus should go to Paradise.

Three crosses having been found by Helena, and the inscription having been detached, a difficulty arose how to identify the true one; but this was removed by placing them by the side of a lady who was dangerously ill, and she was immediately restored to health on the application of the real cross. She gave the nails and part of the cross to her son, and founded a church at Rome, where she placed the remainder, with the inscription. Constantine, it is said, placed one of the nails on the bridle of his war-horse, and one on his sword, and the third was cast into a dangerous gulf of the sea, to appease a storm.

According to Fabian, Athelstan had in his possession one of the nails, with part of the cross; and another part with a nail; and the crown of thorns, were said to have been at

Nôtre Dame, in Paris; and portions of it claimed to be preserved in other churches.

There is a curious story on the subject, related in Harl. MS. 2252 (temp. Hen. 8), entitled, "A grete myracle of a knyghte, callyde Syr Roger Wallysborow." Being in the Holy Land, he wished to bring off privily a piece of the cross, and praying to that effect, his thigh opened miraculously, and received it. He then returned to Cornwall, his native country, having in the course of his voyage, by virtue of the fragment of the cross, appeased the elements, and prevented shipwreck. On his arrival, his thigh opened to liberate the precious relic, of which he gave part to the parish church where this happened, hence called Cross parish, and the remainder to St. Buryan, where his lands were.

The slaughter of the Innocents is referred to in several carols, and there are some written expressly for Innocents' Day; the day of the week on which it falls being considered unlucky throughout the year by many. Brand mentions a custom in Roman Catholic countries of running through all the rooms of a house, making a pretended search in and under the beds, in commemoration of Herod's search for the children; and there is a tradition that his own son was killed among them, which made Augustus say, that it was better to be Herod's hog than his son, referring to his being a Jew, and therefore forbidden to kill swine, playing also on the Greek words, υν (un) a hog, and υιον (uion) a son. Some carols, or Christmas songs, refer to the bringing in of the boar's head; and in the old carol of St. Stephen's Day, before mentioned, St. Stephen, who is stated to be in king Herod's service, is, somewhat inconsistently with such service, introduced as bringing in a boar's head.

"Stevyn out of kechon cam w^t boris hed on honde,
He saw a sterr was fayr and bryzt ou^r bedlem stonde,
He kyst a down the bors hed and went into the halle,
I forsak the kyng herowds and thi werks alle,
I forsak the kyng herowds and thi werks alle,
Ther is a chyd in bedlem born is bet^r than we alle."

It is difficult to say whether the boar's head was first introduced at Christmas as a kind of anti-judaical test, because the Jews would not eat it—something like pork was said to be eaten at Easter, together with tansy pudding (a corruption from athanasia);—but as the boar's head seems to have been a favourite at all great feasts, at least, from the time of that greatest of boars, Scrymer, it is probable that it thus became a "chief service" at the greatest of feasts.

There are several ancient MS. carols in the British Museum, particularly in Sloane MS. 2593 and Harl. MS. 5396, Additional MSS. 5465 and 5665 and Cotton MS. Vespasian A, xxv, of which several, and probably the best, have been printed in Christmas carols, edited by Mr. Wright, for the Percy Society, in 1811, and in the collection of Christmas carols, by the author of the present work, in 1833. There is also a curious collection of songs and carols, supposed to have been a minstrel's book of the fifteenth century, edited, in 1817, for the Percy Society, by Mr. Wright, whose ability in all matters connected with the history, customs, and antiquities of our country, are so well known; old carols may also be found in the libraries of the Universities. The oldest printed collection of carols was by Wynkyn de Worde, in 1521, which contains one on bringing in the boar's head. Another rare collection was printed by Richard Kele, in the Poultry, between 1546 and 1552.

In 1562, John Tysdale had a license for printing 'Certayne goodly carowles to be songe to the glory of God;' and, in the same year, Rowlande Hall had one for 'Crestenmas carroles auctorysshed by my lorde of London.' In 1563, John Day printed some carols of Thomas Becon; and, in 1569, Richard Jonnes and James Robertes, each printed a collection; the last being by Christopher Payne. About the same time Tusser wrote a carol, as well as other poetry, illustrative of Christmas-tide. In 1579, J. Alder had a license for 'a Godly Hymn or Carol for Christmas,' and in 1580, for 'Godly Carols, Hymns, and Spiritual Songs.' In 'Songs of Sundry natures,' by William Byrd, 1589, there is a Christmas carol which has been printed by Mr. J. Payne Collier, the distinguished editor of Shakespeare, in Lyrical Poems, for the Percy Society. In 1597 was published at Edinburgh, 'Ane Compendioos Booke of Godly and Spirituall Songs,' which contains some carols; these with the other songs were adapted to popular tunes, the intention being to supersede the use of profaner ballads: it was reprinted in 1801. In 'Ancient Scottish Poems,' Dunbar has inserted one from the Bannatyne MS. In 1630, 'Certaine of David's Psalmes, intended for Christmas carolls, fitted to the most common but solempne tunes, everywhere familiarly used, by William Slatyr,' was printed by Robert Young, and a similar work in 1642. There is one also at the end of Aylett's 'Eclogues and Elegies.' In Herrick's 'Noble Numbers,' 1640, there are five carols, or songs in the nature of carols, some of which were set to music by Henry Lawes, and were sung before the court, and there are many poems connected with Christmas customs in his other works.

In 1661 was published a collection called 'New Carolls for this Merry Time of Christmas, to sundry pleasant Tunes, with new Additions, never before printed, to be sung to delight the Hearers; printed by H. B., for Andrew Kemb.' In the title-page was a print of the Wise Men discovering the Star. There were likewise 'Christmas carols, fit also to be sung at Easter,' and 'New Christmas Carols,' in 1688. Some of these collections were encouraged by the puritans, to drive away those of a lighter description; and, in 1684, 'A Small Garland of Pious and Godly Songs,' of this nature, was printed at Ghent, for the purpose of superseding the popular ballad, and may be assumed to have contained serious carols for the same purpose.

We must not omit to mention Milton's 'Ode and Hymn on the Nativity.'

"It was the winter wild,
While the heaven-born child,
All meanly wrapt, in the rude manger lies;"

and single hymns or carols may be found in other writers, to name which would only be to swell this, already I fear, too tiresome list. Lewis's 'Presbyterian Eloquence,' 1720, contains a catalogue of Presbyterian books, in which is the following: 'A Cabinet of Choice Jewels; or, the Christian's Joy and Gladness: set forth in sundry pleasant new Christmas carols, viz. a carol for Christmas Day, to the tune of Over Hills and High Mountains; for Christmas Day, at night, to the tune of My Life and my Death; for St. Stephen's Day, to the tune of O, cruel bloody Tale; for New Year's Day, to the tune of Caper and Firk it; for Twelfth Day, to the tune of O Mother Roger.' Several of Poor Robin's Almanacs contain carols or Christmas poems.

In the broadside and other lists of chap books, ballads, &c. published about 150 years ago, the names of several well known carols occur, as, 'When Jesus Christ was twelve years old,' 'Joseph an aged man truly,' 'Jury came to Jerusalem,' 'Angel Gabriel,' 'Christus natus est,' &c. There is also a small collection printed, about the same time, by William Thackery, at the Angel, in Duck Lane. The carol, 'Christians awake, salute the happy morn,' is said to have been written by Mr. Greatorex, the father of the late organist, about a century since, and it is stated that Mr. Webbe, the composer, set one. The late Mr. Hone, in his work on Mysteries, 1823,—where, as well as in his 'Every Day Book,' 'Year Book,' and 'Table Book,' much interesting information may be found relating to Christmas customs—gives a list of eighty-nine recent carols, and mentions one by Francis Hoffman, in 1729, with the curious title of '*A Christmas Carol on Pekoe Tea*; or, a Sacred Carol, which like tea that is perfectly good and fine, will be most useful and grateful all the year round, from Christmas to Christmas, for ever; humbly addressed to Queen Caroline, and the princess Carolina, and all the Royal Family.' Perhaps, if this could be seen, it might turn out to be a tea-dealer's puff, for even now with all our worldly experience, we are occasionally taken in to read a puff from its innocent and unassuming appearance. There have been frequent publications of carols, from time to time, for use, according to the demand, partly in broadsides and partly in the nature of chap publications, and in a popular form down to the present time, which need not, and indeed cannot, be enumerated; and the account given of the old collected publications is not presumed to be perfect.

In 1822 the late Mr. Davies Gilbert published twelve favourite western carols, with the tunes, and in 1823 a second edition, containing twenty, with a few old ballads, &c. In

1833, the author of the present work published a collection of eighty carols, ancient and modern, with seventeen tunes; and a copy of the Christmas play of St. George and the Dragon, with an introduction relating to Christmas customs, the essential part of which has been embodied in these pages. Mr. Parker, in 1838, printed sixteen original carols, of a devout nature, with tunes adapted; and Mr. Chappell introduced some carols in his collection of National English Airs.

In 1847 Mr. Sharpe published eleven Christmas carols, with good illustrations; and in the same year, Dr. Rimbault, a great musical antiquary, edited, in a tasteful form, five old carols, with six tunes. In 1841, as before mentioned, Mr. Wright edited a collection of forty-nine old Christmas carols, for the Percy Society; and in 1847, songs and carols for the same Society; they are seventy-six in number, of which about half may be considered carols; there was an illustrated collection by Mr. Cundell, in 1846, and there are probably others which have not come to my knowledge.

Mr. Hervey, in 1836, published the 'Book of Christmas,' containing a good deal of information in a pleasing style, with illustrations; and two years since a very elegant work was edited by Mr. H. Vizetelly, called 'Christmas with the Poets,' being a selection of poetical pieces, including some carols from the thirteenth century to the present time, forming an interesting collection, embellished with fine woodcuts.

Besides the several broadside carols, and printed collections in town and country, before referred to, there have been various collections of Welsh carols; several are among the Myvyrian MSS., belonging to the Cymmrodorion: No. 14, written about the year 1640, contains thirty-two; and No. 15, of about the same date, has two. The *Llfyr Carolau*, or

'Book of Carols,' fourth edition, Shrewsbury, 1740, comprises sixty-six carols for Christmas, and five summer carols; and *Blodeugerdd Cymric*, or the 'Anthology of Wales,' Shrewsbury, 1779, contains forty-eight Christmas carols, nine summer carols, three May carols, one winter carol, one nightingale carol, and a carol to Cupid, which might interest my readers, if I could translate it.

The carols printed in the following pages, are taken from a collection of several hundred English, including the broadside publications for the last thirty years; and French, including several editions in the *patois*. Some of the English, according to reputation, have been known in Cornwall for nearly three hundred years past, and these, with others, have been obtained from old manuscript copies now in my possession, or oral tradition from the singers themselves, and the tunes have been procured in the same way, though I am indebted to my friend, Mr. Wm. Chappell, for the harmonies.

I have selected, out of several versions of the western Christmas play of 'St. George and the Dragon,' that which seemed best adapted for the purpose. Specimens have been printed in Hone's 'Every Day Book,' the 'Gentleman's Magazine,' and the 'Popular Rhymes' of Mr. Halliwell, who has applied his store of reading to the illustration of our poetical literature. There is a version also in that dialect with some description, in Jan Trenoodle's 'Specimens of Cornish Provincial Dialect,' a small work for which I am answerable, and therefore, perhaps, ought not to refer to it, but I know no other of the sort.

The play of 'Alexander and the King of Egypt,' is a representation of the northern Christmas play, and is taken from a rare printed copy in my possession. It consists of six pages, with very common paper and type, the title-page being, 'Alexander and the King of Egypt. A mock play, as it is acted by the mummers every Christmas. Newcastle: Printed in the year 1788.' It is given here verbatim, with two or three slight omissions, necessary for modern ears. The great similarity between the northern and western plays will immediately be seen, showing the common origin; but these performances must be seen to be properly appreciated.

The mummers, in several parts of the country where they do not go to the extent of acting the old Christmas play, are generally dressed somewhat in the manner described for 'St. George and the Dragon,' one of the party being the clown or buffoon of the set; and they have some doggrel lines, of which a few show symptoms of the same antiquity as the plays; for rhymes, that appear to have been the *ad libitum* production of some modern rustic wit, will be introduced, with "A room! a room! a gallant room!" or some such line, and the characters are then introduced in the style of the plays, and this style, as before referred to, is as old as the Mysteries; take, for example, a specimen from the sixth of the Chester Plays, where the Nuntius says,—

"Make rombe, lordinges, and geve us waie,
And lette Octavian come and plaie;
And Syble the Sage, that well fayer maye,
To tell you of propheseye."

Two or three specimens of these mummers' songs are given by Mr. Dixon, in his 'Collection of Ballads and Songs of the Peasantry of England,' edited for the Percy Society in 1846. These mummings, as well as the plays and carol singings, end in an appeal to the box, and right enough too; for, do not we all, when we have given our services for any purpose, carry round the box, in some shape or other, whether the clergyman for his tithes, the lawyer and physician for their fees, the soldier for his pay, or the statesman for his salary?

In the selection of Carols, I have tried to vary them in age, style, and subject, as far as the materials would permit, without making it too long; and trust that I may, throughout this work, have succeeded in my endeavour to gratify, and not to satiate my readers. I have to express my thanks to Mr. James Stephanoff, for the interest he has taken in the subjects entrusted to his pencil, and the skill and spirit with which he has treated them. The design for the binding has been given by my brother, Mr. Sampson Sandys; and from the well-known zeal and ability of the publisher and printer, I am placed in this awkward predicament, that any failure must rest with myself; and I am fully aware that it can be no excuse, that the work was undertaken as a relief, from the pressure of repeated domestic losses of the severest nature: but I can unaffectedly say, "If I have done well, and as is fitting the story, it is that which I desired; but, if slenderly and meanly, it is that which I could attain unto."

Carols.

1.

SEIGNORS, ore entendez à nus,
De loinz sumes venuz à vous,
    Pur quere noël;
Car l'em nus dit que en cest hostel,
Soleit tenir sa feste anuel,
    Ahi, cest jur.
        Deu doint à tuz icels joie d'amurs,
        Qui à danz noël ferunt honors!

Seignors, jo vus dis por veir,
Ke danz noël ne velt aveir,
    Si joie non;
E repleni sa maison,
De payn, de char, e de peison,
    Por faire honor.
        Deu doint à tuz ces joie d'amur!

Seignors, il est crié en l'ost,
Que cil qui despent bien, e tost,
    E largement;
E fet les granz honors sovent,
Deu li duble quanque il despent,
    Por faire honor.
        Deu doint à . . . .

Seignors, escriez les malveis,
Car vuz nel les troverez jameis
　　De bone part;
Botun, batun, ferun, groinard,
Car tot dis a le quer cunard,
　　Por faire honor.
　　　　Deu doint....

Noël beyt bien li vin Engleis,
E li Gascoin, e li Franceys,
　　E l'Angevin;
Noël fait beivere son veisin,
Si qu'il se dort, le chief enclin,
　　Sovent le jor.
　　　　Deu doint à tuz cels....

Seignors, jo vus di par noël,
E par li sires de cest hostel,
　　Car bevez ben;
E jo primes beverai le men,
E pois après chescon le soen,
　　Par mon conseil;
Si jo vus di trestoz, 'Wesseyl!'
Dehaiz cit qui ne dirra, 'Drincheyl!'

II.

LORDINGS, from a distant home,
To seek old Christmas we are come,
  Who loves our minstrelsy:
And here, unless report mis-say,
The grey-beard dwells, and on this day,
Keeps yearly wassel, ever gay,
  With festive mirth and glee.
To all who honour Christmas, and commend our lays,
Love will his blessings send, and crown with joy their days.

Lordings list, for we tell you true,
Christmas loves the jolly crew
  That cloudy care defy:
His liberal board is deftly spread
With manchet loaves and wastel-bread;
His guests with fish and flesh are fed,
  Nor lack the stately pye.

Lordings, you know that far and near,
The saying is, "Who gives good cheer,
  And freely spends his treasure;
On him will bounteous Heaven bestow
Twice treble blessings here below;
His happy hours shall sweetly flow,
  In never-ceasing pleasure."

Lordings, believe us, knaves abound,
In every place are flatterers found,
  May all their arts be vain!

But chiefly from these scenes of joy,
Chase sordid souls that mirth annoy,
And all who with their base alloy,
    Turn pleasure into pain.

Christmas quaffs our English wines,
Nor Gascoigne juice, nor French declines,
    Nor liquor of Anjou:
He puts th' insidious goblet round,
Till all the guests in sleep are drown'd
Then wakes 'em with the tabor's sound,
    And plays the prank anew.

Lordings, it is our host's command,
And Christmas joins him hand in hand,
    To drain the brimming bowl:
And I'll be foremost to obey:
Then pledge me, sirs, and drink away,
For Christmas revels here to day,
    And sways without controul.
Now wassel to you all, and merry may ye be!
But foul that wight befall, who drinks not health to me!

III.

WELCŪ ȝole in good array,
    In worship of þe holiday,
Welcū be þᵘ heuē kyng,
Welcū þᵘ born ī on mornyng,
Welcū to þe now wil we syng,
Welcū ȝole for eu^r & ay,

Welcũ be þᵘ mare myld,
Welcũ be þᵘ & þⁱ child,
Welcũ fro þᵉ fynd þᵘ as schilde,
Welcũ ȝole for eưʳ & ay,
Welcũ be ȝᵉ stenẽ & ione,
Welcũ childrn cũechone,
Welcũ thomas, martʳ, all on,
Welcũ ȝole for eưʳ & ay,
Welcũ be þᵘ good newyere,
Welcũ þe xij days efere,
Welcũ be ye all þᵗ bene here,
Welcũ ȝole for ewʳ & ay,
Welcũ be ȝᵉ lord and lady,
Welcũ be ȝᵉ all þis cũpane,
ffore ȝolis love makis mere,
Welcũ ȝole fore ewʳ & ay.

IV.

NAY iuy, nay, hyt shall not be I wys,
Let holy hafe þᵉ maystry as þᵉ maner ys.

Holy stond in þᵉ hall fayre to behold,
Iuy stond wᵗ out þᵉ dore, she ys ful sore a cold.
       Nay iuy, &c.

Holy and hys mery men þey dawnsyn & þey syng,
Iuy and her maydenys þey wepyn & þey wryng.
       Nay, &c.

Iuy hath a lyve she laghtyt w^t þe colde,
So mot þey all ha fae þ^t w^t jvy hold.
                    Nay iuy, nay, hyt, &c.

Holy hat berys as rede as any rose,
The foster þe hunters kepe hem fro þe dos.
                    Nay iuy, nay, hyt, &c.

Iuy hath berys as blake as any slo,
Ther com þe oule & ete hym as she goo.
                    Nay iuy, nay, hyt, &c.

Holy hath byrdys a ful fayre flok,
The nyghtyngale þe perpyinguy, þe gayntyl lauyrok.
                    Nay, &c.

Gode iuy what byrdys ast þ^u?
Non but þe howlat þ^t kreye how how.
                    Nay iuy, nay, hyt shal not, &c.

V.

NOW ys Crystemas y-cum,
   Fadyr and Son togedyr in oon,
Holy Goste, as ye be oon,
            in fere-a,
God sende us a good n(e)w yere-a.

I wolde yow synge for and I mygʒhgt,
Off a chylde ys fayre in syghgʒt,
Hys modyr hym bare thys yndyrs nyghʒt
      so stylle-a,
And as yt was hys wylle-a.

There cam iij kynges fro Galylee
Into Bethleem, that fayre cytee,
To seke hym that ever shulde be
      by ryghʒt-a
Lorde and kynge and knyghʒt-a.

As they cam forth with there offrynge,
They met with Herode that mody kynge,
      thys tyde-a,
And thys to them he sayde-a.

" Off wens be ye, yow kynges iij. ?
Off the Este, as ye may see,
To seke hym that ever shulde be
      by ryghgʒt-a
Lorde and kynge and knyghʒt-a."

" Wen yow at thys chylde have be,
Cum home aʒeyne by me,
Tell me the syghʒtes that yow have see,
      I praye yow;
Go yow no nodyr way-a."

They toke her leve both olde and yonge
Off Herode that mody kynge;
They went forth with there offrynge
    by lygh3th-a,
By the sterre that shoone so brygh3t-a.

Tyll they cam in to the place
There Jhesu and hys modyr was,
Offryd they up with grete solace
    in fere-a
Golde and sence and myrre-a.

The fadyr of hevyn an awngylle down sent,
To thyke iij kynges that made presente
    thys tyde-a,
And thys to them he sayd-a.

"My lorde have warnyd yow everychone,
By Herode kynge yow go not home;
For and yow do, he wylle you slone
    and strye-a,
And hurte yow wondyrly-a."

Forthe them wente thys kynges iij,
Tylle they cam home to there cuntré
Glade and blyth they were alle iij,
Off the sygh3tes that they had see,
    by-dene-a,
The cumpany was clene-a.

Knele we now here a-down,
Pray we in good devocioun
To the kynge of grete renown,
        of grace-a,
In hevyn to have a place-a.

VI.

NOWELL, nowell, nowell, nowell,
  Tydyng gode y thyngke to telle.

The borys hede, that we bryng here,
Betokeneth a prince withoute pere,
Ys born this day to bye us dere,
        Nowell.

A bore ys a souerayn beste,
And acceptable in eury feste,
So mote thys lord be to moste and leste,
        Nowell.

This borys hede we bryng wt song,
In worchyp of hym that thus sprang
Of a virgyne to redresse all wrong.
        Nowell.

VII.

NOWELL, nowell, nowell, nowell.
Who ys there that syngith so nowell, nowell?

I am here, syre Cristsmasse;
Well, come, my lord s^r Crstsmasse,
Welcome to vs all bothe more & lasse,
      Com ner, nowell.

Dievs wous garde brewe s^{rs} tydyge y ʒow bryng.
A mayde hath borne a chylde full ʒong,
The weche causeth ʒew for to syng,
      Nowell.

Criste is now born of a pure mayde,
In an oxe stalle he ys layde,
Wher'for syng we alle atte abrayde,
      Nowell.

Bevvex bien par tutte la company,
Make gode chere and be ryght mery,
And syng w^t vs now ioyfully,
      Nowell.

VIII.

A Bonne God wote!
Stickes in my throate,
Without I have a draught
 Of cornie aile,
 Nappy and staile,
My lyffe lyes in great wauste.
 Some ayle or beare,
 Gentill butlere,

Some lycoure thou hus showe,
    Such as you mashe,
    Our throates to washe,
The best were that yow brew.

    Saint, master, and knight,
    That Saint Mault hight,
Were prest betwen two stones;
    That swet humour
    Of his lycoure
Would make us sing at once.
    Mr. Wortley,
    I dar well say,
I tell you as I thinke,
    Would not, I say,
    Byd hus this day,
But that we shuld have drink.

    His men so tall
    Walkes up his hall,
With many a comly dishe;
    Of his good meat
    I cannot eate,
Without a drink i-wysse;
    Now gyve hus drink,
    And let eat wynke,
I tell you all at once,
    Yt stickes so sore,
    I may sing no more,
Tyll I have dronken once.

IX.

Nowel el el el, now is wel that erere was woo.

A BABE is born al of a may,
In the savasyoun of us,
To hem we syngyn bothe ny3ht and day,
Veni creator spiritus.

At Bedlem that blyssid pas,
The chylde of blysse born he was,
Hym to serve, go 3eve us gras,
O lux beata trinitas.

Ther come thre kynges out of the est,
To worchepe the Kyng that is so fre,
With gold and myrre and francincens,
A solis ortus cardine.

The herdes herdyn an aungele cry,
A merye song then sungyn he,
Qwy arn 3e so sore a-gast?
Jam ortus solis cardine.

The aungele comyn down with on cry,
A fayr song then sungyn he,
In the worchepe of that chyld,
Gloria tibi, Domine.

X.

> Make we myrth,
> For Crystes byrth,
> And syng we ȝole tyl Candelmes.

THE fyrst day of ȝole have we in mynd,
How God was man born of owre kynd;
For he the bondes wold onbynd
    Of all owre synnes and wykednes.

The secund day we syng of Stevene,
That stoned and steyyd up even
To God that he saw stond in hevyn,
    And erounned was for hys prouesse.

The iij day longeth to sent Johan,
That was Cristys darlyng, derer non,
Whom he betok, whan he shuld gon,
    Hys moder der for hyr clennesse.

The iiij day of the chyldren ȝong,
That Herowd to deth had do with wrong,
And Crist thei coud non tell with tong,
    But with ther blod bar hym wytnesse.

The v day longeth to sent Thomas,
That, as a strong pyller of bras,
Held up the chyrch, and selayn he was,
    For he sted with ryȝtwesnesse.

The viij day tok Jhesu hys name,
That saved mankynd fro syn and shame,
And circumsysed was for no blame,
   But for ensample of meknesse.

The xij day offerd to hym kynges iij,
Gold, myr, and cense, thes gyftes free,
For God, and man, and kyng was he,
   Thus worschyppyd thei his worthynes.

On the xl day cam Mary myld,
Unto the temple with hyr chyld,
To shew hyr clen that never was fylyd,
   And therwith endyth Crystmes.

XI.

BLYSSID be that lady bryght,
 That bare a chyld off great myght,
Withouten peyne, as it was right,
   Mayd mother Marye.

Goddys sonne is borne, his moder is a maid,
Both aftur and beforne, as the prophyey said,
   With ay;
 A wonder thyng it is to se,
 How mayden and moder on may be;
 Was there nonne but she,
   Maid moder Marye.

The great lord of heaven our servant is becom,
Thorow Gabriels stevyn, owr kynd have benom,
    With ay;
  A wonder thyng it is to se,
  How lord and servant on may be;
  Was ther never nonne but he,
    Born off maid Marye.

Two sons togyther they owght to shyne bryght;
So did that fayer ladye, whan Jesu in hir light,
    With ay;
  A wonder thyng is fall,
  The lord that bought fre and thrall,
  Is found in an assis stall,
    By his moder Mary.

The shepherdes in her region thei lokyd into Heaven,
Thei se an angell commyng down, that said with myld steven.
    With ay;
  Joy be to God almyght,
  And pece in yerth to man is dyte,
  Fore God was born on Chrismes nyght,
    Off his moder Marye.

Thre kynges off great noblay, whan that chyld was born,
To hym they tok the redy way, and kneled hym beforn,
    With ay;
  Thes iij kynges cam fro farre,
  Thorow ledyng of a stare,
  And offered hym gold, encence, and mure,
    And to hys moder Mary.

XII.

HEY, hey, hey, hey, the borrys hede is armyd gay.
The boris hede in hond I bryng,
With garlond gay in porttoryng,
I pray yow alle with me to synge,
        With hay.

Lordys, kny3ttes, and skyers,
Persons, prystis, and wycars,
The boris hede ys the furt mes,
        With hay.

The boris hede, as I yow say,
He takis his leyfe, and gothe his way,
Gone after the xij, theyl flyt day,
        With hay.

Then commys in the secunde kowrs with mykylle pryde,
The crannus, the heyrrouns, the bytteris by ther syde,
The pertrychys and the plowers, the wodcokus and the snyt,
        With hay.

Larkys in hot schow, ladys for to pyk,
Good drynk therto, lycyus and fyne,
Blwet of allmayne, romnay and wyin,
        With hay.

Gud bred alle and wyin dare I welle say,
The boris hede with musterd armyd soo gay ;
Furmante to pottage, with wennissun fyne,
And the hombuls of the dow, and all that ever commis in ;
Cappons i-bake, with the pesys of the roow,
Reysons of corrons, with odyre spysis moo.

XIII.

Caput afri differo
Reddens laudes domino.

THE bore's heed in hand bring I,
   With garlans gay and rosemary,
I pray you all synge merely
              Qui estis in convivio.

The bore's heed, I vnderstande,
Is the chefe seruyce in this lande ;
Loke, where euer it be fande,
              Seruite cum cantico.

Be gladde lordes, bothe more and lasse,
   For this hath ordeyned our stewarde,
To chere you all this Christmasse,
   The bores heed with mustarde.

XIV.
In Betheleem.

BE we mery in this feste,
  In quo saluator natus est.

In Betheleem, that noble place,
As by prophesy sayd it was,
Of the vyrgyn Mary, full of grace,
  Saluator mundi natus est.
      Be we mery, &c.

On Chrystmas nyght, an angel it tolde
To the shephardes, kepyng theyr folde,
That into Betheleem with bestes wolde,
  Saluator mundi natus est.
      Be we mery, &c.

The shephardes were cōpassed ryght,
About them was a great lyght,
Drede ye nought, sayd the angell bryght,
  Saluator mundi natus est.
      Be we mery, &c.

Beholde to you we brynge great ioy,
For why, Jesus is borne this day
(To vs) of Mary, that mylde may,
  Saluator mundi natus est.
      Be mery, &c.

And thus in fayth fynde it ye shall,
Lyenge porely in an oxe stall.
The shephardes than lauded God all,
   Quia Saluator mundi natus est.
Be mery, &c.

XV.

Sung to the Tune of "Essex Last Good Night."

ALL you that in this house be here,
   Remember Christ that for us dy'd,
And spend away with modest cheere,
   In loving sort this Christmas tide.

And whereas plenty God hath sent,
   Give frankly to your friends in love :
The bounteous mind is freely bent,
   And never will a niggard prove.

Our table spread within the hall,
   I know a banquet is at hand,
And friendly sort to welcome all
   That wil unto their tacklings stand.

The maids are bonny girles I see,
   Who have provided much good cheer,
Which at my dame's commandment be
   To set it on the table here.

For I have here two knives in store,
  To lend to him that wanteth one;
Commend my wits, good lads, therefore,
  That comes now hither having none.

For if I schuld, no Christmas pye
  Would fall, I doubt, unto my share;
Wherefore I will my manhood try,
  To fight a battle if I dare.

For pastry-crust, like castle walls,
  Stands braving me unto my face;
I am not well until it falls,
  And I made captain of the place.

The prunes so lovely look on me,
  I cannot chuse but venture on:
The pye-meat spiced brave I see,
  The which I must not let alone.

Then, butler, fill me forth some beer,
  My song hath made me somewhat dry:
And so again to this good cheer,
  I'le quickly fall couragiously.

And for my master I will pray,
  With all that of his household are,
Both old and young, that long we may
  Of God's good blessings have a share.

XVI.

REMEMBER, O thou man, O thou man!
Remember, O thou man!
Thy time is spent;
Remember, O thou man, how thou art dead and gone,
And I did what I can, therefore repent;
Remember Adam's fall,
   O thou man, O thou man!

Remember Adam's fall,
From heaven to hell;
Remember Adam's fall,
How we were condemned all,
In hell perpetuall
   Therefor to dwell.
Remember God's goodnesse,
   O thou man, man, O thou man!

Remember God's goodnesse,
And his promise made,
Remember God's goodnesse,
How he sent his sonne doutlesse,
Our sinnes for to redresse,
   Be not affraid.

The angels all did sing,
O thou man, O thou man!
The angels all did sing,
Vpon the shepheardes hill.

The angels all did singe,
Praises to our heauenly King,
And peace to man liuing,
   With a good will.

The shepheards amazed was,
O thou man, O thou man!
The shepheards amazed was,
To heare the angels sing;
The shepheards amazed was,
How it should come to passe,
That Christ, our Messias,
   Should be our King.

To Bethlem did they goe,
O thou man, O thou man!
To Bethlem did they go,
The shepheards three;
To Bethlem did they goe,
To see where it were so or no,
Whether Christ were borne or no,
   To set man free.

As the angels before did say,
O thou man, O thou man!
As the angels before did say,
So it came to passe;
As the angels before did say,
The found a babe where it lay,
In a manger wrapt in hay,
   So poor he was.

In Bethlem he was borne,
O thou man, O thou man!
In Bethlem he was borne,
For mankind sake;
In Bethlem he was borne,
For vs that were forlorne,
And therefore tooke no scorne,
  Our flesh to take.

Giue thanks to God always,
O thou man, O thou man!
Giue thanks to God always,
With heart most ioyfully;
Giue thankes to God always,
For this our happy day:
Let all men sing and say,
  Holy, holy.

XVII.

JESUS Christ of Nazareth,
He is born of a maiden pure,
Wherein God is blessed.

All the angels of the kingdom of Heaven,
And all the shepherds of earth
They sung, they had great joy.

When Herod became aware
That a little child was born,
Then had he in his heart great spite.

He had search made here and there,
For young children of two years,
All of which he deprived of life.

When our Lady heard this,
And that Herod was thus massacring infants,
She felt in her heart great grief.

She spoke to Joseph without delay;
Get you ready, we must away,
We should be gone, 'tis more than time.

All the angels of the kingdom of Heaven,
And all the clergy of the earth,
They all delighted were and glad!

Jesus Christ of Nazareth,
He is born of a maiden pure,
Wherein God is blessed.

XVIII.

IN those twelve days, and in those twelve days, let us be glad,
For God of his power hath all things made.

What is that which is but one?
We have but one God alone,
In Heaven above sits on his throne.

What are they which are but two?
Two Testaments, as we are told,
The one is New and the other Old.
     And in those, &c.

What are they that are but three?
Three persons in the Trinity,
To Father, Son, and Ghost Holy.
     And in those, &c.

What are they that are but four?
Four Gospels written true,
John, Luke, Mark, and Matthew.
     And in those, &c.

What are they that are but five?
Five senses we have to tell,
God grant us grace to use them well.
     And in those, &c.

What are they that are but six?
Six ages this world shall last,
Five of them are gone and past.
     And in those, &c.

What are they that are but seven?
Seven days in the week have we,
Six to work and the seventh holy.
     And in those, &c.

What are they that are but eight?
Eight beatitudes are given,
Use them well and go to Heaven.
     And in those, &c.

What are they that are but nine?
Nine degrees of angels high,
Which praise God continually.
     And in those, &c.

What are they that are but ten?
Ten commandments God hath given,
Keep them right and go to Heaven.
     And in those, &c.

What are they that are but eleven?
Eleven thousand virgins did partake,
And suffered death for Jesus' sake.
     And in those, &c.

What are they that are but twelve?
Twelve apostles Christ did chuse,
To preach the Gospel to the Jews.
     And in those, &c.

XIX.

JOSEPH was an old man, and an old man was he,
When he wedded Mary, in the land of Galilee;
When Joseph and Mary walked in the garden good,
There was cherries and berries as red as the blood.

O then bespoke Mary, so meek and so mild,
Pluck me some cherries, Joseph, for I am with child;
O then bespoke Joseph, with words so unkind,
Let him pluck the cherries that brought thee with child.

O then bespoke Jesus in his mother's womb,
Bow down then the tallest tree, that my mother may have some;
Then bowed down the tallest tree, it bent to Mary's hand,
Then she cried, See, Joseph, I have cherries at command.

O then bespoke Joseph, I have done Mary wrong,
But cheer up, my dearest, and be not cast down;
Then Joseph and Mary did to Bethlehem go,
And with travels were weary walking to and fro.

They sought for a lodging, but the inns were fill'd all,
They, alas! could not have it, but in an ox's stall;
But before the next morning our Saviour was born,
In the month of December, Christmas Day in the morn.

XX.

A CHILD this day is born,
   A child of high renown,
Most worthy of a sceptre,
   A sceptre and a crown.
         Novels, novels, novels,
            Novels, sing all we may,
            Because the King of all kings
               Was born this blessed day.

The which the holy prophets
   Spake of long time before,
That from the fall of Adam
   He should us all restore.
            Novels, &c.

This child, both God and man,
   From Heaven down to us came,
He is the King of all kings,
   And Jesus is his name.
            Novels, &c.

These tidings shepherds heard,
   In field watching their fold,
Were by an angel unto them,
   That night reveal'd and told.
            Novels, &c.

Who standing near by them,
   To them shined so bright,
That they amazed were
   At that most glorious sight.
                   Novels, &c.

To whom the angel spoke,
   Saying, Be not afraid,
Be glad, poor silly shepherds,
   Why are you so dismayed?
                   Novels, &c.

For lo! I bring you tidings
   Of gladness and of mirth,
Which cometh to all people by
   This holy infant's birth.
                   Novels, &c.

Him hath God lifted up,
   As light and shepherd's horn,
Which in the city of David,
   This present time was born.
                   Novels, &c.

The only Son of God was he,
   The Lord and God most highest;
And He is the true shepherd,
   The young child Jesus Christ.
                   Novels, &c.

Then was there with the angel,
    An host incontinent
Of heavenly bright soldiers,
    Which from the highest was sent.
                      Novels, &c.

Lauding the Lord our God,
    And his celestial king;
All glory be in Paradise,
    This heavenly host did sing.
                      Novels, &c.

Glory be unto our God,
    That sitteth still on high,
With praises and with triumph great,
    And joyful melody.
                      Novels, &c.

But when this holy army
    Of heavenly soldiers bright,
Was unto God returned,
    And vanish'd out of sight.
                      Novels, &c.

The shepherds' hearts joyful,
    At this great glorious news,
That the King of all kings
    Was risen amongst the Jews.
                      Novels, &c.

Without the least of hinderance,
    Anon they went in then,
And found the young child, Jesus Christ,
    Thus born in Bethlehem.
                        Novels, &c.

And as the angel told them,
    So to them did appear;
They found the young child, Jesus Christ,
    With Mary, his mother dear.
                        Novels, &c.

Now such a place it was,
    Where this was come to pass,
For want of room this child was laid
    Betwixt an ox and ass.
                        Novels, &c.

Not sumptuously, but simply,
    Was this young King array'd;
A manger was the cradle,
    Where this young child was laid.
                        Novels, &c.

No pride at all was found
    In this most holy child,
But he being void of all sin,
    The lamb of God most mild.
                        Novels, &c.

His body unto bitter pains
  He gave to set us free;
He is our Saviour, Jesus Christ,
  And none but only he.

Novels, &c.

To Father, Son, and Holy Ghost,
  All glory be therefore,
To whom be all dominion
  Both now and evermore.

Novels, &c.

XXI.

AS I passed by a river side,
  And there as I did reign,
In argument I chanced to hear
  A carnal and a crane.

The carnal said unto the crane,
  If all the world should turn,
Before we had the Father,
  But now we have the Son.

From whence does the Son come?
  From where and from what place?
He said, In a manger,
  Between an ox and ass!

I pray thee, said the carnal,
   Tell me before thou go,
Was not the mother of Jesus
   Conceived by the Holy Ghost?

She was the purest virgin,
   And the cleanest from sin;
She was the handmaid of our Lord,
   And mother of our King.

Where is the golden cradle
   That Christ was rocked in?
Where are the silken sheets
   That Jesus was wrapt in?

A manger was the cradle
   That Christ was rocked in;
The provender the asses left,
   So sweetly he slept on.

There was a star in the West land,
   So bright it did appear,
Into king Herod's chamber,
   And where king Herod were.

The wise men soon espied it,
   And told the king on high,
A princely Babe was born that night,
   No king could e'er destroy.

If this be true, king Herod said,
  As thou tellest unto me,
This roasted cock that lies in the dish
  Shall crow full fences three.

The cock soon freshly feather'd was,
  By the work of God's own hand,
And then three fences crowed he,
  In the dish where he did stand.

Rise up, rise up, you merry men all,
  See that you ready be,
All children under two years old
  Now slain they all shall be.

Then Jesus, ah! and Joseph,
  And Mary, that was so pure,
They travell'd into Egypt,
  As you shall find it sure.

And when they came to Egypt's land,
  Amongst those fierce wild beasts,
Mary, she being weary,
  Must needs sit down to rest.

Come sit thee down, says Jesus,
  Come sit thee down by me,
And thou shalt see how these wild beasts
  Do come and worship me.

First, came the lovely lion,
    Which Jesus's grace did spring,
And of the wild beasts in the field,
    The lion shall be king.

We'll choose our virtuous princes,
    Of birth and high degree,
In every sundry nation,
    Where'er we come and see.

Then Jesus, ah! and Joseph,
    And Mary, that was unknown,
They travelled by a husbandman,
    Just while his seed was sown.

God speed thee, man! said Jesus,
    Go fetch thy ox and wain,
And carry home thy corn again,
    Which thou this day hast sown.

The husbandman fell on his knees,
    Even before his face;
Long time hast Thou been looked for,
    But now Thou art come at last.

And I myself do now believe
    Thy name is Jesus called;
Redeemer of mankind thou art,
    Though undeserving all.

The truth, man, thou hast spoken,
  Of it thou mayest be sure,
For I must lose my precious blood
  For thee and thousands more.

If any one should come this way,
  And enquire for me alone,
Tell him that Jesus passed by
  As thou thy seed did sow.

After that there came king Herod,
  With his train so furiously,
Enquiring of the husbandman
  Whether Jesus passed by.

Why the truth it must be spoke,
  And the truth it must be known,
For Jesus passed by this way,
  When my seed was sown.

But now I have it reapen,
  And some laid on my wain,
Ready to fetch and carry
  Into my barn again.

Turn back, says the captain,
  Your labour and mine's in vain,
It's full three quarters of a year
  Since he his seed has sown.

So Herod was deceived,
  By the work of God's own hand,
And further he proceeded
  Into the Holy Land.

There's thousands of children young,
  Which for his sake did die;
Do not forbid those little ones,
  And do not them deny.

The truth now I have spoken,
  And the truth now I have shown;
Even the blessed virgin,
  She's now brought forth a Son.

XXII.

AS it fell out one May morning,
  And upon one bright holiday,
Sweet Jesus asked of his dear mother,
  If He might go to play.

To play, to play, sweet Jesus shall go,
  And to play pray get you gone,
And let me hear of no complaint,
  At night when you come home.

Sweet Jesus went down to yonder town,
　　As far as the Holy Well,
And there did see as fine children
　　As any tongue can tell.

He said, God bless you every one,
　　And your bodies Christ save and see;
Little children, shall I play with you,
　　And you shall play with me?

But they made answer to him, No!
　　They were lords' and ladies' sons;
And He, the meanest of them all,
　　A maiden's child, born in an oxen's stall.

Sweet Jesus turned him around,
　　And he neither laugh'd nor smil'd,
But the tears came trickling from his eyes,
　　Like water from the skies.

Sweet Jesus turned him about,
　　To his mother's dear home went he,
And said, I have been in yonder town,
　　As after you may see.

I have been down in yonder town,
　　As far as the Holy Well,
And there did I meet as fine children
　　As any tongue can tell.

I bid God bless them every one,
    And their bodies Christ save and see;
Little children, shall I play with you,
    And you shall play with me?

But they made answer to me, No!
    They were lords' and ladies' sons,
And I, the meanest of them all,
    A maiden's child, born in an ox's stall.

Though you are but a maiden's child,
    Born in an ox's stall,
Thou art the Christ, the King of Heaven,
    And the Saviour of them all.

Sweet Jesus go down to yonder town,
    As far as the Holy Well,
And take away those sinful souls
    And dip them deep in hell.

Nay, nay, sweet Jesus said,
    Nay, nay, that may not be,
For there are too many sinful souls
    Crying out for the help of me.

O then spoke the angel Gabriel,
    Upon one good Saint Stephen,
Altho' you're but a maiden's child,
    You are the King of Heaven.

XXIII.

A VIRGIN most pure as the prophets do tell,
Hath brought forth a babe, as it hath befell,
To be our Redeemer from death, hell, and sin,
Which Adam's trangression had wrapt us all in.
    Rejoice and be you merry, set sorrow aside,
    Christ Jesus our Saviour was born on this tide.

In Bethlehem city, in Jury it was,
Where Joseph and Mary together did pass,
And there to be taxed with many one more,
For Cæsar commanded the same should be so.
    Rejoice, &c.

But when they had entered the city so far,
The number of people so mighty was there,
That Joseph and Mary whose substance was small,
Could get in the city no lodging at all.
    Rejoice, &c.

Then they were constrained in a stable to lie,
Where oxen and asses they used to tie;
Their lodging so simple, they held it no scorn,
But against the next morning our Saviour was born.
    Rejoice, &c.

The King of all Glory to the world being brought,
Small store of fine linen to wrap him was bought ;
When Mary had swaddled her young son so sweet,
Within an ox manger, she laid him to sleep.
      Rejoice, &c.

Then God sent an angel from heaven so high,
To certain poor shepherds in fields where they lie,
And bid them no longer in sorrow to stay,
Because that our Saviour was born on this day.
      Rejoice, &c.

Then presently after the shepherds did spy
A number of angels appear in the sky,
Who joyfully talked and sweetly did sing,
To God be all glory, our Heavenly King.
      Rejoice, &c.

Three certain wise princes, they thought it most meet,
To lay their rich offerings at our Saviour's feet ;
Then the shepherds consented and to Bethlehem did go,
And when they came thither, they found it was so.
      Rejoice, &c.

XXIV.

GOD rest you, merry gentlemen,
  Let nothing you dismay,
For Jesus Christ our Saviour
  Was born upon this day,
To save us all from Satan's power
  When we were gone astray.
O tidings of comfort and joy,
For Jesus Christ our Saviour was born on Christmas Day.

In Bethlehem, in Jury,
  This blessed babe was born,
And laid within a manger
  Upon this blessed morn;
The which his mother Mary
  Did nothing take in scorn.
      O tidings, &c.

From God, our Heavenly Father,
  A blessed angel came,
And unto certain shepherds
  Brought tidings of the same,
That there was born in Bethlehem
  The Son of God by name.
      O tidings, &c.

Fear not then, said the Angel,
 Let nothing you affright,
This day is born a Saviour
 Of a pure Virgin bright;
So frequently to vanquish all
 The friends of Satan quite.
      O tidings, &c.

The shepherds at these tidings
 Rejoiced much in mind,
And left their flocks a feeding
 In tempest, storm, and wind,
And went to Bethlehem straightway,
 This blessed Babe to find.
      O tidings, &c.

But when they came to Bethlehem,
 Where our dear Saviour lay,
They found Him in a manger,
 Where oxen fed on hay;
His mother, Mary, kneeling,
 Unto the Lord did pray.
      O tidings, &c.

Now to the Lord sing praises
 All you within this place,
And with true love and brotherhood
 Each other now embrace;
This holy tide of Christmas
 All others doth deface.
      O tidings, &c.

XXV.

GOD'S dear Son without beginning,
    Whom the wicked Jews did scorn;
The only wise without all sinning
    On this blessed day was born.
To save us all from sin and thrall,
    When we in Satan's chains were bound,
And shed his blood to do us good,
    With many a purple bleeding wound.

At Bethlehem, king David's city,
    Mary's Babe had sweet creation,
God and Man endu'd with pity,
    And a Saviour of each nation.
Yet Jewry land with cruel hand,
    Both first and last his power envy'd;
Where He was born, they did Him scorn,
    And shew'd Him malice when He died.

No princely palace for our Saviour,
    In Judea could be found,
But blessed Mary's meek behaviour,
    Patiently upon the ground,
Her babe did place in vile disgrace,
    Where oxen in their stalls did feed;
No midwife mild had this sweet Child,
    Nor woman's help at mother's need.

No kingly robes nor golden treasure
    Deck'd the birth-day of God's Son;
No pompal train at all took pleasure
    To this King of kings to run.
No mantle brave could Jesus have,
    Upon His cradle for to lye;
No musick's charms in nurse's arms,
    To sing the Babe a lullaby.

Yet as Mary sat in solace,
    By our Saviour's first beginning,
Hosts of angels from God's palace
    Sounded sweet from Heaven singing;
Yea, heaven and earth, for Jesus' birth,
    With sweet melodious tunes abound,
And every thing for Jewry's King,
    Upon the earth gave chearful sound.

Then with angel's love inspired,
    The wise princes from the East,
To Bethlehem as they desired,
    Came whereas the Lord did rest:
And there they laid before the maid,
    Before her Son, our God and King,
Their offerings sweet, as was most meet,
    Unto so great a power to bring.

Now to Him that us redeemed,
    By His precious death and passion;
And us sinners so esteemed
    To buy us dearly thus salvation;

Yield lasting fame that still the name
Of Jesus may be honored here;
And let us say that Christmas Day
Is still the best day in the year.

XXVI.

I SAW three ships come sailing in
  On Christmas Day, on Christmas Day;
I saw three ships come sailing in
  On Christmas Day in the morning.

And what was in those ships all three,
  On Christmas Day, on Christmas Day?
And what was in those ships all three,
  On Christmas Day in the morning?

Our Saviour Christ and his lady,
  On Christmas Day, on Christmas Day;
Our Saviour Christ and his lady,
  On Christmas Day in the morning.

Pray whither sailed those ships all three,
  On Christmas Day, on Christmas Day;
Pray whither sailed those ships all three,
  On Christmas Day in the morning.

O, they sailed into Bethlehem,
  On Christmas Day, on Christmas Day;
O, they sailed into Bethlehem,
  On Christmas Day in the morning.

And all the bells on earth shall ring,
    On Christmas Day, on Christmas Day;
And all the bells on earth shall ring,
    On Christmas Day in the morning.

And all the angels in Heaven shall sing,
    On Christmas Day, on Christmas Day;
And all the angels in Heaven shall sing,
    On Christmas Day in the morning.

And all the souls on earth shall sing,
    On Christmas Day, on Christmas Day;
And all the souls on earth shall sing,
    On Christmas Day in the morning.

Then let us all rejoice amain,
    On Christmas Day, on Christmas Day;
Then let us all rejoice amain,
    On Christmas Day in the morning.

XXVII.

THE first nowell the angel did say
Was to three poor shepherds in the fields as they lay;
In fields where they lay keeping their sheep,
In a cold winter's night that was so deep.
        Nowell, nowell, nowell, nowell,
        Born is the King of Israel.

They looked up and saw a star
Shining in the east, beyond them far,
And to the earth it gave great light,
And so it continued both day and night.
       Nowell, &c.

And by the light of that same star,
Three wise men came from country far;
To seek for a King was their intent,
And to follow the star wherever it went.
       Nowell, &c.

This star drew nigh to the north-west,
O'er Bethlehem it took its rest,
And there it did both stop and stay
Right over the place where Jesus lay.
       Nowell, &c.

Then did they know assuredly
Within that house the King did lie;
One entered in then for to see,
And found the Babe in poverty.
       Nowell, &c.

Then enter'd in those wise men three,
Most reverently upon their knee,
And offer'd there, in His presence,
Both gold, and myrrh, and frankincense.
       Nowell, &c.

Between an ox-stall and an ass,
This child truly there born He was;
For want of clothing they did Him lay
All in the manger, among the hay.
        Nowell, &c.

Then let us all, with one accord,
Sing praises to our Heavenly Lord,
That hath made Heaven and earth of nought,
And with His blood mankind hath bought.
        Nowell, &c.

If we in our time shall do well,
We shall be free from death and hell;
For God hath prepared for us all
A resting-place in general.
        Nowell, &c.

XXVIII.

THE Lord at first had Adam made
 Out of the dust and clay,
And in his nostrils breathed life,
 E'en as the Scriptures say;
And then in Eden's Paradise
 He placed him to dwell,
That he within it should remain,
 To dress and keep it well.
    Now let good Christians all begin
     An holy life to live,
    And to rejoice and merry be,
     For this is Christmas Eve.

And thus within the garden he
    Commanded was to stay;
And unto him in commandment
    These words the Lord did say:
"The fruit that in the garden grows
    To thee shall be for meat,
Except the tree in the midst thereof,
    Of which thou shalt not eat.
                  Now let good, &c.

"For in that day thou dost it touch,
    Or dost it then come nigh,
And if that thou dost eat thereof,
    Then thou shalt surely die."
But Adam he did take no heed
    To that same only thing,
But did transgress God's holy laws,
    And sore was wrapp'd in sin.
                  Now let good, &c.

Now mark the goodness of the Lord,
    Which He to mankind bore;
His mercy soon he did extend
    Lost man for to restore;
And then, for to redeem our souls
    From death, and hell, and thrall,
He said his own dear Son should come
    The Saviour of us all.
                  Now let good, &c.

Which promise now is brought to pass,
   Christians believe it well,
And by the coming of God's Son,
   We are redeem'd from hell.
And if we truly do believe,
   And do the thing that's right,
Then by His merits we at last
   Shall live in Heaven bright.
                  Now let good, &c.

Now, for the benefits that we
   Enjoy from Heaven above,
Let us renounce all wickedness,
   And live in perfect love.
Then shall we do Christ's own command,
   Even his written word;
And when we die, in Heaven we shall
   Enjoy our living Lord.
                  Now let good, &c.

And now the tide is nigh at hand,
   In which our Saviour came;
Let us rejoice and merry be,
   In keeping of the same.
Let's feed the poor and hungry sort,
   And such as do it crave;
And when we die, in Heaven be sure
   Our reward we shall have.
                  Now let good, &c.

XXIX.

TO-MORROW shall be my dancing day,
 I would my true love did so chance
To see the legend of my play,
 To call my true love to my dance.
Sing, oh! my love, oh! my love, my love, my love;
This have I done for my true love.

 Then was I born of a virgin pure,
  Of her I took fleshly substance;
 Thus was I knit to man's nature,
  To call my true love to my dance.
   Sing, oh! &c.

 In a manger laid and wrapp'd I was,
  So very poor, this was my chance,
 Betwixt an ox and a silly poor ass,
  To call my true love to my dance.
   Sing, oh! &c.

 Then afterwards baptized I was,
  The Holy Ghost on me did glance,
 My Father's voice heard from above,
  To call my true love to my dance.
   Sing, oh! &c.

Into the desert I was led,
    Where I fasted without substance;
The Devil bade me make stones my bread,
    To have me break my true love's dance.
        Sing, oh! &c.

The Jews on me they made great suit,
    And with me made great variance,
Because they lov'd darkness rather than light,
    To call my true love to my dance.
        Sing, oh! &c.

For thirty pence Judas me sold,
    His covetousness for to advance;
Mark whom I kiss, the same do hold,
    The same is he shall lead the dance.
        Sing, oh! &c.

Before Pilate the Jews me brought,
    Where Barabbas had deliverance,
They scourg'd me and set me at nought,
    Judged me to die to lead the dance.
        Sing, oh! &c.

Then on the cross hanged I was,
    Where a spear to my heart did glance,
There issued forth both water and blood,
    To call my true love to my dance.
        Sing, oh! &c.

Then down to hell I took my way
  For my true love's deliverance,
And rose again on the third day,
  Up to my true love and the dance.
      Sing, oh! &c.

Then up to Heaven I did ascend,
  Where now I dwell in sure substance,
On the right hand of God, that man
  May come unto the general dance.
      Sing, oh! &c.

XXX.

NOW when Joseph and Mary
  Were to Bethlehem bound,
They with travelling were weary,
  Yet no lodging they found
In the city of David,
  Tho' they sought o'er all;
They, alas! could not have it,
  But in an oxes stall.

The place was no braver
  But as mean as might be,
Our Redeemer and Saviour,
  The great King of Glory,

Then the sweet Babe of Heaven
　　Was born there we find,
Whose sweet life was once given
　　For the sins of mankind.

Whilst the shepherds were feeding
　　Of their flocks in the fields,
The birth of our Saviour
　　Unto them was revealed;
Many angels assembling,
　　In their glory appeared,
Whilst the shepherds were trembling,
　　Being smitten with fear.

O forbear to be fearful,
　　We have reason to sing;
Then rejoice and be chearful,
　　We glad tidings do bring:
There is born in the city
　　Of David, therefore,
Such a Saviour of pity,
　　Whom we all do adore.

He's the Prince of Salvation,
　　Then be not afraid,
And with this salutation
　　To the shepherds they said,
Be no longer a stranger,
　　For in mean swadling clothes
He is laid in a manger;
　　Then the shepherds arose.

Being resolved together
   They to Bethlehem go,
And when they came thither
   They found it was so;
They with duty adore him,
   Coming where he was laid—
Strait they fell down before him,
   This obedience they made.

Nay, the wise men, whose prudence
   Had discovered the star,
Came to pay their obedience
   When they travell'd from far;
Bringing with them the choicest
   That their land did afford,
Of gold, myrrh, and spices,
   To present to the Lord.

Their example engages
   Every Christian to be,
Ever since in all ages,
   Both noble and free;
Then rejoice and be merry,
   In a moderate way,
Never, never be weary,
   To honour this day.

Which afforded a blessing
   To the race of mankind,
Far beyond all expressing
   Therefore let us mind;

Whilst on earth he was dwelling,
    He was still doing good,
Nay, his love more excelling,
    For he shed his own blood.

To redeem us and save us
    From the guilt of our sins,
For His love he would have us
    A new life to begin;
Then remember the season,
    Be you kind to the poor,
It's no more than is reason,
    We have blessings in store.

XXXI.

THIS new Christmas carol, let us cheerfully sing,
To the honor and glory of our Heavenly King;
Who was born of a virgin, blessed Mary by name,
For poor sinners' redemption, to the world here He came.

The mighty Jehovah, by the prophets foretold,
That the sweet Babe of Heaven mortal eyes should behold;
Both King, Prince, and Prophet, nay, our Saviour beside,
Let His name through all ages be ever glorified.

Now, when Joseph and Mary was espoused, we find,
Having seen her condition, he was grieved in mind;
Aye, and thought to dismiss her, whom he loved so dear,
But an angel from Heaven did her innocence clear.

He declared in a vision, that a Son she should have,
By the Father appointed, fallen mortals to save;
And the same should be called blessed Jesus by name,
From the high court of Heaven this Ambassador came.

Then the righteous man, Joseph, believed the news,
And the sweet Virgin Mary he did no wise refuse;
Thus the blest amongst women, did bear and bring forth
A sweet Prince of Salvation, both in Heaven and Earth.

When the days of her travail did begin to draw nigh,
Righteous Joseph and Mary went immediately
To the city of David, to be taxed indeed,
E'en as Cæsar Augustus had firmly decreed.

Being come to the city, entertainment they crave,
But the inns were so filled they no lodging could have,
For the birth of our Saviour, though he was Prince of all,
He could have there no place but a poor oxes stall.

Now the proud may come hither, and perfectly see,
The most excellent pattern of humility;
For, instead of a cradle, deckt with ornaments gay,
Here, the great King of Glory, in a manger He lay.

As the shepherds were feeding their flocks in the field,
The sweet birth of our Saviour unto them was revealed,
By blest angels of glory, who those tidings did bring,
And directed the shepherds to their heavenly King.

When the wise men discover'd the bright heavenly star,
Then with gold and rich spices, straight they came from afar,
In obedience to worship with a heavenly mind,
Knowing that He was born for the good of mankind.

Let us learn of those sages, who were wise, to obey;
Nay, we find through all ages they have honoured this day,
Ever since our Redeemer's bless'd nativity,
Who was born of a virgin to set sinners free.

XXXII.

WHEN Cæsar did the sceptre sway,
   Of Roman state God's word did say,
That all the world should out of hand,
Be taxed by his great command.
     Noel, noel, we may rejoice
     To hear the angel Gabriel's voice—Noel, noel.

In David's city, in Bethlehem,
Great store of people thither came,
According to the king's decree,
In Jury land taxed to be.
                 Noel, noel, &c.

Then Joseph with his virgin bright,
Came with the rest at that same tide,
And their substance being but small,
Could get in the inn no lodging at all.
       Noel, noel, &c.

At length a stable room they had,
In which the virgin was full glad;
And in that stable so forlorn
The world's Redeemer there was born.
       Noel, &c.

No palace nor a costly inn
Was found to put our Saviour in;
No costly robes of silver and gold,
To wrap Him in as reason would.
       Noel, &c.

No music nor sweet melody,
But glorious angels from on high,
Declare to shepherds where they lay,
That Jesus Christ was born this day.
       Noel, &c.

Thus Jesus Christ, in humble wise,
Appeared thus to human eyes;
Then may we all both more and less
Cast off the bands of wickedness.
       Noel, &c.

Let variance, strife, and all debate,
'Twixt neighbours now be out of date,
That peace may spread throughout earth then,
There shall be good will with men.
Noel, &c.

Rejoice, rejoice, in sober wise,
And praise the Lord who rules the skies,
Who for our sakes thought it no scorn
To give command now Christ is born.
Noel, &c.

XXXIII.

SAINT Stephen was an holy man,
  Endued with heavenly might,
And many wonders he did work
  Before the people's sight.
And by the blessed Spirit of God,
  Which did his heart inflame,
He spared not in every place
  To preach Christ Jesus' name.
    O man, do never faint nor fear,
      When God the truth shall try,
    But mark how Stephen for Christ's sake
      Was willing for to die.

Which doctrine seem'd most wond'rous strange
    Among the faithless Jews,
And for the same despitefully
    Good Stephen they accused.
Before the elders was he brought
    His answer for to make,
But they could not his spirit withstand,
    Whereby this man did speak.
                      O man, &c.

And then false witness did appear,
    And looked him in the face,
And said he spake blasphemous words
    Against that holy place;
And how he said that Jesus Christ
    The temple would destroy,
And change the laws which they so long
    From Moses did enjoy.
                      O man, &c.

Whilst this was told, the multitude
    Beholding him aright,
His comely face began to shine
    Most like an angel bright.
The high priest then to them did say,
    And bid them tell at large,
If this was true, which at that time
    They laid unto his charge.
                      O man, &c.

Then Stephen did put forth his voice,
    And he did first unfold
The wond'rous works that God hath wrought,
    Even from their fathers old;
That they thereby might plain perceive
    Christ Jesus should be he,
That from the burthen of the law
    Should save us frank and free.
                  O man, &c.

But, oh! quoth he, you wicked men,
    Which of the prophets all
Did not your fathers persecute
    And keep in woeful thrall;
Who told the coming of the just
    In prophecies most plain;
Who here amongst you was betray'd
    And most unjustly slain?
                  O man, &c.

But when they heard him so to say,
    Their hearts in sunder clave,
And gnashing on him with their teeth,
    Like mad men they did rave;
And with a shout most loud and shrill,
    Upon him they all ran,
And then without the city gates
    They ston'd this holy man.
                  O man, &c.

Then he most meekly on his knees,
    To God did pray at large,
Desiring that He would not lay
    This sin unto their charge;
Then yielding up his soul to God,
    Who had it dearly bought,
He lost his life, whose body then
    To grave was seemly brought.
                  O man, &c.

XXXIV.

HARK! the herald Angels sing,
    Glory to the new-born King;
Peace on earth, and mercy mild,
God and sinner reconcil'd.
            Hark! the herald angels sing,
            Glory to the new-born King.

Joyfull all ye nations rise,
Join the triumph of the skies,
With the angelic host proclaim,
Christ is born in Bethlehem.
                Hark! the herald, &c.

Christ by highest Heaven ador'd,
Christ the everlasting Lord!
Late in time behold Him come,
Offspring of a virgin's womb.
                Hark! the herald, &c.

Hail the heaven-born Prince of Peace!
Hail the Sun of Righteousness!
Light and life to all He brings,
Risen with healing on His wings.
      Hark! the herald, &c.

Mild he lays his glory by,
Born that man no more may die,
Born to raise the sons of earth,
Born to give them second birth.
      Hark! the herald, &c.

XXXV.

Su l'ar "Ma Mere mariez-moi."

GUILLÔ, pran ton tamborin ;
Toi, pran tai fleùte, Robin.
Au son de cés instruman,
Turelurelu, patapatapan ;
Au son de cés instruman
Je diron Noci gaiman.

C' étó lai môde autrefoi
De loüé le Roi dé Roi,
Au son de cés instruman,
Turelurelu, patapatapan ;
Au son de cés instruman,
Ai nos an fau faire autan.

Ce jor le Diale at ai cu,
Raudons an graice ai Jésu,
Au son de cés instruman,
Turclurelu, patapatapan,
Au son de cés instruman,
Fezon lai nique ai Satan.

L'homme & Dei son pu d'aicor
Que lai fleûte & le tambor.
Au son de cés instruman,
Turclurelu, patapatapan,
Au son de cés instruman,
Chanton, danson, sautons-an.

XXXVI.

Per le jour des Reys.

Un Paston ben de Hiérusalém & dits a sons Coumpaignons.

DE noubélos Efans, en benen de la bilo
E' bist passá tres Reys d'uno faysso gentilo,
E' demandon per tout l'hostalet benazit
Que le Rey d'Israel per palays a cauzit.

Qualqu'un a decelat que porton per estrenos,
Tres Brustietos d'Encens, d'Or, é de Myrro plenos
Que li ban humblomen ufri, digomendiu,
Que confesson deja qu'el es Rey, home, Diu.

Elis parlon sampa de l'Efantet aymable
Que nous aus l'autre jour troubeguen à l'estable,
A qui Peyret dounée un Aignelet pla fayt,
E' jou sense reprochi, un picharrou de layt.

Posco doune oüey metis uno ta bélo troupo
Hurousomen trouba le bél efan de poupo,
Mentre que de nous aus quadun le pregara
De nous salba l'esprit quand le cos mourira.

XXXVII.

TRES Rei de l'Orian
Son conduit per un Astre
Ver lou nouvel Enfan,
Qu'an adoura lei Pastre
Venouen sensen
Creigne aucũ desastre,
L'Astre avancen
S'arreste en Bethlehem.

S'isten, vount 'ei l'Enfan,
Fixa l'astre admirable,
Intron dessu lou chan,
Trouvon Jesus aimable.
Descouvron qu'ei
Lou sul Dieou veritable,
Qu'es homme, & rei ;
Chacun lou recounei.

A ginoux, à sei pé
Entoura de sei pagé
Em'un profond respé,
Liaguen fa seis houmage
Lisfron perlor
Aquelei pious mage
De sei tresor
L'encen, la mirrhe, & l'or.

Fasen nostei presen
A Jesus, qui nous amou,
Oufren li nostei ben,
Nostei cor, nosteis amou.
Enfan tan doux,
Vost'amour nous enflamou,
Nou charma tous ;
Voulen ama que vous.

XXXVIII.
Sur un chant joyeux.

QUAND Dieu naquit á Noël
 Dedans la Judeé,
On vit ce jour solemnel
 La joie inondée ;
Se n'etoit ni petit ni grand
Qui n'apportât son présent,
Et n'o, n'o, n'o, n'o,
Et n'offrit, frit, frit,
Et n'o, n'o, & n'offrit,
Et n'offrit sans cesse Toute sa richesse.

L'un apportoit un agneau
　　Avec un grand zele,
L'autre un peu de lait nouveau
　　Dedans une écuelle ;
Tel, sous ses pauvres habits,
Cachoit un peu de pain bis,
Pour la, la, la, la,
Pour la, sain, sain, sain,
Pour la, la, pour la sain,
Pour la Ste Vierge et Joseph Concierge.

Ce bon Père putatif
　　De Jesus mon Maitre,
Que le pasteur plus chétif
　　Desiroit connaitre,
D'un air obligeant & doux,
Recevoit les dons, de tous,
Sans cé, cé, cé, cé,
Sans céré, ré, ré,
Sans cé, cé, sans céré,
Sans cérémonie, Pour le fruit de vie.

Il ne fut pas jusqu' aux Rois
　　Du rivage Maure,
Qui joint au nombre de trois,
　　Ne vinssent encore ;
Ces bons Princes d'Orient.
Offrirent en le priant,
L'en, l'en, l'en, l'en, l'en,
Cens, cens, cens, cens, cens,
L'en, l'en, l'en, cens, cens, cens,
L'encens & la myrrhe et l'or qu'on admire.

Quoiqu'il n'en eût pas besoin,
  Jesus notre Maitre,
Il en prit avecque soin
  Pour faire connoitre
Qu'il avoit les qualités
Par ces dons représentés,
D'un vrai, vrai, vrai, vrai,
D'un Roi, Roi, Roi, Roi,
D'un vrai, vrai, d'un Roi, Roi,
D'un vrai, Roi de Gloire en qui l'on doit croire.

Plaise à ce divin Enfant
  Nous faire la grâce,
Dans son sejour triomphant
  D'avoir une place :
Si nous y sommes jamais,
Nous goûterons une paix
De lon, lon, lon, lon,
De gue, gue, gue, gue,
De lon, lon, de gue, gue,
De longue durée dans cet empircé.

XXXIX.

Sur l'air " Ver lou Pourtaou San-Laze."

LON de la gran carriere,
  Ver lou Pourtaou-Limber,
Ay vis parcisse en l'air
  Un Ange de lumiere,
Cridavou de per-tout,
Bergié, reveillas-vous.

Ere su ma mounture,
D'abord sicou descendu,
Et m'a dit, beou Moussu,
   Ay, la belle aventure,
Es na lou Fis de Dieou,
Toun Mestre amay lou micou.

Foou quitta ta famille,
Vay-t'en en Bethelem,
Trouvaras l'Inoucen
   A cent pas de la ville,
Portou-ye quaouquouren,
Es lougea paouramen.

Ay poursui moun vouyage,
Ay vis veni de gen,
Qu'eroun touteis ensen,
   Em'un grand equipage,
Erou trés gran Seignour,
Eme toutou sa cour.

Chascun avié sei Page,
Eme sei Gardou- cor,
Me sicou pensa d'abor,
   Qu'éroun leis trés Rei Mage,
Que venien adoura
Lou gran Rei nouveou na.

Me sicou més à n'un cayre,
Per lei leissa passa,
Et puis ay demanda
　A seis homes d'affayre,
Si van en Bethelem
Veire lou Dieou neissen.

Yá un d'aquelei Garde
Que má brutalisa,
Su lou cham m'a douna
　Un bon co d'halabarde :
Si m'espouffesse pa,
Me venié may piqua.

Yeou ay suivi la foulou,
Sen me descouragea,
La doulour m'a passa,
　Ou bout d'une miéchourou,
Sicou ana eme lou trin
Jusquo ver lou Douphin.

Avien de dromadairou,
Quantita de charrios,
Et de cameou fort gros,
　La suite érou fort bellou,
Jamay yeou n'ay ren vi
Eme tant de plesi.

Un astre lei guidave,
Plus brillan qu'un souleou,
Jamay ren de tant beou,
　Tout lou mounde badave :
Lou tem m'a ren dura,
Tant ére esmerveilla.

Aprés dex jour de marche,
L'astre s'es arresta
Sur un lio tout trouca,
　Ben plus precioux que l'Arche,
Aqui lou Tout-puissan
Parei coum'un enfan.

XL.

Sur l'ayre, "QUAND JE ME LEVE LE MATIN."

L'AN mil siés cens quaranto cinc,
　Repassen per nostro memorio,
Coussi Jousép en paure trinc
　Acoumpaignée le Réy de Glorio,
Quand demourabo dins les réns
De Mario la piucélo préns.

Jousép é Mario maridats
　En Béthléhen sén ban amaço,
Nou soun pas fort amounedats.
　Més bé soun de Rouyalo raço,
E l'efan és Rey dins les réns,
De Mario la piucélo préns.

Sense gran argen al paquét
  N'an pas un trinc de grand parado,
Non menoun que le bourriquét
  Dambé le bioou soun camarado,
Diu mentretan és dins les réns,
De Mario la piucélo préns.

Aprép un penible cami
  Sant Jousép é la santo méro,
Que nou saben pas oun dourmi,
  Ban beilha dins uno feignéro,
Oun l'efan que Diu sort des réns
Nou laysso plus sa méro préns.

Aqui la paillo lour fa liéyt
  Sense cousseno ni courtino,
Oun las estelos de la néyt
  Bezen ajayre lour Regino,
E' naysse l'efan de sous réns
Piucélo toutjour é nou préns.

XLI.

J'ANTAN po no ruë,
  Passai lé menétrei,
Acouté come ai juë.
Su los hauboi dé noei ;
No devan le feù
Po le meù,
Chantons an jeusqu'ai méneù.

An Deçanbre on trezeule,
Dé noci tô lé jor;
Dé chantre fot-an-gueule,
An antone é carrefor;
No devan le feù, &c.

Lé borgei dan lai grainge
Voù grullô le Pòpon,
Chantire ai sai loüainge
Dé noci de tô lé ton;
No devan le feù, &c.

Lé bone jan disire
De noci bé dévo,
Ma quant ai lé chantire,
Ai n'aivein pa lé pié chau;
No devan le feù, &c.

Dans lo froide chambrôte,
Lé none an ce sain moi,
Faute d'autre émusôte,
Chante noci queique foi;
No devan, &c.

Lé próve laivandeire,
Au son de lo rullô,
An chante ai lai riveire,
Lai téte au van, lé pié mô!
No devan, &c.

Qui montre au feù sé cucùsse
Trepille de chantai,
Qui sòfle dan sé peùce,
Nán di pa noei si gai';
No devan, &c.

XLII.

I HEAR along our street
   Pass the minstrel throngs :
Hark ! they play so sweet,
On their hautboys, Christmas songs !
   Let us by the fire
   Ever higher
Sing them till the night expire !

In December ring,
   Every day the chimes ;
Loud the gleemen sing,
In the streets, their merry rhymes.
        Let us, &c.

Shepherds at the grange,
   Where the Babe was born,
Sang with many a change,
Christmas carols until morn.
        Let us, &c.

These good people sang,
Songs devout and sweet,
While the rafters rang,
There they stood with freezing feet.
    Let us, &c.

Nuns in frigid cells,
At this holy tide,
For want of something else,
Christmas songs at times have tried.
    Let us, &c.

Washerwomen old,
To the sound they beat,
Sing by rivers cold,
With uncovered heads and feet.
    Let us, &c.

Who by the fireside stands,
Stamps his feet and sings;
But he who blows his hands,
Not so gay a carol brings.
    Let us by the fire
    Ever higher
Sing them till the night expire.

A Mock Play.

Act I.—Scene I.
Enter Alexander.—Alexander *speaks.*

SILENCE, brave gentlemen; if you will give me an eye,
Alexander is my name, I'll sing the Tragedy;
A ramble here I took, the country for to see,
Three actors here I've brought so far from *Italy;*
The first I do present, he is a noble king,
He's just come from the wars, good tidings he doth bring;
The next that doth come in, he is a docter good,
Had it not been for him, I'd surely lost my blood:
Old *Dives* is the next, a miser you may see,
Who, by lending of his gold, is come to poverty.
So, gentlemen, you see four actors will go round;
Stand off a little while, more pastime shall be found.
[Exeunt.

Act I.—Scene II.
Enter Actors.

Room, room, brave gallants, give us room to sport,
For in this room we have a mind to resort—
Resort, and to repeat to you our merry rhyme,
For remember, good sirs, this is *Christmas* time;
The time to cut up goose pies now doth appear,
So we are come to act our merry mirth here:

At the sounding of the trumpet, and beating of the drum,
Make room, brave gentlemen, and let our actors come.
We are the merry actors that traverses the street;
We are the merry actors that fight for our meat;
We are the merry actors that show the pleasant play:
Step in, thou king of *Egypt*, and clear the way. [appear,

    King of Egypt. I am the king of *Egypt*, as plainly doth
And Prince *George* he is my only son and heir:
Step in, therefore, my son, and act thy part with me,
And shew forth thy praise before the company. [bold,

    Prince George. I am Prince *George*, a champion brave and
For with my spear I've won three crowns of gold;
'Twas I that brought the Dragon to the slaughter,
And I that gain'd the *Egyptian* monarch's daughter.
In Egypt's fields I prisoner long was kept,
But by my valour I from them soon 'scap'd:
I sounded at the gates of a divine,
And out came a giant of no good design;
He gave me a blow, which almost struck me dead,
But I up with my sword, and did cut off his head.

    Alexander. Hold, Stacker, hold, pray do not be so hot,
For on this spot thou knowest not who thou's got;
'Tis I that's to hash thee and smash thee as small as flies,
And lend thee to *Satan* to make minch pies:
Minch pies hot, minch pies cold—
I'll send thee to Satan ere thou be three days' old.
But, hold, Prince *George*, before thou go away,
Either thou or I must die this bloody day;
Some mortal wounds thou shalt receive by me,
So let us fight it out most manfully. [*Exeunt.*

Act II.—Scene I.

Alexander *and* Prince George *fight: the latter is wounded, and falls.*

King of Egypt *speaks.*

Curs'd Christian, what is this thou hast done?
Thou hast ruin'd me by killing my best son.

Alex. He gave me a challenge—why should I him deny?
How high he was, but see how low he lies!

K. of Egypt. O Sambo! Sambo! help me now,
For I never was in more need;
For thou to stand with sword in hand,
And to fight at my command.

Doct. Yes, my liege, I will thee obey,
And by my sword I hope to win the day:
Yonder stands he who has kill'd my master's son;
I'll see if he be sprung from royal blood,
And through his body make an ocean flood.
Gentleman, you see my sword-point is broke,
Or else I'd run it down that villain's throat.

K. of Egypt. Is there never a doctor to be found,
That can cure my son of his deadly wound?

Doct. Yes, there is a doctor to be found,
That can cure your son of his deadly wound.

K. of Egypt. What diseases can he cure?

Doct. All diseases, both within and without,
Especially the itch, ..., palsy, and the gout;
Come in, you ugly, nasty, dirty . . . .,
Whose age is threescore years or more,

Whose nose and face stands all awry,
I'll make her very fitting to pass by.
I'll give a coward a heart, if he be willing,
Will make him stand without fear of killing.
And any man that's got a scolding spouse,
That wearies him with living in his house,
I'll ease him of his complaint, and make her civil,
Or else will send her headlong to the devil.
Ribs, legs, or arms, when any's broke, I'm sure
I presently of them will make a cure;
Nay, more than this by far, I will maintain,
If you should break your neck, I'll cur't again.
So here's a doctor rare, who travels much at home,
Here take my pills, I cure all ills, past, present, and to come:
I in my time many thousands have directed,
And likewise have as many more dissected.
To cure the love-sick maid, like me there's none,
For with two of my pills the job I've done;
I take her home, and rubs her o'er and o'er,
Then if she dies ne'er believe me more.
To cure your son, good sir, I do fear not,
With this small bottle, which by me I've got.
The balsam is the best which it contains,
Rise up, my good Prince *George*, and fight again.

Exeunt.

Act II. — Scene II.

Prince George *arises.*—Prince George *speaks.*

O, horrible! terrible! the like was never seen—
A man drove out of seven senses into fifteen;
And out of fifteen into fourscore!
O, horrible! terrible! the like was ne'er before. [stranger.
   Alex. Thou silly ass, that lives by grass, dost thou abuse a
I live in hopes to buy new ropes, and tie thy nose to the
   Pr. Geo. Sir, unto you I bend. [manger.
   Alex. Stand off, thou slave, I think thee not my friend.
   Pr. Geo. A slave, sir! that is for me by far too base a
That word deserves to stab thy honour's fame. [name,
   Alex. To be stab'd, sir, is the least of all my care,
Appoint your time and place, I'll meet you there.
   Pr. Geo. I'll cross the water at the hour of five.
   Alex. I'll meet you there, sir, if I be alive. [and young,
   Pr. Geo. But stop, sir,—I'd wish you to a wife, both lusty
She can talk both *Dutch, French,* and the *Italian* tongue.
   Alex. I'll have none such.
   Pr. Geo. Why, don't you love your learning?
   Alex. Yes, I love my learning as I do my life,
I love a learned scholar, but not a learned wife,
Stand off, had I as many hussians, shusians, chairs, and stools,
As you have had sweethearts, boys, girls, and fools;
I love a woman, and a woman loves me,
And when I want a fool I'll send for thee.

K. of Egypt. Sir, to express thy beauty, I am not able,
For thy face shines like a very kitchen table;
Thy teeth are no whiter than the charcoal,
And thy breath stinks like the . . . . !
  Alex. Stand off, thou dirty dog, for by my sword thou's die,
I'll make thy body full of holes, and cause thy buttons flie.
[*Exeunt.*

Act. III. — Scene I.

King of Egypt fights, and is killed.

Enter Prince George.

Oh! what is here? Oh! what is to be done?
Our king is slain, the crown is likewise gone;
Take up the body, bear it hence away,
For in this place no longer shall it stay.

The Conclusion.

Bounser Buckler, velvet's dear,
And *Christmas* comes but once a year,
Though when it comes, it brings good cheer,
But farewell *Christmas* once a year.
  Farewell, farewell, adieu! friendship and unity,
I hope we have made sport, and pleas'd the company;
But, gentlemen, you see, we're but young actors four,
We've done the best we can, and the best can do no more.

Christmas Play of St. George and the Dragon.

AS REPRESENTED IN THE WEST OF ENGLAND.

Enter Father Christmas.

HERE come I, old Father Christmas,
Welcome, or welcome not,
I hope old Father Christmas
Will never be forgot.

I am not come here for to laugh or to jeer,
But for a pocketfull of money, and a skinfull of beer;
To show some sport and pastime,
Gentlemen and ladies in the Christmas time.
If you will not believe what I do say,
Come in the Turkish Knight—clear the way.

Enter the Turkish Knight.

Open your doors, and let me in,
I hope your favors I shall win;
Whether I rise, or whether I fall,
I'll do my best to please you all.
St. George is here, and swears he will come in,
And if he does, I know he'll pierce my skin.
If you will not believe what I do say,
Come in the King of Egypt—clear the way.

Enter the King of Egypt.

Here I, the King of Egypt, boldly do appear,
St. George, St. George, walk in, my son and heir.
Walk in, my son St. George, and boldly act thy part,
That all the people here may see thy wondrous art.

Enter Saint George.

Here come I, St. George, from Britain did I spring,
I'll fight the Dragon bold, my wonders to begin.
I'll clip his wings, he shall not fly;
I'll cut him down, or else I die.

Enter the Dragon.

Who's he that seeks the Dragon's blood,
And calls so angry, and so loud?
That English dog, will he before me stand?
I'll cut him down with my courageous hand.
With my long teeth, and scurvy jaw,
Of such I'd break up half a score,
And stay my stomach, till I'd more.

[St. George *and the* Dragon *fight: the latter is killed.*]

Father Christmas.

Is there a doctor to be found
   All ready, near at hand,
To cure a deep and deadly wound,
   And make the champion stand?

Enter Doctor.

Oh! yes, there is a doctor to be found
   All ready, near at hand,
To cure a deep and deadly wound,
   And make the champion stand.

Fa. Chr. What can you cure?
Doct. All sorts of diseases,
    Whatever you pleases,
      The phthisic, the palsy, and the gout;
    Whatever disorder, I'll soon pull him out.
Fa. Chr. What is your fee?
Doct. Fifteen pounds, it is my fee,
    The money to lay down;
    But as 'tis such a rogue as he,
      I'll cure him for ten pound.
    I have a little bottle of Elicumpane,
      Here, Jack, take a little of my flip-flop,
      Pour it down thy tip-top:
    Rise up, and fight again.
      [*The* Doctor *gives his medicine:* St. George *and the* Dragon *again fight, and the latter is again killed.*]

St. George.

Here am I, St. George, that worthy champion bold,
And with my sword and spear I've won three crowns of gold:
I fought the fiery dragon, and brought him to the slaughter;
By that I've won fair Sabra, the King of Egypt's daughter.

    The Turkish Knight *advances.*

Here come I, the Turkish Knight,
Come from the Turkish land to fight.
I'll fight St. George, who is my foe,
I'll make him yield before I go:
He brags to such a high degree,
He thinks there's none can do the like of he.

St. George.

Where is the Turk that will before me stand?
I'll cut him down with my courageous hand.

> [*They fight: the* Knight *is overcome, and falls on one knee, saying—*]

Oh! pardon me, St. George, pardon of thee I crave,
Oh! pardon me this night, and I will be thy slave.

St. George.

I'll never pardon a Turkish Knight;
So rise thee up again, and try thy might.

> [*They fight again, when the* Knight *is killed, and a scene with* Father Christmas *and the* Doctor *occurs as before, and the* Knight *is cured. The* Doctor *then, according to the stage direction, has a basin of girdy grout given him, and a kick, and is driven out. Sometimes the* Giant Turpin *is introduced, but his part is little more than a repetition of the* Turkish Knight. *If there is a fair* Sabra, *she is generally a mute, and now comes forward to* Saint George.]

Father Christmas.

Now ladies and gentlemen, your sport is just ended,
So prepare for the box, which is highly commended.
The box it would speak, if it had but a tongue:
Come, throw in your money, and think it no wrong.

INDEX TO CAROLS.

I had hoped to have inserted a Carol by the Rev. R. S. Hawker, of Moorwenstow, Cornwall, but it was previously engaged for the Christmas number of 'Household Words.' I must, however, take the opportunity of correcting a mistake in 'Trenoodle's Specimens of Cornish Dialect,' where the song of 'The Trelawney Rising' is treated as an old ballad. This spirited composition is the production of Mr. Hawker.

No.		PAGE
1.	Seignors, ore entendez à nus	215
	From Douce's Illustration of Shakespeare (MS. Reg. 16. E. viii, 13th century).	
2.	Lordings, from a distant home . . .	217
	Translation of the same, from Douce's Illustrations	
3.	Welcñ ȝole in good array .	218
	Douce MS., 302. 15th century.	
4.	Holy stond in þe hall fayre to behold	219
	Harln. MS., 5396. Temp. Hen. 6	
5.	Now ys Crystemas y-cum . .	220
	Wright's Carols (Harln. MS., 541. Temp. Hen. 7).	
6.	The borys hede, that we bryng here .	223
7.	I am here, syre Cristsmasse . .	224
	Both from Additional MS., 5665. Temp. Hen. s	
8.	A bonne God wote! . .	224
	Wright's Carols, Cotton MS., Vespasian, A, xxv	
9.	A Babe is born al of a may . .	226
	The same, Sloane MS., 2593.	
10.	The fyrst day of ȝole have we in mynd	227
11.	Blyssid be that lady bryght . .	228
	Both from Wright's Songs and Carols	
12.	Hey, hey, hey, hey, the borrys hede is arnyd gay	230
	Wright's Carols.	
13.	The bore's heed in hand bring I	231
	Ritson's Ancient Songs.	
14.	In Betheleem, that noble place . .	232
	Bibliographical Miscellanies (Kele's Christmas Carolles.)	
15.	All you that in this house be here .	233
	Wright's Carols (New Carols, 1661).	

	PAGE
16. Remember, O thou man, O thou man!	235
Melismata, 1611.	
17. Jesus Christ of Nazareth	237
Translated from Hoffman's Horæ Belgicæ, part 2, p. 16.	
18. What is that which is but one?	238
19. Joseph was an old man, and an old man was he	241
20. A child this day is born	242
21. As I passed by a river side	246
22. As it fell out one May morning	251
23. A Virgin most pure, as the prophets do tell	254
24. God rest you, merry gentlemen	256
25. God's dear Son without beginning	258
26. I saw three ships come sailing in	260
27. The first nowell the angel did say	261
28. The Lord at first had Adam made	263
29. To-morrow shall be my dancing day	266
30. Now when Joseph and Mary	268
31. This new Christmas Carol, 'Let us cheerfully sing'	271
32. When Cæsar did the sceptre sway	273
33. Saint Stephen was a holy man	275
34. Hark! the herald angels sing	278
This and the sixteen preceding are from manuscript copies, several of which are also printed as broadsides.	
35. Guillô pran ton tamborin	279
Noei Bourguignon.	
36. De noubelos Efans en benen de la bilo	280
Recueil de Poetes Gascons, 1700.	
37. Tres Rei de l'Orian	281
Nouveaux Cantiques Spirituels Provençaux, 1750.	
38. Quand Dieu naquit a Noel	282
Noels Vieux & Nouveaux.	
39. Lon de la gran carriero	284
Recueil de Noels Provençaux, 1791.	
40. L'An mil sies cens quaranto cinc	287
Recueil de Poetes Gascons.	
41. J'antan po no rué	288
Noei Bourgignon.	
42. I hear along the street	290
Translation of No. 41, by Longfellow.	
Christmas Play of Alexander	292
The like of St. George	298

INDEX TO PRINCIPAL MATTERS.

	PAGE
Ale Christmas, account of	35
Boar's head and brawn	30, 32
Boy Bishop, referred to	80
Carol singing	173
Carols, list of	207
Carol, Merry, tale of	185
Carol, Cherry Tree, account of	200
Carol singing in France	192
Christmas block	113
Christmas boxes	149
Christmas plays	153
Christmas tree	151
Cross, account of	204
Epiphany, offerings on	37, 42, 55
Evergreens, practice of decorating with	11, 127
Feasts of fools and asses	13
Fools, domestic, referred to	121
Gray's Inn, Christmas feast	93
Gray's Inn, Serjeant Roe's play at	76
Inns of Court, revels	73
King of the bean	39, 42, 164, 166
Lord of Misrule	60, 86, 91, 121-2
Minced pies	138
Misletoe	12
Mysteries and miracle plays	48
New year's gifts	37, 39, 42, 47, 59, 78, 90, 99, 110, 123, 133, 143
Noël, description of term	190
Pageants, revels, and mummings	40, 41, 48, 65-70, 86, 106
Pantomime, Christmas	152
Star-song	171
Temple Christmas feasts	92, 122
Thirty pieces of silver, legend of	169
Three Kings, history of	159

Turkeys at Christmas	112
Twelfth cake	. 166
Twelfth Night—Epiphany	. 164
Twelfth Night at sea	. 132
Waits .	. 83, 96, 116
Wassail bowl .	18, 55
Yule, explanation of	5

INDEX OF REFERENCES.

To avoid encumbering the pages with foot-notes, all references requiring them have been omitted, but the principal works and passages referred to will be found in this Index, excepting those that already appear in the body of the work.

Many of the **old Chronicles** have been inspected for historical facts, but it has **not** been thought necessary to specify them, except in a few instances; and where one is cited, the fact is frequently corroborated by two **or three** others. Hickes's 'Thesaurus,' vol. i, pp. 209-14, and Gebelin's 'Allegories Orientales,' contain a good deal of learning about **Yule** or Gule, and the former as to midwinter. Du Cange's 'Glossary,' in voce Festum, gives many particulars respecting the **Feasts of Asses and Fools.** The Wardrobe Accounts, temp. Edw. First, have entries connected with that time; and Mr. Collier's 'Annals of the Stage, and History of Dramatic Poetry,' and the 'Account of Revels,' by Mr. Peter Cunningham, both works containing much valuable information, the Privy **Purse Expenses** of Elizabeth **of York,** of Henry the Eighth, and of the Princess Mary, the 'Northumberland **Household Book,**' and Nichols's ' Progresses of **Queen** Elizabeth **and** King James,' are the authorities for many of the plays and masks, and the **particulars of the accounts** connected with them, and the New Year's Gifts from **the** time of Henry the Seventh to that of James the First; and many additional particulars may be found in them. Brady's 'Clavis Calendaria' contains much information respecting the early history of **Christmas,** and Mosheim's 'Ecclesiastical History,' may also be consulted. Spelman's '**Glossary,**' voce Xenia, and Boulanger, 'l'Antiquité Devoilée,' iv, 16, 17, a work however **not to** be recommended, speak of the ancient New Year's Gifts. Madox's ' **History of** the Exchequer' states the movements of our early

— 307 —

monarchs, mentioning for a long series of years where they kept their Christmasses; and Turner's, Henry's, and Lingard's 'Histories of England,' and the 'Pictorial History,' may be referred to also, by those wishing to look further into the subject. Many facts taken from these books do not appear to require more than this general reference to them.

PAGE	LINE	
3	29	Nehemiah, viii, 10.
15	31	Rabelais, vol. i, 478, n. ed. 1823.
20	22	Lingard's Hist. Eng. ed. 1837, vol. i, 259.
21	22	John of Brompton. Twysden, X Scriptores.
25	26	Archæologia, vol. xi, 13 (from Wilkins's Concil.).
27	26	Blount, Fragmenta Antiq., by Beckwith, 50.
30	13, 21	Madox's Hist. Exchequer, 258.
33	13	The Woman's Prize, Fletcher, iv, 2.
34	9	Hamlet i, 1.
36	18, 29	Baker's Chronicle, 82, 83.
37	31	Théâtre Français au moyen Age, 1842, p. 118.
38	20	Cronica Jocelini de Brakelonda, 46.
39	21	Archæologia, xxvi, 342.
40	21, 30	Archæologia, xxxi, 37, 38, 43, 122.
42	9	Cotton MS. Nero, C. viii.
—	15	Petitôt Mémoires, 1st Ser. vi, 66.
—	22	Monstrelet, ed. 1840, i, 153.
44	11	Warton, Hist. of Poetry, 8vo, ii, 71, 72.
45	—	Henry V, i, 1.
46	24	Archæologia, xxi, 66. Old Poem on Siege of Rouen.
—	31	Petitôt Mémoires, 1st Ser. viii, 35.
47	26, 31	Excerpta Historica, 148, 150.—(Cotton MS. Cleopatra, F. iv.)
—	28	Proceedings of Privy Council, iii, 285.
48	4	Fairholt's History of Costume.—(Harl. MS. 2278.)
—	11	Proceedings of Privy Council, v, 114.
—	14	Rymer's Fœdera, x, 387.
—	30	Collier, Hist. Dram. Poetry, ii, 127.
50	17	King John, ii, 1.
51	28	Harl. MS. 5931.
52	3	Fabliaux et Contes du xii et xiii siècles, i, 329, &c.
54	29	Additional MS. 6113.

PAGE LINE
55 25 Antiquarian Repertory, i, 328.
56   4 Hamlet, i, 4.
—   7 Love's Labour Lost, v, 2.
57 31 Ritson's Ancient Songs, 304. (From New Christmas Carols.)
58 15 Midsummer Night's Dream, ii, 1.
—   24 Herrick's Works, ii, 92.
59 25 Ordinances of Royal Household, 120.
61 14 Archæologia, xxv, 319-27.
66   6 Hall's, Holinshed's, and Baker's Chronicles may be consulted for this
       and most of the Christmas revels in the time of Henry VIII; also
       Collier's Annals of the Stage, for many particulars of payments
       and gifts.
72 29 Henry VIII, i, 4.
76 18 Hall's Chronicle.
78 14 Ellis's Original Letters, i, 271.—(Cotton MS. Vespasian, F. xiii.)
79 16 Cotton MS. Appendix, xxviii.
80 27 Strutt's Sports, &c. 305.
81   8 Archæologia, xxv, 422.
82   4 Leland's Itinerary, iv, 182.
83   7 Camden's Remains, 262.
—   18 Archæological Journal, No. 4, 367.
—   24 Kalendars of the Exchequer, i, 269.
89 10 Particulars of George Ferrer's Misrule will be found in Stow's Annals,
       Baker's Chronicle, Loseley MS. 45, &c. and Machyn's Diary, 13, &c.
90 10 Loseley MS. 90.
91 17 Machyn's Diary, 162.
92   4 Machyn's Diary, 222.
93 19 Dugdale Origines Jurid.
—   24 Account of Revels, 28.
95   — See Collier, i, 196, &c., for this page.
96 13 Lansdowne MS. 71.
—   22 Ben Jonson's Conversations with Drummond, 23.
102 — See Archæologia, i, 9; Ditto, xix, 292; Nichols's Progresses; Sloane
       MS. 4827; Ditto, 814, Additional MS. 5751;—for particulars
       of New Year's Gifts in this and preceding pages.
103 6 Account of Revels, 204.
108 12, 22 Pictorial History of England, iii, 88.

PAGE	LINE	
110	25	Nichols's Progresses, i, xl, n.
—	30	Account of Revels, xi.
111	30	Lansdowne MS. 92.
112	26	Doblado's Letters.
113	17	Introduction to Canto 6, Marmion.
—	28	Romeo and Juliet, i, 4.
114	4	Westward Ho, ii, 3.
115	6	Horace, lib. i, od. 9.
—	19	Michaelmas Term, ii, 3.
—	23	Promptorium Parvulorum, 238.
116	2	Johnes's Translation, vol. iii, c. 7.
—	16	Herrick's Works, ii, 124.
—	30	Witty Fair One, iv, 2.
118	27	Nichols's Illustrations of Manners and Expenses, 53.
121	25	Archæologia, xviii, 335.
122	6	Curiosities of Literature, iii, 269.
124	6	Hone's Every Day Book, i, 9. (Banquet of Jests, 1634.)
125	29	Petitôt Mémoires, 47, 101.
136	17	Percy's Reliques, ed. 1840, 169.
—	28	Evans's Ballads, iii, 262.
137	15	Evans's Ballads, i, 146.
138	15	City Madam, ii, 1.
144	23	Roper's Life of Sir T. More, 73.
146	17	Cowley's Anacreontiques, No. 2.
147	9	Wine and Walnuts, ii, 157.
—	30	New Year's Day, by Hartley Coleridge.
149	30	Brady Clavis Calendaria, ii, 316, 17.
154	20	In Wily Beguiled.
155	22	Collier's Annals of the Stage, i, 22.
157	18	Malcontent, by Marston, iv, 2.
158	—	Dr. Macculloch's Proofs and Illustrations of the Attributes of God, i, 358, a work of remarkable learning and information joined to sincere and unaffected piety—the production of a gifted and accomplished man, whose death will ever be regretted by those who, in his lifetime, enjoyed his friendship.
160	25	Milton's Ode on the Nativity.
161	25	Sandys's Travels, 141.

PAGE	LINE	
162	12	Harl. MSS. 437, 619.
—	16	Apocryphal New Testament, 2, 3.—Infancy, iii, 2.
—	29	Burton's Anatomy of Melancholy, 1638, 225.
163	16	Diary of Philip Henslowe, 70.
—	22, 28	Hone's Every Day Book, i, 46.
165	16	Fabliaux et Contes, par Barbazan et Meon, ii, 285.
—	18	Strutt's Sports and Pastimes, 8vo, 344.
166	12	Archives Curieuses de l'Histoire de France, 2 Series, v, 392.
168	13	Warton's History of Poetry, 8vo, ii, 91 n.
—	16	Harl. MS. 5931.
170	9	French Mystery of the 15th Century, 'Le Geu des trois Rois.'
171	13	MS. Bibl. Reg. 5 F. xiv, 7. Ib. 18 A, x, 8. Harl. MS. 1704-11.
—	14	Harl. MS. 2407, 13.
178	24	This reference should be 'Popular Rhymes and Nursery Tales.'
179	12	Barzaz-Breiz, Chants Populaires de la Bretagne, i, 1, 25.
180	2	Description of Patent Rolls, by T. D. Hardy, 129.
183	6	Privy Purse Expenses of Princess Mary, Introduction, xxvii.
—	7	Privy Purse Expenses of Elizabeth of York, 83.
184	25	Barnaby Googe, translation of Naogeorgus.
185	11	Pictorial History of England, iii, 446 (address by Mr. John Davison to General Assembly in Scotland, 1596).
186	25	Old Ballads, 1723, p. 69.
188	11	Batt upon Batt, 1711, p. 6.
191	6	Bibliothèque de l'Ecole des Chartes, i, 250.
—	20	Rabelais, vi, 209, n. (liv. 4, c. 22).
—	26	Pasquier les Recherches de la France, 383-4.
—	30	Ménage Diction. Etymol., voce Noël.
192	3	Archæologia, 22.
—	17	Fabliaux et Contes, iv, 80, 99.
194	1	Laborde's Essai, i, 118, n.
200	27	Notes and Queries, v, 7, communication by Mr. Thoms.
203	8	Introduction to Scotch songs, i, 104.
206	2	See French mystery of fifteenth century, La Nativité, edited by Jubinal, ii, 19, Cornish play of Creation of the World, and poem of Mount Calvary, for further particulars.
—	26	Horne's introduction to the Scriptures, i, 629.
213	2	Maccabees, 15, 38.

Music to Carols.

A VIRGIN MOST PURE.

A CHILD THIS DAY IS BORN.

THE LORD AT FIRST HAD ADAM MADE.

THE FIRST NOWELL.

The first Now-ell that the Angels did say Was to cer-tain poor shepherds in field as they lay, In fields where they lay, keep-ing their sheep In a cold winter's night that was so deep. Now-ell, Now-ell, Now-ell, Now-ell, Born is the King of Is-ra-el.

THIS NEW CHRISTMAS CAROL.

GOD REST YOU, MERRY GENTLEMEN.

SAINT STEPHEN

GOD'S DEAR SON.

God's dear Son without be-gin-ning, Whom the wick-ed Jews did scorn, The only wise without all sinning, On this bles-sed day was born, To save us all From sin and thrall, Whilst we in Satan's chains are bound, And shed his blood to do us good with many a bleeding purple wound

TO-MORROW SHALL BE MY DANCING DAY.

I SAW THREE SHIPS.

JOSEPH WAS AN OLD MAN.

IN THOSE TWELVE DAYS.

In those twelve days let us be glad, In those twelve days let us be glad, For God by his pow'r hath all things made. What is that which is but one? What is that which is but one? We have but one God a-lone, In hea-ven a-bove sits on his throne.

E. TUCKER, PRINTER, PERRYS PLACE, OXFORD STREET.

www.ingramcontent.com/pod-product-compliance
Lightning Source LLC
Chambersburg PA
CBHW020243240426
43672CB00006B/621